How to revise and practice

Also by Dr McPherson

Indo-European Cognate Dictionary

Beginning Ancient Greek: A Visual Workbook

Easy Russian Alphabet: A Visual Workbook

Effective Notetaking (3rd ed.)

Mnemonics for Study (2nd ed.)

Mnemonics for Study with Spanish glossary

Mnemonics for Study with Italian glossary

How to learn: The 10 principles of effective revision and practice

Successful Learning Simplified: A Visual Guide

How to Approach Learning: What teachers and students should know about succeeding in school

My Memory Journal

Planning to Remember: How to remember what you're doing and what you plan to do

Perfect Memory Training

The Memory Key

How to revise and practice

2nd Edition

Fiona McPherson, PhD

Wayz Press
Wellington, New Zealand

Contents

A note about this workbook

This workbook is a revised edition of my book *How to learn: The 10 principles of effective revision and practice*. That book was quite research-heavy, describing the experimental studies behind the principles I lay out. This revised edition has relegated such details to an appendix, and expanded greatly the section on practical applications. Some chapters remain essentially the same (the first two chapters, the short review chapter 7, the final chapter), with the addition of review questions and exercises. Other chapters (3, 4, 5, 6) have been heavily cut and edited, although there is still mention of various research studies, when the descriptions provide useful examples of tasks and strategies, as well as strengthening confidence in the recommended strategies. Chapters 8-14 are expanded versions of chapters 8 and 9, with lots of exercises. All chapters (with the exception of Chapter 7) have review questions. There are a number of exercises.

Note that numbers in square brackets, like this [3.1], refer to an entry in the Chapter Notes, which will expand on the research referred to for those interested in more details. If there is no further discussion of the research, there will simply be a normal study citation (e.g., Kornell 2019). The full reference can then be found in the References, at the end of the book. My apologies if doing these citations (rather than inserting a number) makes the text appear a little too academic for some readers, but I feel it makes it much easier to read if you know without checking the Chapter Notes whether I indeed have more to say on the subject, or am simply citing the source research.

What you need to know about memory

To understand how to practice or revise effectively, you need to understand some basic principles about how memory works. This chapter covers:

- the 8 basic principles of memory

- how neurons work

- what working memory is and why it's so important

- what consolidation is and why it matters

'Practice' (a term I use to cover both revision of information and the practice of skills) is a deceptively simple concept. Everyone thinks they know what it means, and what they think it is, basically, is repetition. When we have to remember an unknown phone number long enough to dial it, we repeat it to ourselves. As children told to learn a poem, we repeated it until we had it memorized. Learning to drive, we repeated the necessary actions over and over again. Repetition is at the heart of learning.

But simple repetition is the least effective learning strategy there is.

How do we reconcile these statements? Well, repetition is crucial to cement a memory, but the untutored way of doing it wastes a great deal of time, and still results in learning that is less durable than more efficient strategies.

In this book, I'm going to tell you the 10 principles of effective repetition, why they work, and how they work. We'll look at examples from science, mathematics, history, foreign language learning, and skill learning. At the end of it, you'll know how to apply these principles in your study and your daily life.

Let's start with a very brief look at how memory works.

The 8 basic principles of memory

The most fundamental thing you need to understand about memory is that it is not a recording. When we put information into our memory, we don't somehow copy the real-world event, as a video camera might, but rather we select and edit the information. For this reason, putting information into memory is called **encoding**. This is why I habitually talk about memory codes rather than memories. It's a reminder that nothing in your memory is a 'pure' rendition, a faithful copy. We create our memory codes, and when we try and retrieve a memory, it is this coded information that we are looking for. (Like a computer, what our brain processes is information — when I use the word 'information', I don't just mean 'facts', but images and skills and events and everything else we file in long-term memory.)

Why does it matter that the information is coded?

Because what you think you are looking for may not be precisely what is there. How easy it is to remember something (retrieve a memory code) depends on the extent to which the code matches what you think you're looking for. For example, say you are trying to remember someone's name. You might think it begins with T, or that it's unusual, or very common, or sounds something like -immy, or that it's old-fashioned, or ... Whatever your idea is, the point is that there *is* an idea, a starting point, a clue (we call it a **retrieval cue**). How likely you are to retrieve the memory code depends on how good a clue it is.

This is because memory codes are linked together in a network. Remembering is about following a trail through the network, following the links. No surprise then that your starting point (the retrieval cue) is crucial.

For example, consider this simplified memory code for Henry VIII:

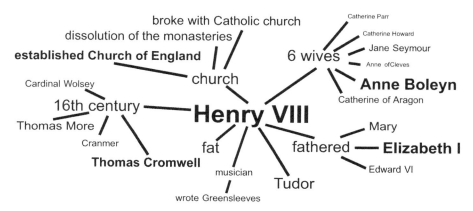

The size of the words reflect how strong those parts of the code are — Anne Boleyn, for example, is for most of us the most memorable of Henry's wives; Elizabeth the most memorable of his children.

Accordingly, it would be a lot easier to retrieve "Henry VIII" if the retrieval cue was "father of Elizabeth I" than if it was "father of Edward VI", or if the cue was "established the Church of England" rather than "Cranmer's king", or, worst of all, "16th century musician". (Do note that information in a memory code is not necessarily true! For example, Henry VIII did not actually write the song *Greensleeves*, but it is a common belief that he did. 'Information' is a blanket word to cover a type of content; the statement "The grass is green" and the statement "The grass is red" contain the same amount of information, although only one of the statements is true.)

The trail through memory resembles a trail through a jungle. Much-travelled paths will be easier and quicker to follow. Paths that have been used recently will be easier to find than old disused trails.

There are eight fundamental principles encompassed in these simple ideas:

1. **code principle**: memories are selected and edited codes.

2. **network principle**: memory consists of links between associated codes.

3. **domino principle**: the activation of one code triggers connected codes.

4. **recency effect**: a recently retrieved code will be more easily found. If you were watching the TV program *The Tudors* last night, it would be much easier to call up Henry VIII's name up again than it would be if you hadn't thought of him since school.

5. **priming effect**: a code will be more easily found if linked codes have just been retrieved.
   Having been thinking of Henry VIII, you will find it easier to retrieve "Walter Raleigh" (linked to Elizabeth I), compared to a situation where you were asked, out of the blue, who that guy was who put his cloak across the puddle for Queen Elizabeth to walk over.

6. **frequency** (or **repetition**) **effect**: the more often a code has been retrieved, the easier it becomes to find.

7. **matching effect**: a code will be more easily found the more closely the retrieval cue matches the code.
   This can be seen in jokes: if you were asked, "What did the tree do when the bank closed?", you'd probably realize instantly that the answer had something to do with "branch", because "branch' is likely to be a strong part of both your "tree" code and your "bank" code. On the other hand, if you were asked, "What tree is made of stone?", the answer (lime tree) is not nearly as easily retrieved, because "lime" is probably not a strong part of either your "tree" code or your "stone" code.

8. **context effect**: a code will be more easily found if the encoding and retrieval contexts match.
   If you learned about Henry VIII from watching *The Tudors* on TV, you will find it easier to remember facts about Henry VIII when

you're sitting watching TV. We use this principle whenever we try and remember an event by imagining ourselves in the place where the event happened.

These principles all affect how practice works and what makes it effective, but three are especially important. The recency and priming effects remind us that it's much easier to follow a memory trail that has been activated recently, but that's not a strength that lasts. Making a memory trail permanently stronger requires repetition (the frequency effect). This is about neurobiology: every time neurons fire in a particular sequence (which is what happens when you 'activate' a memory code), it makes it a little easier for them to fire in that way again.

The frequency effect is at the heart of why practice is so important. The recency and priming effects are at the heart of why most people don't practice effectively.

How neurons work

Let's take a very brief look at this business of neurons firing. Neurons are specialized brain cells. We might think of them as nodes in the network. Neurons are connected to each other through long filaments, one long one (the **axon**) and many very short ones (**dendrites**). It is the long axon that carries the outgoing signal from the neuron. The dendrites receive the incoming signals, and they do this through specialized receptors called **synapses**. For here's the thing: neurons aren't physically connected. Messages are carried through the network by electrical impulses along the filaments, which induce chemical responses at the synapses. Specialized chemicals called **neurotransmitters** travel the very short gap between the synapses on one neuron to those on a nearby one.

In other words, information is carried within the neuron in the form of electrical impulses (as it is in your radio and television), is then transformed into a chemical format so that it can cross the gap between neurons, and then translated back into electrical impulses in the receiving neuron.

Being carried as an electrical signal has an important implication: how fast we think (and how well, as we'll see in the next section) depends on how fast the signals are flowing. The speed of the electrical signal depends on the wiring. As with the wiring in your home, the 'wires' (axons) are sheathed in insulation. The better insulated, the less 'loss' in the signal, the faster the signal can travel. In the brain, this insulation is called **myelin**. Because myelin is white(ish), and the cell bodies are gray, we commonly refer to 'gray matter' and 'white matter'.

Myelin tends to degrade over time, and this degradation is one of the factors implicated in cognitive decline in old age. Myelin degradation can also occur in certain medical conditions (multiple sclerosis being the prime example).

But how quickly the signals move is only part of the story — the other part is how far the signals have to travel. Axons can be very long, but information moves more quickly when the connection between two neurons is very short. Consider how many neurons you need to activate to have a coherent thought, and you'll realize that you'll do your best thinking when the neurons you need are all clustered tightly together.

Here's the last crucial concept: a neuron doesn't care what information it carries; a neuron, like your brain, is flexible. However, if you keep sending the same (or similar) information through, a small network of closely arranged neurons will develop to carry that specific information. With practice (the frequency effect), the connections between the neurons will grow 'stronger' — more used to carrying that information across particular synapses, more easily activated when triggered.

Working memory — a constraining factor

It seems incredible that we can store all the memories we accumulate in such a system, but we have some 200 billion neurons in our brain, and each neuron has about 1000 synapses on average. These are unimaginable numbers. But although our memory store is vast, as in a real jungle we can't see very much of it at a time. In fact, it's quite remarkable how little we can 'see' at any point, and this limitation is one of the critical constraints on our learning and our understanding.

We call the tiny part of memory that we are aware of, **working memory**. When you put information into your memory, the encoding takes place in working memory. When you drag it out of your memory, you pull it into working memory. When you read, you are using working memory to hold each word long enough to understand the complete sentence. When you think, it is working memory that holds the thoughts you are thinking.

As we all know to our cost, working memory is very small. Try and hold an unfamiliar phone number in your mind long enough to dial it and you quickly realize this. Probably the most widely known 'fact' about working memory is that it can only hold around seven **chunks** of information (between 5 and 9, depending on the individual). But we know now that working memory is even smaller than that. The 'magic number 7' (as it has been called) applies to how much you can hold if you actively maintain it — that is, repeat it to yourself. In the absence of this deliberate circulation, it is now thought that working memory can only hold around four chunks (between three and five), of which only one can be attended to at any one time (that is, only one is 'in focus').

Although it sounds like a small difference, the difference between having a working memory capacity of three chunks or one that can hold five chunks has significant effects on your cognitive abilities. Your working memory capacity is closely related to what is now called **fluid intelligence**, meaning the part of an IQ test that has nothing to do with knowledge but depends almost entirely on your ability to reason and think quickly.

While working memory capacity may seem to be a 'fixed' attribute, something you are born with, it does increase during childhood and adolescence, and tends to decrease in old age. There have been a number of attempts to increase people's working memory capacity through training, some of which have had a certain amount of success, but most of this success has been with people who have attention difficulties. It is much less clear that training can increase the working memory capacity of an individual without cognitive disabilities.

At a practical level, however, differences in working memory capacity have a lot to do with how well we form our memory codes — with our skill in leaving out irrelevant material, and our skill at binding together the important stuff into a tightly-bound network. This is implicit in the word 'chunks'.

Although working memory can hold only a very small number of chunks, 'chunks' is the escape clause, as it were — for what constitutes a chunk is a very flexible matter. For example, 1 2 3 4 5 6 7 are seven different chunks, if you remember each digit separately (as you would if you were not familiar with the digits, as a young child isn't). But for those of us who are well-versed in our numbers, 1 through to 7 could be a single chunk. Similarly, these nine words:

1. brown

2. the

3. jumps

4. dog

5. over

6. quick

7. lazy

8. the

9. fox

could be nine chunks, or, in a different order ("the quick brown fox jumps over the lazy dog"), one chunk (for those who know it well as an example used in typing practice). At a much higher level of expertise, a chess master may have whole complex sequences of chess moves as single chunks.

Think back to what I said about how clusters of neurons become more strongly and closely connected with practice, and you'll see why practice is the key to functionally increasing your working memory capacity. The key is your chunks. A chunk is a very tight cluster. Such clusters enable you to increase how much information you can 'hold' in working memory.

I said that working memory contains a certain number of chunks, but to a large extent this way of thinking about it is a matter of convenience. It's more precise to say that the amount of information you can hold depends on how fast you are moving it. Because here's the thing about working memory — nothing stays in it for more than a couple of seconds, if you're not consciously keeping it active. This is why you have to keep repeating that phone number: you have to bring each digit back into 'focus' before its time is up and it fades back into the long-term store.

Let's go back to my earlier statement that the 'magic number 7' has now been reduced to 4 in the absence of deliberate repetition. We can reconcile these two numbers through another concept: that working memory (the 'inner circle') is surrounded by an outer area, in which, say, 3 items that have recently been in working memory can hover for a while, ready to be pulled back in easily.

Let's see that at work in a simple equation. Say you were given this problem to solve:

$$(38 \times 4) \div 3$$

How you solve this will depend on your mathematical expertise, but a common way would be to break it down to:

$30 \times 4 = 120$

$8 \times 4 = 32$

$120 + 32 = 152$

$150 \div 3 = 50$

$2 \div 3 = \frac{2}{3}$

$50 + \frac{2}{3} = 50\frac{2}{3}$

Now think of the working memory flow needed to achieve this. First, you separate 38 into 30 and 8, moving your focus from 38 to 30, between 30 and 4 as you produce a new number (120) which briefly becomes the focus as you update working memory (30 and 4 can be discarded, replaced by this new number). Now you pull the waiting 8 into focus, perform the updating operation on it (multiply by 4), and replace it with the new number, 32. Now you must pull 120 back into focus as you add it to 32 and update working memory again, replacing 32 and 120 with the new number 152. Now you need the "divide by 3" (I hope it's still waiting! It all depends how fast you've been.) And so on.

Let's think about what you have to hold in working memory while you perform this fairly simple calculation:

30 x 4 = 120 (while performing this operation you need to hold in mind that 30 is just part of 38 and that you'll need to multiply the 8 by 4 and then add the two sums together to get a new sum that will then need to be divided by 3)

8 x 4 = 32 (performing this operation while holding in mind: the previous sum (120); the need to add the two sums together; the later need to divide by 3)

120 + 32 = 152 (holding in mind the division by 3)

150 ÷ 3 = 50 (holding in mind the 2 left over)

2 ÷ 3 = ⅔ (holding in mind the 50)

50 + ⅔ = 50 ⅔

On the next page, you can see a visual of the first step (the numbers floating in the space beyond the rings represent information in your long-term memory store).

You can see working memory is already filling up, but if you're not skilled at math, each of these operations may involve a little more work, especially if you don't know your tables well, so that "32" doesn't come instantly to mind when you see "8 x 4". In such a case, there'll be even less space available for those other parts of the equation that you're holding in mind.

Moreover, if you suffer from 'math anxiety', you might also have other thoughts cluttering up the space — thoughts like "oh I'm hopeless at math", memories of failure, and the like.

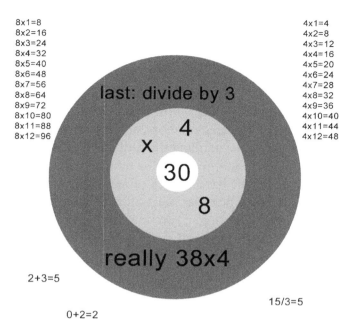

8x1=8
8x2=16
8x3=24
8x4=32
8x5=40
8x6=48
8x7=56
8x8=64
8x9=72
8x10=80
8x11=88
8x12=96

4x1=4
4x2=8
4x3=12
4x4=16
4x5=20
4x6=24
4x7=28
4x8=32
4x9=36
4x10=40
4x11=44
4x12=48

last: divide by 3

x   4

30

8

really 38x4

2+3=5

15/3=5

0+2=2

On the other hand, you might have approached the equation this way:

38 doubled is 76 (at this point, you're holding in mind the intention to double it again, and to divide the answer by 3)

76 doubled is 152 (at this point, you only need to hold in mind the intention to divide the answer by 3)

152 ÷ 3 is 50 with 2 left over

50 ⅔

Because working memory is fundamentally time-based, a lot comes down to how quickly you can perform basic operations — which is simply another way of saying how accessible the information is. Because I had a teacher at school who used to put a number on the board and tell us to keep doubling (or halving) until he returned to the room, I have no trouble instantly transforming 38 to 76, 76 to 152. It would be a different story if I had to laboriously say to myself: $70 + 70 = 140$, $6 + 6 = 12$, $140 + 12 = 152$.

This is why you can functionally (i.e., for practical purposes) increase your working memory capacity in specific areas by making your long-term knowledge more readily accessible — it all comes down your level of expertise, or to put it another way: practice.

Understanding that memory codes flow between long-term memory, the focus, the inner ring of working memory, and the outer ring of working memory, is critical for understanding the fundamental principles of effective practice. The flow is governed by time and attention. Once an item is out of focus, it only has a couple of seconds before it will retire out of the inner ring into the outer ring, unless you bring it back into focus. Once it's in the outer ring, it can only stay there a short time before it will fade back into the vast sea of long-term memory — unless, of course, you bring it back into focus.

It is by keeping the information moving, therefore, that you keep it in working memory. Fast speakers, and fast thinkers, have an advantage.

Understanding the limits of your working memory capacity helps you work out the most effective approach to your own practice, in particular, how much information you should try and handle at one time. It also helps you recognize when a particular learning task might be more demanding of your working memory.

The demands any cognitive task put on working memory we call **cognitive load**. Being able to assess the cognitive load of a task gives you the opportunity to reduce the load where necessary. Often, the reason a student has trouble understanding or performing a task is because the cognitive load is too much for them. Note that the cognitive load of a task is not a fixed amount, but varies for the individual, because, of course, it depends on the chunks (that is, on your long-term memory codes).

To a large extent, then, cognitive load is reflected in task difficulty.

Here are some factors to consider when trying to assess cognitive load:

- **how much information there is**

- **how complex the information is**

How difficult it is to craft it into a tightly-bound cluster — that is, how hard it is for you to connect the information together and make sense of it.

- **how often you have to shift your focus**
  For example, if you are trying to do more than one task at a time (writing an essay and checking your Facebook page), then you are appreciably adding to your cognitive load; if you are trying to translate a text in a foreign language and have to keep diverting to the dictionary and a grammar book, then this will add considerably to the cognitive load (as compared to being able to translate without needing to check vocabulary and grammar points).

- **whether information already in focus has to be altered and how much time and effort is needed to change it**
  For example, in the math example above, you were performing calculations that 'updated' the number in focus.

There are basically two approaches to reducing cognitive load:

- break the task into smaller components

- practice the task or parts of the task until they are so easily retrieved from long-term memory that they are essentially automatic.

Thus, to reduce the cognitive load of dual essay-writing and Facebook-checking, you simply stop doing one activity and focus on the other. To reduce the cognitive load of trying to translate while constantly checking words and grammar, you need to practice your vocabulary and grammar until they are readily accessible.

Practice, then, is at the heart of reducing cognitive load and functionally improving your working memory capacity.

The role of consolidation in memory

But putting your code together in working memory is not all there is to encoding. Before your memory code can take its place in long-term memory, you need to **consolidate** it.

Memory consolidation is the final concept we need to understand how and why practice works.

Consolidation is aptly named. It's a process that takes place over time, and in a sense never truly ends. Your memories are always in a state of flux, vulnerable to change — every time you remember something, you change the memory code, even if only a little. But such changes can be thought of as *re*-consolidation. The initial stage in the consolidation process involves stabilizing the memory code, and this takes place over several hours. This is a crucial point when it comes to practicing effectively, because new memories are particularly vulnerable to being lost during this period.

The second stage of the memory-cycle is consolidation, and a lot of that occurs during sleep. During consolidation, the memory is edited — bits deemed unimportant may be dropped; important bits emphasized; connections made stronger or cut.

The time it takes to stabilize and consolidate new learning is why you often do better (perform a new skill better, or remember more) the next day.

It's also why it really helps if you run over any new learning in the evening before bed. If you learn in the morning, you have all your subsequent experiences and new information interfering with that earlier learning. New memory codes that haven't yet been consolidated are particularly vulnerable to interference, so they may well be over-written or corrupted by the time your sleeping brain looks over the day's events to see what is worthy of being kept.

Some types of information are more easily lost than others. For example, contextual details — such as knowing where you met a person; remembering the gender of the voice which spoke the foreign words you are trying to learn; remembering where a particular section is in a textbook — are particularly vulnerable. While such details might seem peripheral and not worth worrying about, context information is vital for source memory (remembering where and when you learned something), and also provides useful retrieval cues. So it's not to be despised, although you shouldn't waste too much attention on it either. The trick is to attend to useful context cues, and ignore less useful ones.

The third and final stage in the consolidation process — again, of particular interest in regard to effective practice — is re-consolidation, and that occurs every time the memory is retrieved from long-term memory. In other words, every time you practice or remember something, you are in effect re-making that memory code. This gives you a chance to improve it, to make it more memorable. Of course, it also means you can damage it — make it less what you want or need.

encoding
initial process of transforming information into code

stabilization
< 6 hours

That's why practice has to be right. If you practice the wrong thing, the wrong information, then you make *that* more memorable, at the cost of the correct information.

consolidation
mostly occurs during sleep

This has been a very brief description of how memory works. I have provided only the most basic concepts that you need to know in order to understand how practice works and how to get the most out of it. If you want to know

reconsolidation
happens every time you retrieve the memory code

more about these principles, I discuss them in much more detail in my books *The Memory Key*, now out-of-print but still available from my store as a digital download, and its revised version *Perfect Memory Training*, available in both print and digitally from online booksellers.

Points to remember

Memory is about two processes: **encoding** (the way you shape the memory when you put it in your database, which includes the connections you make with other memory codes already there) and **retrieving** (how easy it is to find in your database). So making a 'good' memory (one that is easily retrieved) is about forming a code that has easily activated connections.

Repetition makes the memory trail stronger.

Recency *appears* to make the memory trail stronger, but this isn't a lasting strength.

Both when you encode and when you retrieve a memory, it enters working memory. Working memory can only hold a very small number of memory codes at a time and to keep a code there for more than 1.5-2 seconds you need to keep shifting it into focus. This affects the content of your practice.

Your working memory capacity affects how big the cognitive load of a task is for you, but you can reduce cognitive load by breaking down the task. You can also reduce it — and functionally increase your working memory capacity — by practicing the task (or parts of the task) until it becomes automatic, or almost so.

Encoding a memory is not enough to get it into long-term memory. The memory needs to be stabilized and consolidated. Stabilization may take as long as six hours, and consolidation mainly occurs during sleep (daytime naps and even short periods of rest can also provide opportunities for some consolidation).

Review Questions

Note that, in all the review questions throughout this book, there will be some questions where more than one answer is correct. Because the purpose of these questions is to make you think about what you've just read, I will not tell you which ones. This helps reduce the guesswork involved!

1. Practice is simply repetition.   Y / N

2. 'Memory' is a term for that part of the brain that

    a. contains faithful copies of things we've learned or experienced

    b. contains consolidated information that has been selected & edited

    c. contains networks of connected memory codes

    d. contains everything you've ever experienced

3. A retrieval cue can be

    a. a question

    b. an image

    c. a smell

    d. a statement that triggers an idea

    e. a word

4. How easily you retrieve information from your memory depends on

    a. how strong the memory code is

    b. how easily the retrieval cue connects to the memory code

    c. how many times you've repeated the information

    d. how strong the connections are that lead from the retrieval cue to the memory code

    e. how long it's been since you last retrieved it

5. Information can be true or false.   Y / N

6. Practice is crucial for learning because

   a. the more often a code has been retrieved, the easier it becomes to find

   b. recent retrievals are remembered better

   c. repetition strengthens the connections between and within memory codes

   d. a code is more easily found if linked codes have just been retrieved

   e. repetition makes the neurons involved more easily activated when triggered

7. Recency permanently strengthens the memory trail. Y / N

8. Information travels in the brain

   a. as electrical signals

   b. in chemical transmitters

   c. along long, insulated filaments

   d. through physically connected neurons

9. How fast information travels depends on

   a. how well insulated the filaments are

   b. how far apart the involved neurons are

   c. how often those neurons are been activated together

   d. how smart you are

10. Working memory is

    a. the only part of memory that you're consciously aware of

    b. what you consciously think with

    c. very very small

    d. fixed in the amount you can hold at one time

    e. equivalent to your IQ

11. Which statement is true?

   a. Information is either in or out of working memory.

   b. Information flows between different working memory states.

12. 'Cognitive load'

   a. means the amount of information to be processed

   b. is a term for how complicated the information is

   c. refers to the demands a task puts on working memory

   d. is something you can measure for any given task

   e. depends in part on the individual doing the task

13. Which of these factors is important in assessing cognitive load?

   a. how hard it is for you to understand the information

   b. how much information there is

   c. how often you have to shift your focus of attention to different aspects of the task or to another activity

   d. how unpracticed you are at the task or aspects of the task

   e. whether the information doesn't connect with or contradicts information you already have

14. You can reduce the cognitive load of a task by

   a. practicing parts of the task until they're more automatic

   b. breaking the information into smaller pieces and learning them separately

   c. reducing distractions

   d. just doing the part of the task that's easy

15. Which of these statements is true?

   a. A memory code is fixed and stable once it enters long-term memory.

   b. Information is encoded in working memory and then passes directly into long-term memory as a permanent record.

c. Memory codes are subject to change every time you retrieve them from long-term memory.

d. Memory codes pass through various editing and stabilizing stages before becoming part of your long-term memory store.

What should you practice?

> If you've ever seriously practiced a skill such as playing a sport or a musical instrument, you'll know very well that half the battle is pinpointing precisely *what* to practice. In this chapter, I discuss this issue in relation to two types of learning situation — the learning of relatively meaningless information (foreign language vocabulary) and the learning of reasonably complex text.

Before we get to the most effective ways of practicing, we need to look at the content of your practice. There is no point in diligently applying the principles of effective practice if you're practicing the wrong thing!

You may think it's self-evident, that of course you would practice what you need to practice. But unfortunately it is not always (or even often) that obvious.

Some examples

Let's start by looking at what would seem to be a very obvious situation. Say you want to learn ten new Italian words:

acqua, water

denti, teeth

fratello, brother

giorno, day

libro, book

nave, ship

pneumatico, tire

risposta, answer

scarpa, shoe

sole, sun

The simplest method is to repeat them 'by rote': you say the pairs over and over again. Bad idea. You waste a lot of time, and get little return.

Or you might be more cunning, tying the words together using a keyword-type mnemonic (if you're not familiar with this, don't worry, I discuss it in the next chapter). Thus, instead of repeating "*scarpa-shoe*", you repeat "sharp shoe".

But here's the thing — what you need to practice is not the word-pairs, but the task you're aiming to master. You need to think about why you want to learn these words. What's your goal?

If you simply want to learn to read Italian, your task is to be able to retrieve the English meaning when you see the Italian word. So that's what your practice needs to be. You want to practice remembering "shoe" when you see "scarpa". That is, you need to practice *retrieving* "shoe"; it is not enough to simply repeat the two together.

If you have the larger requirement of wanting to be able to communicate in Italian — which means being able to read, write, speak, and understand Italian when spoken —then you need to practice both directions. That is, you need to practice retrieving the English when you see the Italian, and retrieving the Italian when you see the English. So you need to practice recalling "shoe" when you see "scarpa", and recalling "scarpa" when you see "shoe". Practicing this in both modalities — the written word and the spoken word — is also a good idea.

This is the principle: **effective practice matches the task you want to master**.

There's another principle that follows from that: the more specific the task, the easier it is to practice; **the more general the task, the more varied your practice will need to be**.

Thus, for example, if you are only ever going to come across the word *giorno* in connection with *libro*, the next word in the list, then it would be fine to only practice retrieving the word *day* as part of this ordered list. But of course that's not going to happen. So you need to practice retrieving your words in different orders / contexts. And that means in completely different contexts. Often you'll learn words that are part of category groups — foods, perhaps, or sports, or words that all relate to the classroom. It's fine (indeed a good idea) to begin with categories. But it's not a good idea to stick with them forever. You want to practice retrieval in all the contexts in which you're likely to encounter the words (or at least a wide diversity of contexts).

Procedural learning — that is, the learning of a skill or procedure — also provides a relatively straightforward task. But again, you need to think about the contexts. Let's take the example of driving a car. Here in New Zealand, a few years ago we changed a road rule governing who gives way to whom. It's a fairly major step changing such an important road rule and widespread chaos was predicted. It didn't, thankfully, eventuate — the change was well-communicated to the public, and perhaps more importantly, it was an improvement on the old road rule. But I noticed one interesting difficulty. Although it was no great trouble to remember the new rule in relatively unfamiliar intersections, it took quite an effort of concentration to remember it at very familiar intersections. The problem is that we develop specific patterns of behavior in response to well-travelled situations, and these are only loosely associated with the more general, abstracted pattern, the 'rule'.

In other words, I needed to practice not only the general principle, but also the specific change in behavior at particular intersections ("when I'm *here* and wanting to turn *there*, I need to wait for any cars coming from *that direction*").

Of course, both vocabulary learning and skill learning provide reasonably cut-and-dried examples of the content you need to practice. The more common situation in academic study is that you have texts of varying complexity and you have to somehow work out what the information is that you need to learn. Consider, for example, this text on ozone and UV radiation:

The Relationship Of Ozone And Ultraviolet Radiation: Why Is Ozone So Important?

In this section, we will explore what is ozone and what is ultraviolet radiation. We then will explore the relationship between ozone and ultraviolet radiation from the sun. It is here that ozone plays its essential role in shielding the surface from harmful ultraviolet radiation. By screening out genetically destructive ultraviolet radiation from the Sun, ozone protects life on the surface of Earth. It is for this reason that ozone acquires an enormous importance. It is why we study it so extensively.

2.1 Ozone and the Ozone Layer

About 90% of the ozone in our atmosphere is contained in the stratosphere, the region from about 10 to 50-km (32,000 to 164,000 feet) above Earth's surface. Ten percent of the ozone is contained in the troposphere, the lowest part of our atmosphere where all of our weather takes place. Measurements taken from instruments on the ground, flown on balloons, and operating in space show that ozone concentrations are greatest between about 15 and 30 km.

Although ozone concentrations are very small, typically only a few molecules O^3 per million molecules of air, these ozone molecules are vitally important to life because they absorb the biologically harmful ultraviolet radiation from the Sun. There are three different types of ultraviolet (UV) radiation, based on the wavelength of the radiation. These are referred to as UV-a, UV-b, and UV-c. UV-c (red) is entirely screened out by ozone around 35 km altitude, while most UV-a (blue) reaches the surface, but it is not as genetically damaging, so we don't worry about it too much. It is the UV-b (green) radiation that can cause sunburn and that can also cause genetic damage, resulting in things like skin cancer, if exposure to it is prolonged. Ozone screens out most UV-b, but some reaches the surface. Were the ozone layer to decrease, more UV-b radiation would reach the surface, causing increased genetic damage to living things.

Because most of the ozone in our atmosphere is contained in the stratosphere, we refer to this region as the stratospheric ozone layer. In contrast to beneficial stratospheric ozone, tropospheric ozone is a pollutant found in high concentrations in smog. Though it too absorbs UV radiation, breathing it in high levels is unhealthy, even toxic. The high reactivity of ozone results in damage to the living tissue of plants and animals. This damage by heavy tropospheric ozone pollution is often manifested as eye and lung irritation. Tropospheric ozone is mainly produced during the daytime in polluted regions such as urban areas. Significant government efforts are underway to regulate the gases and emissions that lead to this harmful pollution, and smog alerts are regular occurrences in polluted urban areas.

2.2 Solar Radiation

To appreciate the importance of stratospheric ozone, we need to understand something of the Sun's output and how it impacts living systems. The Sun produces radiation at many different wavelengths. These are part of what is known as the electromagnetic (EM) spectrum. EM radiation includes everything from radio waves (very long wavelengths) to X-rays and gamma rays (very tiny wavelengths). EM radiation is classified by wavelength, which is a measure of how energetic is the radiation. The energy of a tiny piece or 'packet' of radiation (which we call a photon) is inversely proportional to its wavelength.

The human eye can detect wavelengths in the region of the spectrum from about 400 nm (nanometers or billionths of a meter) to about 700 nm. Not surprisingly, this is called the visible region of the spectrum. All the colors of light (red, orange, yellow, green, blue, and violet) fall inside a small wavelength band. Whereas radio waves have wavelengths on the order of meters, visible light waves have wavelengths on the order of billionths of a meter. Such a tiny unit is called a nanometer (1 nm= 10-9 m). At one end of the visible 'color' spectrum is red light. Red light has a wavelength of about 630 nm. Near the opposite end of the color spectrum is blue light, and at the very opposite end is violet light. Blue light has a wavelength of about 430 nm. Violet light has a wavelength of about 410 nm. Therefore, blue light is more energetic than red light because of its shorter wavelength, but it is less energetic than violet light, which has an even shorter wavelength. Radiation with wavelengths shorter than those of violet light is called ultraviolet radiation.

The Sun produces radiation that is mainly in the visible part of the electromagnetic spectrum. However, the Sun also generates radiation in ultraviolet (UV) part of the spectrum. UV wavelengths range from 1 to 400 nm. We are concerned about ultraviolet radiation because these rays are energetic enough to break the bonds of DNA molecules (the molecular carriers of our genetic coding), and thereby damage cells. While most plants and animals are able to either repair or destroy damaged cells, on occasion, these damaged DNA molecules are not repaired, and can replicate, leading to dangerous forms of skin cancer (basal, squamous, and melanoma).

2.3 Solar Fluxes

Solar flux refers to the amount of solar energy in watts falling perpendicularly on a surface one square centimeter, and the units are watts per cm² per nm. Because of the strong absorption of UV radiation by ozone in the stratosphere, the intensity decreases at lower altitudes in the atmosphere. In addition, while the energy of an individual photon is greater if it has a shorter wavelength, there are fewer photons at the shorter wavelengths, so the Sun's total energy output is less at the shorter wavelengths. Because of ozone, it is virtually impossible for solar ultraviolet to penetrate to Earth's surface. For radiation with a wavelength of 290 nm, the intensity at Earth's surface is 350 million times weaker than at the top of the atmosphere. If our eyes detected light at less than 290 nm instead of in the visible range, the world would be very dark because of the ozone absorption!

2.4 UV Radiation and the Screening Action by Ozone

To appreciate how important this ultraviolet radiation screening is, we can consider a characteristic of radiation damage called an action spectrum. An action spectrum gives us a measure of the relative effectiveness of radiation in generating a certain biological response over a range of wavelengths. This response might be erythema (sunburn), changes in plant growth, or changes in molecular DNA. Fortunately, where DNA is easily damaged (where there is a high probability), ozone strongly absorbs UV. At the longer wavelengths where ozone absorbs weakly, DNA damage is less likely. If there was a 10% decrease in ozone, the amount of DNA damaging UV would increase by about 22%. Considering that DNA damage can lead to maladies like skin cancer, it is clear that this absorption of the Sun's ultraviolet radiation by ozone is critical for our well-being.

While most of the ultraviolet radiation is absorbed by ozone, some does make it to Earth's surface. Typically, we classify ultraviolet radiation into three parts, UV-a (320-400 nm), UV-b (280-320 nm), and UV-c (200-280 nm). Sunscreens have been developed by commercial manufacturers to protect human skin from UV radiation. The labels of these sunscreens usually note that they screen both UV-a and UV-b. Why not also screen for UV-c radiation? When UV-c encounters ozone in the mid-stratosphere, it is quickly absorbed so that none reaches Earth's surface. UV-b is partially absorbed and UV-a is barely absorbed by ozone. Ozone is so effective at absorbing the extremely harmful UV-c that sunscreen manufacturers don't need to worry about UV-c. Manufacturers only need to eliminate skin absorption of damaging UV-b and less damaging UV-a radiation.

The screening of ultraviolet radiation by ozone depends on other factors, such as time of day and season. The angle of the Sun in the sky has a large effect on the UV radiation. When the Sun is directly overhead, the UV radiation comes straight down through our atmosphere and is only absorbed by overhead ozone. When the Sun is just slightly above the horizon at dawn and dusk, the UV radiation must pass through the atmosphere at an angle. Because the UV passes through a longer distance in the atmosphere, it encounters more ozone molecules and there is greater absorption and, consequently, less UV radiation striking the surface.

[adapted from NASA's Stratospheric Ozone Electronic Textbook, http://www.ccpo.odu.edu/SEES/ozone/oz_class.htm]

What should you do, faced with this dense text? How can you turn it into an information set that is 'learnable'?

One tried-and-true piece of advice is to find the 'main idea' in each paragraph. But this is rarely as straightforward as it sounds, and many students find this too difficult. They might instead decide to take the first (or last) sentence of each paragraph. Let's look at the 'learnable points' (that is, a set of points that you can use for revision) that would be generated from such a strategy.

first-sentence summary

1. 90% of the ozone is in the stratosphere

2. the stratosphere is the region from about 10 to 50-km (32,000 to 164,000 feet) above Earth's surface

3. ozone concentrations are very small

4. ozone is vital because it absorbs harmful ultraviolet radiation from the Sun

5. human eyes can see only part of the spectrum: from about 400 nm to 700

6. Sun's radiation is mainly visible to us

7. Solar flux refers to the amount of solar energy in watts falling perpendicularly on a surface one square centimeter, and the units are watts per cm2 per nm. — definition

8. something called an action spectrum is a characteristic of radiation damage

9. most but not all UV radiation is absorbed by ozone

10. ozone's effectiveness depends on time of day and season

last-sentence summary

1. ozone concentrations are greatest between about 15 and 30 km

[presumably above the Earth's surface]

2. reduction of ozone layer would increase UV-b radiation reaching the surface

3. UV-b radiation causes genetic damage to living things

4. The energy of a tiny piece or 'packet' of radiation (which we call a photon) is inversely proportional to its wavelength. — definition

5. Radiation with wavelengths shorter than those of violet light is called ultraviolet radiation. — definition

6. the damage to DNA can usually be fixed, but when it isn't it can lead to skin cancer

7. only UV-b, and to a lesser extent UV-a, matter

There are 10 paragraphs (not counting the introductory one) in the original text. A 'main idea' summary would therefore be presumed to produce 10 learnable points, which indeed is what the first-sentence summary produces. The last-sentence summary, on the other hand, only produces 7 learnable points, because the last sentences in three of the paragraphs produced no learnable point (that is, they contained no important information). This suggests that the first-sentence summary is 'better', but think about this: if both sets of learnable points provide important information, then if you only have one point from each paragraph, you must be missing some important information.

So let's try instead to pick out the most important sentences regardless of where they are in the text, and not restricting ourselves to only one in each paragraph:

• By screening out genetically destructive ultraviolet radiation from the Sun, ozone protects life on the surface of Earth.

• About 90% of the ozone in our atmosphere is contained in the stratosphere, the region from about 10 to 50-km (32,000 to 164,000 feet) above Earth's surface.

• Ten percent of the ozone is contained in the troposphere, the lowest part of our atmosphere

- ozone concentrations are greatest between about 15 and 30 km.

- ozone molecules are vitally important to life because they absorb the biologically harmful ultraviolet radiation from the Sun. There are 3 different types of ultraviolet (UV) radiation, based on the wavelength of the radiation. These are referred to as UV-a, UV-b, and UV-c.

- It is the UV-b radiation that can cause sunburn and that can also cause genetic damage,

- In contrast to beneficial stratospheric ozone, tropospheric ozone is a pollutant found in high concentrations in smog.

- The high reactivity of ozone results in damage to the living tissue of plants and animals.

- The Sun produces radiation at many different wavelengths.

- EM radiation is classified by wavelength, which is a measure of how energetic is the radiation.

- The energy of a tiny piece or 'packet' of radiation (which we call a photon) is inversely proportional to its wavelength.

- The human eye can detect wavelengths in the region of the spectrum from about 400 nm (nanometers or billionths of a meter) to about 700 nm.

- Violet light has a wavelength of about 410 nm.

- Radiation with wavelengths shorter than those of violet light is called ultraviolet radiation.

- We are concerned about ultraviolet radiation because these rays are energetic enough to break the bonds of DNA molecules (the molecular carriers of our genetic coding), and thereby damage cells.

- Solar flux refers to the amount of solar energy in watts falling perpendicularly on a surface one square centimeter, and the units are watts per cm^2 per nm.

- An action spectrum gives us a measure of the relative effectiveness of radiation in generating a certain biological response over a range of wavelengths.

- If there was a 10% decrease in ozone, the amount of DNA damaging UV would increase by about 22%.

- we classify ultraviolet radiation into three parts, UV-a (320-400 nm), UV-b (280-320 nm), and UV-c (200-280 nm).

- When UV-c encounters ozone in the mid-stratosphere, it is quickly absorbed so that none reaches Earth's surface. UV-b is partially absorbed and UV-a is barely absorbed by ozone.

- The angle of the Sun in the sky has a large effect on the UV radiation.

Unfortunately, this still manages to occasionally miss out some important details that help us understand and remember. This is the problem with using verbatim text — the author doesn't always put the important information in the precise sentences you want; sometimes the information you want is spread across two or more sentences, but to include all the sentences that contain some useful nugget, you would end up with a text that's not that much shorter than your original text! No, your aim should be to get *all* the vital information, but *only* the vital information. To do that, you need to paraphrase.

Here's my paraphrased summary:

Ozone is important because it shields the surface from harmful ultraviolet radiation.

About 90% of the ozone in our atmosphere is contained in the stratosphere (the ozone layer), and 10% in the troposphere, the lowest part of our atmosphere where all of our weather takes place.

There are three different types of ultraviolet (UV) radiation, based on the wavelength of the radiation: UV-a (longest), UV-b, and UV-c (shortest). UV-c is entirely screened out by the ozone layer, and UV-a is not as damaging, so the main problem is UV-b.

Tropospheric ozone is a pollutant found in high concentrations in smog. The high reactivity of ozone results in damage to the living tissue of plants and animals, and is often felt as eye and lung irritation.

The Sun produces radiation at many different wavelengths. Electromagnetic radiation is classified by wavelength, which is a measure of how energetic is the radiation.

The visible part of the electromagnetic spectrum ranges from 400 nanometers to 700 nm. Red light has a wavelength of about 630 nm; violet light about 410 nm. Radiation with wavelengths shorter than those of violet light is called ultraviolet radiation.

Ultraviolet rays are energetic enough to break the bonds of DNA molecules, and thereby damage cells. While our bodies can repair this most of the time, sometimes damaged DNA molecules are not repaired, and can replicate, leading to skin cancer.

Solar flux refers to the amount of solar energy in watts falling perpendicularly on a surface one square centimeter, and the units are watts per cm^2 per nm. The strong absorption of UV radiation in the ozone layer reduces the intensity of solar energy at lower altitudes. More energetic photons (ones with shorter wavelengths) are also less common.

The action spectrum measures the relative effectiveness of radiation in generating a certain biological response (such as sunburn) over a range of wavelengths. Because ozone is most protective on the most dangerous wavelengths, a 10% decrease in ozone would increase the amount of DNA-damaging UV by about 22%.

Time and season affect how much UV radiation is absorbed by ozone because the angle of the sun affects how long the radiation takes to pass through the atmosphere (the path is shorter when the sun is directly overhead, so the radiation meets fewer ozone molecules).

This is still quite lengthy (380 words compared to our original text of 1400 words), but now that we have all the important information, we can turn it into a good learnable set. To do that, you need to reduce the summary further, and the more you already know about the topic, the more you can reduce it. Here's my learnable set, assuming a little knowledge of electromagnetic radiation:

- Ozone is important because it shields the surface from harmful ultraviolet radiation.

- The stratosphere holds 90% of the ozone in our atmosphere (the ozone layer).

- The troposphere holds 10%.

- The ozone layer protects us; tropospheric ozone is a pollutant found in high concentrations in smog.

- Radiation with wavelengths shorter than those of violet light (at the short end of the visible spectrum) is called ultraviolet radiation. UV waves are dangerous because they're energetic enough to break the bonds of DNA molecules.

- Of the three different types of ultraviolet (UV) radiation, the shortest (UV-c) is entirely screened out by the ozone layer, while the longest (UV-a) is not so damaging, so the main problem is UV-b.

- Because ozone is most protective on the most dangerous wavelengths, a 10% decrease in ozone would increase the amount of DNA-damaging UV by about 22%.

- Time and season affect how much UV radiation is absorbed by ozone because the angle of the sun affects how long the radiation takes to pass through the atmosphere (the path is shorter when the sun is directly overhead, so the radiation meets fewer ozone molecules).

- Measurement:

  - Solar flux = the amount of solar energy in watts falling perpendicularly on a surface one square centimeter.

  - The action spectrum measures the relative effectiveness of radiation in generating a certain biological response (such as sunburn) over a range of wavelengths.

We've now reduced our original text to a mere 240 words, and the learnable set can easily be transformed into a Q & A format, perfect for practice:

Q: Why is ozone important?

A: Because it shields the surface from harmful ultraviolet radiation.

Q: What proportion of the atmosphere's ozone is in the stratosphere?

A: 90%

Q: In the troposphere?

A: 10%

Q: Is ozone always protective?

A: No. The ozone layer protects us, but tropospheric ozone is a pollutant found in high concentrations in smog.

Q: What is ultraviolet radiation?

A: Radiation with wavelengths shorter than those of violet light (at the short end of the visible spectrum).

Q: Why is it dangerous?

A: Because it's energetic enough to break the bonds of DNA molecules.

Q: Which of the three different types of ultraviolet radiation is most dangerous and why?

A: UV-b. Because the shortest (UV-c) is entirely screened out by the ozone layer, and the longest (UV-a) is not so damaging.

Q: How much would a 10% decrease in ozone increase the amount of DNA-damaging UV?

A: By about 22%.

Q: Why does time of day and season affect how much UV radiation is absorbed by ozone?

A: Because the angle of the sun affects how long the radiation takes to pass through the atmosphere (the path is shorter when the sun is directly overhead, so the radiation meets fewer ozone molecules).

Q: What is solar flux?

A: The amount of solar energy in watts falling perpendicularly on a surface one square centimeter.

Q: What does the action spectrum measure?

A: The relative effectiveness of radiation in generating a certain biological response (such as sunburn) over a range of wavelengths.

Now, your learnable points may not be the same as the ones I've produced, because what's appropriate will depend on both your existing knowledge and your goals (affected by the extent of your interest in this topic, and the relevance of it to your other work and interests). But the point of this exercise is not to provide the 'correct' set of important points, but to demonstrate that the first and most important principle of effective practice is to work out exactly *what* you should be practicing, and to show that this isn't always intuitively obvious.

If you want more help with this very difficult skill, my books on note-taking cover this situation in considerable detail.

Points to remember

Effective practice matches the task you want to master.

The more specific the task, the easier it is to practice; the more general the task, the more varied your practice will need to be.

For complex text, you need to produce a set of learnable points for revision. This involves a 3-step process:

1. Highlight important information in the text that is unknown to you.

2. Re-organize and reduce the information, using your own words, to create a summary that succinctly captures what is important to you.

3. Transform your learnable set into a Q & A format.

Exercise 2.1

2.1 Produce a set of learnable points for the following text, using the first two steps of the 3-step process described above. (My own rendering produced 12 learnable points, but my points, which you can see in the Answers section, are provided as a guide only — remember that learnable points are based on what *you* need to learn.)

Theories About Motivation

William James (1842–1910) was an important contributor to early research into motivation, and he is often referred to as the father of psychology in the United States. James theorized that behavior was driven by a number of instincts, which aid survival. From a biological perspective, an instinct is a species-specific pattern of behavior that is not learned. There was, however, considerable controversy among James and his contemporaries over the exact definition of instinct. James proposed several dozen special human instincts, but many of his contemporaries had their own lists that differed. A mother's protection of her baby, the urge to lick sugar, and hunting prey were among the human behaviors proposed as true instincts during James's era. This view—that human behavior is driven by instincts—received a fair amount of criticism because of the undeniable role of learning in shaping all sorts of human behavior. In fact, as early as the 1900s, some instinctive behaviors were experimentally demonstrated to result from associative learning (recall when you learned about Watson's conditioning of fear response in "Little Albert") (Faris, 1921).

Another early theory of motivation proposed that the maintenance of homeostasis is particularly important in directing behavior. You may recall from your earlier reading that homeostasis is the tendency to maintain a balance, or optimal level, within a biological system. In a body system, a control center (which is often part of the brain) receives input from receptors (which are often complexes of neurons). The control center directs effectors (which may be other neurons) to correct any imbalance detected by the control center.

According to the drive theory of motivation, deviations from homeostasis create physiological needs. These needs result in psychological drive states that direct behavior to meet the need and, ultimately, bring the system back to homeostasis. For example, if it's been a while since you ate, your blood sugar levels will drop below normal. This low blood sugar will induce a physiological need and a corresponding drive state (i.e., hunger) that will direct you to seek out and consume food. Eating will eliminate the hunger, and, ultimately, your blood sugar levels will return to normal. Interestingly, drive theory also emphasizes the role that habits play in the type of behavioral response in which we engage. A habit is a pattern of behavior in which we regularly engage. Once we have engaged in a behavior that successfully reduces a drive, we are more likely to engage in that behavior whenever faced with that drive in the future (Graham & Weiner, 1996).

Extensions of drive theory take into account levels of arousal as potential motivators. As you recall from your study of learning, these theories assert that there is an optimal level of arousal that we all try to maintain. If we are underaroused, we become bored and will seek out some sort of stimulation. On the other hand, if we are overaroused, we will engage in behaviors to reduce our arousal (Berlyne, 1960). Most students have experienced this need to maintain optimal levels of arousal over the course of their academic career. Think about how much stress students experience toward the end of spring semester. They feel overwhelmed with seemingly endless exams, papers, and major assignments that must be completed on time. They probably yearn for the rest and relaxation that awaits them over the extended summer break. However, once they finish the semester, it doesn't take too long before they begin to feel bored. Generally, by the time the next semester is beginning in the fall, many students are quite happy to return to school. This is an example of how arousal theory works.

So what is the optimal level of arousal? What level leads to the best performance? Research shows that moderate arousal is generally best;

when arousal is very high or very low, performance tends to suffer (Yerkes & Dodson, 1908). Think of your arousal level regarding taking an exam for this class. If your level is very low, such as boredom and apathy, your performance will likely suffer. Similarly, a very high level, such as extreme anxiety, can be paralyzing and hinder performance. Consider the example of a softball team facing a tournament. They are favored to win their first game by a large margin, so they go into the game with a lower level of arousal and get beat by a less skilled team.

But optimal arousal level is more complex than a simple answer that the middle level is always best. Researchers Robert Yerkes (pronounced "Yerk-EES") and John Dodson discovered that the optimal arousal level depends on the complexity and difficulty of the task to be performed. This relationship is known as Yerkes-Dodson law, which holds that a simple task is performed best when arousal levels are relatively high and complex tasks are best performed when arousal levels are lower.

(excerpted from the OpenStax Psychology textbook, figures excluded. Download for free at https://cnx.org/contents/Sr8Ev5Og@12.2:MLADqXMi@11/10-1-Motivation)

Exercise 2.2

Produce a set of learnable points for the following text, using the first two steps of the 3-step process described above. (As a guide, my own rendering produced 12 learnable points.) Note that the figure included in this text is also part of the text.

Classifying Matter

Matter can be classified into several categories. Two broad categories are mixtures and pure substances. A pure substance has a constant composition. All specimens of a pure substance have exactly the same makeup and properties. Any sample of sucrose (table sugar) consists of 42.1% carbon, 6.5% hydrogen, and 51.4% oxygen by mass. Any sample of sucrose also has the same physical properties, such as melting point, color, and sweetness, regardless of the source from which it is isolated.

Pure substances may be divided into two classes: elements and compounds. Pure substances that cannot be broken down into simpler substances by chemical changes are called elements. Iron, silver, gold, aluminum, sulfur, oxygen, and copper are familiar examples of the more than 100 known elements, of which about 90 occur naturally on the earth, and two dozen or so have been created in laboratories.

Pure substances that can be broken down by chemical changes are called compounds. This breakdown may produce either elements or other compounds, or both. Mercury(II) oxide, an orange, crystalline solid, can be broken down by heat into the elements mercury and oxygen. When heated in the absence of air, the compound sucrose is broken down into the element carbon and the compound water. (The initial stage of this process, when the sugar is turning brown, is known as caramelization— this is what imparts the characteristic sweet and nutty flavor to caramel apples, caramelized onions, and caramel). Silver(I) chloride is a white solid that can be broken down into its elements, silver and chlorine, by absorption of light. This property is the basis for the use of this compound in photographic films and photochromic eyeglasses (those with lenses that darken when exposed to light).

The properties of combined elements are different from those in the free, or uncombined, state. For example, white crystalline sugar (sucrose) is a compound resulting from the chemical combination of the element carbon, which is a black solid in one of its uncombined forms, and the two elements hydrogen and oxygen, which are colorless gases when uncombined. Free sodium, an element that is a soft, shiny, metallic solid, and free chlorine, an element that is a yellow-green gas, combine to form sodium chloride (table salt), a compound that is a white, crystalline solid.

A mixture is composed of two or more types of matter that can be present in varying amounts and can be separated by physical changes, such as evaporation (you will learn more about this later). A mixture with a composition that varies from point to point is called a heterogeneous mixture. Italian dressing is an example of a heterogeneous mixture. Its composition can vary because it may be prepared from varying amounts of oil, vinegar, and herbs. It is not the same from point to point throughout the mixture—one drop may be mostly vinegar, whereas a different drop may be mostly oil or herbs because the oil and vinegar separate and the herbs settle. Other examples of heterogeneous mixtures are chocolate chip cookies (we can see the separate bits of chocolate, nuts, and cookie dough) and granite (we can see the quartz, mica, feldspar, and more).

A homogeneous mixture, also called a solution, exhibits a uniform composition and appears visually the same throughout. An example of a solution is a sports drink, consisting of water, sugar, coloring, flavoring, and electrolytes mixed together uniformly. Each drop of a sports drink tastes the same because each drop contains the same amounts of water, sugar, and other components. Note that the composition of a sports drink can vary—it could be made with somewhat more or less sugar, flavoring, or other components, and still be a sports drink. Other examples of homogeneous mixtures include air, maple syrup, gasoline, and a solution of salt in water.

Although there are just over 100 elements, tens of millions of chemical compounds result from different combinations of these elements. Each compound has a specific composition and possesses definite chemical and physical properties that distinguish it from all other compounds. And, of course, there are innumerable ways to combine elements and compounds to form different mixtures. A summary of how to distinguish between the various major classifications of matter is shown below.

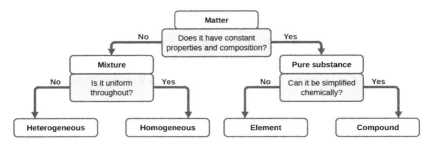

Eleven elements make up about 99% of the earth's crust and atmosphere. Oxygen constitutes nearly one-half and silicon about one-quarter of the total quantity of these elements. A majority of elements on earth are found in chemical combinations with other elements; about one-quarter of the elements are also found in the free state.

(excerpted from the OpenStax textbook, Chemistry: Atoms First 2e, some figures excluded. Download for free at https://openstax.org/books/chemistry-atoms-first-2e/pages/1-2-phases-and-classification-of-matter)

Principles of Retrieval Practice

In the following four chapters, I discuss the crucial strategy of retrieval practice in detail, describing how to do it effectively, how often you need to repeat your practice, and how you should space out your practice.

Retrieval practice

The reason for including 'revision' under the term 'practice' now becomes obvious. This chapter introduces the concept of 'retrieval practice' — the single most useful learning strategy there is. In this chapter, I explain what retrieval practice is and how it compares with other learning strategies. I also discuss whether mistakes matter.

I said earlier that effective practice matches the task you want to master. In the most general sense, the essence of that task is usually that you want to retrieve information from your long-term memory (the exception is if you are only interested in recognizing the correct information — recognition is a different process from retrieval). For the most part, though, when you practice or revise something, what you need to be doing is practicing retrieving the information. This is, unsurprisingly, called **retrieval practice**. The vital thing to remember is that it is not the same as repetition or rehearsal. The idea is not to simply *repeat* the correct information, but to try and *retrieve* it.

Clearly retrieval practice is a form of testing, and the effectiveness of retrieval practice as a means of learning is the main reason why repeated testing is valuable (far more clearly valuable than repeated testing as a means of assessment).

The basic memory principles I have discussed makes it clear why retrieval practice is so powerful — every time you retrieve the information, you make the trail to it stronger. But you must truly be retrieving it from long-term memory — if the information is still in working memory, you are simply keeping it active (in the same way that repeating a phone number to yourself keeps it in working memory), not retrieving it.

Retrieval practice is the single most powerful learning strategy there is.

By comparison, re-reading is the most common study strategy used by students, and about the worst strategy (for long-term learning) there is [3.1]. Re-reading is excellent at giving you the immediate *illusion* that you've learned the material. However, the material will be forgotten much more quickly, and is very unlikely to remain with you in the long term. (Which is why every student dreams of having a 'photographic' memory! The dream itself is an acknowledgement that reading a text is not sufficient for long-term memory.)

The problem is that re-reading a text makes it very familiar, and familiarity is the rule of thumb we use to judge whether we know something. So repeated reading leads you to strongly believe you'll remember the information. But if you have made no effort to test your ability to retrieve it, you really don't have any idea how hard that might be.

Retrieval practice cannot be the whole of your study strategy, however. There are aspects to its use — how many times you should retrieve the information to be learned; how often and how widely separated your retrieval sessions should be — that I'll discuss in later chapters, but there are also wider issues regarding how you choose what to practice, and the form in which you practice its retrieval.

Keyword mnemonic

In the previous chapter, I mentioned the keyword mnemonic. If you're learning another language, or new technical words, this is an excellent strategy to have at your hand. The essence of the keyword mnemonic (I discuss it later in more detail) lies in the choosing of an intermediary word that binds what you need to remember to something you already know well. So, to remember that the Spanish word *carta* means *letter* (the sort you post), you select an English word that sounds as close to *carta* as you can get, and you make a mental picture that links that word to the English meaning — for example, a letter in a cart.

Results from using the keyword method have been dramatic. For example, in the classic study, over a third of 120 Russian words were remembered more than 80% of the time in the keyword condition, compared to only *one* item in the control condition (*glaz* for *eye* — a mnemonic link so obvious I am sure most of the control participants used it even without explicit direction). Moreover, only seven words were remembered less than half the time in the keyword condition, compared to 70 in the control ("use your own method") condition! [3.2]

The keyword method is the most-studied mnemonic method there is, and there have been many experiments demonstrating its effectiveness, especially when measured against rote repetition, but also when compared with the popular context method (experiencing the word to be learned in several different meaningful contexts; guessing the meaning from the context) [3.3].

Retrieval practice has been shown to be as effective, and sometimes even better, than the keyword method. But more to the point, retrieval practice can make the keyword mnemonic substantially more effective. For example, in one study, using Swahili-English pairs, those who practiced retrieval of the keyword mnemonics performed almost *three times* better on the final test compared to those who simply 'studied' (i.e., read) the keyword mnemonics: 40% correct vs 14%. Further investigation revealed that a big advantage of using the two strategies together was that retrieval failures encouraged the students to come up with better keywords [3.4].

In other words, retrieval practice supports the keyword method not simply because the path to the keywords has become stronger, but also because failures during testing are likely to encourage you to create better keywords. When you practice retrieval, you can see whether the keyword is a good one for you; if you're having trouble remembering the keyword, you know to try and find a better one.

This advantage of retrieval practice extends beyond the keyword method, of course. When you test yourself, you give yourself the opportunity to see how hard the material is to remember. This shows you when you need to augment retrieval practice with other methods, such as the keyword method or concept mapping (below). Or, if you're already using such strategies, when you need to tweak (the keyword; the map) to make it more memorable.

It cannot be said often enough that students, when asked to use different strategies, almost always rate retrieval practice poorly. You cannot judge the value of a strategy by your feelings at the time of learning — our judgment on such matters rests on rules of thumb that include how familiar the material now feels and how quickly we recall it. But the information is not yet secured in long-term memory, and may never be. Until you've slept, you won't know if it has been consolidated into long-term memory, and until you've observed how quickly you can retrieve it from *long-term memory* (not working memory), you are in no position to assess how well you've learned it.

Concept maps

Another very effective learning strategy, for a different type of learning situation, involves constructing concept maps. A concept map is a diagram that attempts to show how facts and ideas are connected to each other, through the use of labeled nodes (representing concepts) and lines connecting them (showing the relationships between the concepts). You are no doubt familiar with one type of concept map — the mind map.

On the next page, you can see an example of a concept map (taken from *Effective notetaking*).

Research comparing concept maps and retrieval practice has found that, in general, retrieval practice produces better learning than concept mapping. That 'in general' is very important! One study comparing the two did what few studies do, and that is, it reported on individual differences. While the vast majority of students performed better after retrieval practice, a few benefited more from concept mapping [3.5]. This

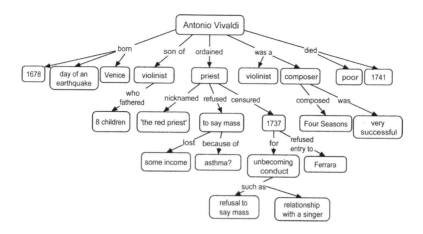

reminds us that however effective a strategy is in general, it's not necessarily the best strategy for everyone.

I would also like to emphasize that these results should certainly not be taken as a slur on concept mapping! Concept mapping is another study strategy I wholeheartedly recommend — but as with any strategy, you need to recognize when it is most useful. I believe the greatest value of concept mapping is to help you gain understanding of a complex topic, and I go into that in great detail in my book *Effective Notetaking*. However, I also believe it has value as an adjunct strategy with retrieval practice, as the keyword mnemonic has. Creating a concept map *without reference to the text* is a very useful form of retrieval practice for complex information.

Mnemonics & concept mapping can support retrieval practice

The big advantage of retrieval practice is of course that it is a very simple, easily learned technique. It also requires much less cognitive effort than, say, the keyword mnemonic, which puts many people off because of the difficulty of finding good keywords, and the effort (which is greater for some than for others) of creating images.

But this is not an either/or situation. In the case of learning new vocabulary, for example, the most effective strategy is to combine retrieval practice and the keyword mnemonic, using the principles of effective retrieval practice in conjunction with the keyword mnemonic, as needed. By 'as needed', I mean that you shouldn't feel the need to use the keyword mnemonic with every word. The effectiveness of retrieval practice on its own is sufficient for many words, and the effort of creating keywords is too great for many people to bother with using the mnemonic unless the word is of proven difficulty to remember. I will discuss this in more detail later.

Similarly, concept mapping can also be used very effectively as a retrieval practice technique. Again, I will discuss this in a later chapter.

Do note the difference between these types of support! Retrieval practice increases the effectiveness of the keyword mnemonic; concept mapping can be used as a method of retrieval practice.

But you can use the keyword mnemonic as a method of retrieval practice — all you need to do is try to come up the keywords without looking at the material you want to learn. Of course, you can only do that once! But, for variety, it is something you could do. While retrieval practice at its most effective, and cognitively demanding, involves free recall (retrieving the information in response to no more cues than the question asking for the information), there are other forms of retrieval practice. Essentially, any method that involves memory recall without looking at the information you're trying to remember, can be a form of retrieval practice.

In fact, there is one technique that is probably more commonly used than free recall: multi-choice practice quizzing. This is common in classrooms and textbooks, where students are given short multiple-choice quizzes.

A less-commonly used strategy is that of test-generation, where you read a text and try to come up with appropriate test questions about it. As long as you do this without looking at the text, this becomes a retrieval practice strategy.

A study compared these four retrieval-based strategies (free recall; multi-choice practice quiz; test-generation; keyword mnemonic) using a 275-word reading comprehension passage (Bae et al. 2019). For the keyword strategy, students were asked to write down a list of five keywords that captured the main ideas of the text.

Based on previous research, the free recall and multi-choice quizzing were expected to be more effective than the last two, and this is indeed what was found. But it's worth noting some of the finer points.

The strategies were compared in a process that involved the students being given seven minutes to read the text, a two-minute multiplication filler task, then another seven minutes to read the text, another filler task, then seven minutes to spend on the retrieval-based strategy, then another filler task. The final test was given a week later.

However, there's a twist. In some conditions, the students had a free recall test in place of the second study period. That meant that not only were the four strategies directly compared on the basis of a single retrieval session, but they were also compared as an adjunct to the free-recall strategy, in a repeated retrieval situation.

Interestingly, there was no benefit for the free-recall retrieval practice in repeating it (in such close proximity to the first instance, and without any feedback). But, while free recall was the most effective of the four strategies in the single retrieval condition, having a multi-choice quiz as the second retrieval session produced the best results of all. In the single-retrieval conditions, test-generation was the least effective retrieval strategy, but as the second session strategy, it did as well as free-recall, and slightly better than the keyword strategy.

All of this should not be taken to mean that the best strategy for you is always to use free recall, followed on later sessions by multi-choice quizzes — although this is a good general approach. But test-generation tends to be hampered by a student's low level of expertise with the topic. It may well be that, if the students had been tested with material that was more familiar to them, they might have done better using that strategy. Similarly, the keyword mnemonic takes practice — students more skilled with its use might have done better with it.

And variety is useful. You will learn better if you are more engaged with the process. Doing the same thing all the time is not engaging. So it is good to have several retrieval-based practice strategies in your toolbox, that you can apply in appropriate situations, and especially when you need a bit of a change to help motivate you.

Benefits for related information

Basically, retrieval practice is about testing yourself. There are two intriguing and unexpected aspects to this testing. One is that it can be of some benefit even when you get no feedback about whether your answer is right or wrong (but of course it's much more effective with feedback). Another is that it can improve your memory for untested material, as long as that untested information is related to the material you've practiced retrieving or appears in close proximity to it in the text.

This, however, only works if you search your mind for related information when retrieving. If you keep a narrow focus on the exact question, retrieval benefits tend to be restricted just to the information retrieved. This is also reflected in time taken — if you're focusing on retrieving information quickly, you probably won't gain related benefits.

For example, a text used in a study exploring this issue included the following paragraph [3.6]:

> But there is one thing they cannot use the large bill for: the construction of tree holes. toucans need such holes for nesting and raising their young. Although they are closely related to woodpeckers, they are not able to construct such holes. toucans depend on natural tree holes or holes constructed by other animals. When toucans sleep, they turn their head so that their long bill rests on their back and their tail is folded over their head. The bird becomes a ball of feathers. Often found in abandoned tree hollows or old woodpecker holes, five or six adults may sleep in one hole!

In this example, the question "Where do toucans sleep at night?" was related to "What other bird species is the toucan related to?" because toucans sleep in the holes created by woodpeckers.

While most related pairs appeared in the same paragraph of the article, knowing the answer to one question wouldn't of itself tell you the answer to the other. Students needed to search their minds for related material in order to gain the wider benefit of having practiced retrieving one of these related facts.

Errorless learning

There's an idea you may have heard of — that retrieving the wrong answer will actively harm your learning. There is some truth in this. Certainly if you repeatedly practice the wrong behavior, or repeatedly call forth the same incorrect answer, you're strengthening something that will interfere with acquiring the correct information or behavior. However, research has shown that a *single* instance of retrieving the wrong information only prevents correct retrieval within a brief time-frame. As long as there's a day's delay between the retrieval practice and the final test, it isn't an issue. (The delay necessary is probably less than that, but we have to go with the comparisons investigated. We know such forgetting can be observed when the test is up to 20 minutes after the retrieval practice; we know it isn't observed when there's a 24-hour delay.)

Additionally, such forgetting of the correct response doesn't occur if you make multiple connections between list items (which is what naturally occurs when you're working through a text — you make multiple connections between the facts and ideas in the text). It's also reduced if you engage in distinctive processing for each word (such as thinking about how it's different from the other words).

In other words, if you integrate your information (as you do when reading a text), or if some time elapses between your retrieval practice and testing, then a single instance of retrieving the wrong answer shouldn't be an issue.

This sort of relational processing is more likely if your learning is motivated by mastery goals, rather than performance goals. With mastery, your goal is to develop your own competence. Performance goals, on the other hand, are more along the lines of "I need to learn this to pass the exam", "I want to get in the top third of the class".

Supporting this, a series of three experiments found that there was no significant retrieval-induced forgetting in a mastery-approach goal condition, but there was in the performance-approach goal condition (Ikeda et al. 2015).

Mastery goals do encourage deeper learning, but that doesn't mean it's always the best approach. When you're taking a number of different subjects, it's too much to apply a mastery approach to all of them. Even within a subject, there are going to be topics that are best approached in a more pragmatic "I need to know this, but no more" way.

So, in the same way that you should have several effective study strategies that you apply appropriately in a considered way, rather than a single go-to strategy, so you should approach your learning in a strategic way, with different goals for different subjects and topics.

And although relational processing is linked with mastery goals, and item-specific processing with performance goals, a thoughtful approach can combine relational processing with performance goals, when appropriate.

Moreover, even in the case where you are learning something like word pairs (such as when practicing foreign vocabulary), 'retrieval-induced forgetting' only seems to occur when items are presented in a random order during retrieval practice. If the same order is maintained during practice as occurred during the original presentation (even if there are gaps from omitted items), then the effect doesn't occur.

In other words, retrieval-induced forgetting, which is used to justify an errorless learning strategy, only appears to occur in a narrow set of circumstances:

- when your learning — retrieval practice and testing — occurs within a very short time period

- when you don't make any attempts to understand or elaborate the material to be learned

- when you practice by mixing up the order of your items (note that this is generally a good idea, just not when the first two factors are in play).

There's also another factor:

* when you're not receiving immediate feedback.

Forced guessing

One question students and teachers often wonder about is whether it's a bad idea to force a guess (that is, even when you have absolutely no idea of the correct answer). A study that explored this question found that forcing a guess did *not* significantly impair learning [3.7].

This result was found both when immediate feedback was offered, and when feedback wasn't offered until the end of the test.

One potentially important factor in these experiments is that, if people are being forced to guess, they probably are well aware that their guesses are likely to be wrong. This is a very different situation from making errors that you genuinely believe are correct. (Note, for example, that in this study only 36% of questions answered wrongly on the first test were corrected on the second.)

Nevertheless, for our purposes here, one thing is clear: guessing, even though it produces incorrect information, doesn't significantly harm learning, and this remains true even when feedback is a little delayed.

However, it's possible that learning tasks that rely heavily on familiarity (such as multi-choice tests that only require recognition) might be more badly affected by errors.

Points to remember

Testing can involve recognition or retrieval. A multi-choice test, for example, involves recognition of the correct answer. A short-answer test requires you to retrieve the correct information from your memory.

Retrieval practice is a study strategy in which you practice retrieving the information from your long-term memory.

In comparison with other study strategies, retrieval practice has consistently been shown to be more effective.

Popularity is generally in inverse relation to effectiveness! The most popular study strategy is re-reading. While this may appear effective at the time, information studied this way is forgotten much faster over time.

Concept mapping *when used in the presence of the text* appears to produce no better learning than re-reading.

The keyword method is a very effective strategy for certain types of information, most particularly for learning vocabulary. It is far superior to rote repetition. However, retrieval practice seems to be even better. Best of all is probably to combine retrieval practice with judicious use of the keyword method.

Individual differences always matter — even though retrieval practice may be the most effective study strategy for most students, some individuals will find another strategy, such as concept mapping, superior. Even so, they would probably find combining their preferred method with retrieval practice even more effective.

Retrieval practice can have benefits that extend beyond the exact information practiced, to information that is related or appears in close proximity to the information practiced. However, this only applies if you spend some time searching your mind for related information, when retrieving.

In certain circumstances, making errors when retrieving can corrupt your memory code (which is rebuilt every time you retrieve it), but this effect is mainly restricted to physical skill learning and simple, relatively meaningless information (such as lists of words). Even then, the effects can be countered by the use of appropriate feedback and practice schedules.

Review Questions

1. Retrieval practice means

   a. rote repetition

   b. re-reading

   c. learning to recognize the correct answer

   d. repeatedly retrieving the correct information from long-term memory

2. The best means of judging how well you've learned information is by how familiar it seems.   Y / N

3. Which strategy is, in general, the most effective for memorizing new vocabulary?

   a. retrieval practice

   b. concept mapping

   c. concept mapping with retrieval practice

   d. rote repetition

   e. keyword mnemonic

   f. keyword mnemonic with retrieval practice

4. Which strategy is, in general, the most effective for learning and remembering complex material

   a. retrieval practice

   b. concept mapping

   c. concept mapping with retrieval practice

   d. rote repetition

   e. keyword mnemonic

   f. keyword mnemonic with retrieval practice

5. Retrieval practice involves

   a. retrieving the same answers to the same cues in the same order over and over again until you get them right

b. varying the cues and their order

c. monitoring the speed and accuracy of your answers, and improving the connections you've made where necessary

d. retrieving the information as quickly as you can, so you don't have a chance to forget the correct response

e. spacing out your practice so you're sure you're retrieving from long-term memory

6. Retrieval practice only works if you

a. get immediate feedback on whether your answer is correct

b. focus on the precise question

c. search your mind for information that is conceptually related or appeared together in the text

d. make it easy enough that you always know the correct answer

e. allow enough time and activity to pass to have pushed the information out of working memory

f. don't guess

7. Retrieval practice works best if you

a. get immediate feedback on whether your answer is correct

b. focus on the precise question

c. search your mind for information that is conceptually related or appeared together in the text

d. make it easy enough that you always know the correct answer

e. don't guess

8. Retrieving the wrong answer interferes with your learning

a. always

b. only if you do it repeatedly

c. if it happens just before a test

d. when you don't understand the material

e. when you don't receive immediate (or slightly delayed) feedback

How often should you practice?

In this brief chapter, I get down to some of the practical aspects of practicing effectively: in particular, the number of times you should practice retrieving an item, both within a learning session and across sessions.

First and foremost among the questions of how to practice effectively is this one: how often do I need to practice? There are two parts to the answer:

- how often you should practice during your first study session

- how many times you should give yourself practice tests after that.

Criterion levels set the number of correct retrievals

Let's start the discussion with a bit of jargon — the concept of 'criterion level'. In psychology experiments, this refers to a specific level of performance that the participant must reach before moving on. In learning experiments, it usually means that the participant must correctly retrieve the information a certain number of times before they are judged to have 'learned' it.

Do pay special attention to that phrase '*correctly* retrieve'! Previously, learning research has tended to vary the number of retrieval *attempts*. Similarly, many students have some rule, such as repeating an item three times. But the vital part of this concept is that *only the correct retrievals count*.

Task difficulty affects optimal criterion level

A couple of studies have played with different criterion levels in an attempt to work out the best number of correct retrievals for efficient learning. In research involving the learning of Lithuanian words, the biggest gains came from having two correct retrievals rather than only one, but the learning benefits continued with each additional correct retrieval, up to four [4.1].

However (and unsurprisingly), the benefits of repeated retrievals were greater for more difficult tasks. Simply recognizing correct English-Lithuanian pairs, for example, is a much easier task than recalling the English word when presented with the Lithuanian, or, (hardest of all), recalling the Lithuanian when presented with the English.

It's also worth noting that in the latter case, although performance plateaued at four correct retrievals (meaning that further retrievals didn't appreciably improve learning), recall was at a much lower level than it was when the student only had to recall the English in response to the Lithuanian. It is in precisely these circumstances that the keyword mnemonic comes into its own.

However, the optimal criterion level isn't only a matter of what theoretically produces the best learning. You also need to take account of the boredom factor. The returns of additional criterion levels may not be great enough to justify the increase in boredom (another reason to use something like the keyword mnemonic, which may add interest, when more practice is needed). This is important because the more boring an activity, the less likely it is that you will repeat it (or pay proper attention to it, if you do). "So much and no more" should be your watchword.

Individual items may demand different criterion levels

This principle is something you should take to heart, and apply to individual items. For example, say you were learning the following German words:

1. der Apfel

2. der Spinat

3. der Kürbis

4. der Kopfsalat

5. der Fisch

6. die Banane

7. die Karotte

8. die Kartoffel

9. die Zitrone

10. die Tomate

Some of these have very obvious English counterparts: Apfel—apple; Spinat—spinach; Fisch—fish; Banane—banana; Karotte—carrot; Tomate—tomato.

Others are less obvious: Kürbis; Kopfsalat; Kartoffel; Zitrone. But Zitrone, meaning lemon, becomes clearer once you replace the 'z' with 'c' — citron, citrus fruit, citric acid. Similarly, if you know the word 'dummkopf!', then you won't find it hard to remember that 'Kopf' is head, and the meaning of 'lettuce' for 'Kopfsalat' (salad head) is quite easy. Kürbis (pumpkin) and Kartoffel (potato), on the other hand, are much less obviously related to their English counterparts.

It seems clear, then, that some of these words are almost a case of recognition, and a criterion level of two correct retrievals should be quite sufficient when that is the case. However, more difficult items should be given a higher criterion level, such as four.

When material is very difficult, an even higher criterion level may be necessary — in which case, you should consider drafting in an additional strategy, such as a mnemonic or mapping technique, to assist.

How do you manage these different criterion levels in the context of a list? The most obvious way is to group your words in terms of the criterion level you've set. Another possibility, if you're using software that can manage it, is to set a default level, but set exceptions for those items that seem particularly easy or difficult.

Individual differences matter

On the subject of individual differences in learning abilities, it's worth noting that results from nearly a quarter of the students in the Lithuanian-words experiment were excluded (32 out of 131) because the students failed to reach a sufficiently high level of performance. In other words, individual differences matter! So these criterion levels are only guides — you need to work out your own optimal levels (taking into account boredom level as well as performance).

How many times should you review?

One way to cope with high criterion levels is through distribution over learning sessions, which brings us to our second question: how many times should you test yourself on the material after that first study session?

That is quite a complicated question as it interacts with another critical factor, namely spacing (which is discussed in the next chapter). But one study has given us an excellent starting point [4.2].

This study included three experiments in which students learned short texts via retrieval practice. The short texts contained eight key terms and their definitions.

In contrast to the Lithuanian-words study, these findings were very clear that going to 4 was wasted effort. I suggest that this has to do with difficulty level. The huge advantage coherent text has over foreign vocabulary is that it makes more sense. As I've discussed many times elsewhere, meaningful information (if you understand it) is much easier to remember than relatively arbitrary information (such as individual words).

But here's what's really interesting: on the six-week test, criterion level made no substantial difference on how well the information was remembered (recall was around 40% at all levels). This suggests that, as long as you remember to carry out revision sessions, you don't need to worry so much about the number of correct retrieval attempts on the first study session.

Having said that, items that had been correctly recalled more than once were re-learned faster than words that had only been correctly recalled once, but there was no significant advantage to having a criterion level greater than two.

How did the review sessions affect learning?

A second experiment showed very clearly the advantage to having three revision sessions rather than just one. Average recall on the final test was less than 40% for items that only had one re-learning session, compared to over 50% for those that had three re-learning sessions. You may think that sounds low, but note that recall of those items that were not revised at all was below 10%!

This experiment also showed a clear benefit to having a criterion level of three compared with only one.

Recommended schedule

What all this shows clearly is that having review sessions is much more important than your criterion level in that initial study session. Nevertheless, the researchers of this study recommended that **students practice recalling concepts to an initial criterion of three correct recalls and then relearn them three times at widely spaced intervals**.

One reason for this recommendation is the protection it gives if you fail to revise on schedule. Additionally, an analysis of total practice trials over all sessions (remember that on each session, the student has to correctly recall an item before it disappears) revealed that a 3 × 3 schedule required fewer retrieval attempts than other schedules producing similar levels of performance. In other words, it was the most efficient schedule if you're weighing time spent against results.

Again, it's worth noting that, across these experiments, some students' results were excluded from analysis either because they were so much better than the others or because they were so much worse. This emphasizes that group studies can only reveal so much — they are guides, not rules. In this context, it's also important to note that these were psychology students studying psychology texts, so the experience was confounded with learning outside the experiment. Indeed, the students reported having met around half the items in class.

One final point: performance on multi-choice tests was little affected by any of this. Multi-choice tests only require recognition, not recall, which is a much easier task.

Points to remember

In your first study session, you should practice retrieving the information a certain number of times. Once is not enough! Three is a good rule of thumb.

Similarly, three is a good rule of thumb for the number of times you subsequently review the information.

Unsuccessful retrieval attempts do not count!

Because you want to avoid getting too bored, it's helpful to have some flexibility about the number of retrievals. Easy material can be limited to two successful retrievals, while harder material should have more.

As always, individual needs will vary — these numbers are a guide, not a rule.

Review Questions

1. 'Criterion level' refers to

   a. the number of times you should repeat the information to be learned

   b. how often you should correctly retrieve the information to be learned

   c. how often you should try to recall the information

   d. repeating your attempts until you get it right

2. The best criterion level

   a. is 2 correct retrievals

   b. is 3 correct retrievals

   c. depends on how difficult the task is

   d. depends on whether you're trying to memorize words, simple facts, or complex information

   e. depends on how difficult you find the task and the material

3. If you have 12 items to learn, and a criterion level of 3, then

   a. you will have a total of 36 retrievals in a session

   b. you will have 48 retrievals in a session

   c. you will have 24 retrievals in a session

   d. you will have at least 36 retrievals in a session

4. Select the most difficult task in each pair

   a. (i) recalling facts vs
   (ii) recognizing the correct answer in a multi-choice test

   b. (i) knowing the English words in response to a list of words in a closely related language vs
   (ii) recalling words in a language unrelated to your own

   c. (i) filling in correct words in spaces in a complex text vs
   (ii) writing a short essay without reference to the text

5. Criterion level can be thought of as within a session only, or within and across sessions.   Y / N

6. Pick which statement is correct

   a. You should use the 'rule of 3'.

   b. You should use the 'rule of 3' as a guide, but be flexible how you apply it.

   c. You should find the best criterion level for you and stick with it.

Spacing your practice

Timing is one of the key tenets of effective retrieval practice. In this chapter, I look at the amount of time you should have between initial study and review, and between subsequent reviews.

Let's begin by establishing that spaced practice is far more effective than massed practice. I'd like to think that everyone knows that, but it's an idea that has taken a while to gain traction in education, and indeed has still not changed many traditional practices that should be changed.

The advantage of spreading out your practice

Since research has shown that most students do not appreciate the power of spacing, let's touch briefly on the 1978 study that first brought this to everyone's attention [5.1]. The study aimed to find the best way of teaching postmen to type. The postmen followed one of four schedules:

- an intensive schedule of two 2-hour daily sessions

- two intermediate schedules involving two hours a day, either as one 2-hour session, or two 1-hour sessions

- a more gradual schedule of one hour a day.

The researchers found quite dramatic differences in learning, with the 1-hour-a-day group learning as much in 55 hours as the 4-hour-a-day group in 80. Moreover, the 1-hour-a-day group remembered their skills better when tested several months later.

But (and this goes a long way to explain just why there's been so much resistance to this simple, now well-established principle), the gradual group were the least happy with the program — for although they learned much more quickly in terms of hours, it took them many more days (80 hours at four hours a day is 20 days, but 55 hours at one hour a day is 55 days).

There's an important message in that, but it's one that's more important for some people than others — for those who need quick returns to stay focused, or if the specific task is one in which you need to see quick returns. This is another aspect where you need to take into account your own personality and circumstance. However, you can take advantage of spacing's benefits without dragging things out so much.

As I've said, the evidence for the benefits of spaced over massed practice is overwhelming, and I'm not going to review three decades' worth of it. Particularly because most of it hasn't done much to tell us what we really want to know — namely, what's the best spacing for learning.

Optimal spacing

On that question, a very large study has finally given us something to work with [5.2]. This study (which took place on the internet, enabling the researchers to have a very diverse range of more than 1350 participants) compared a wide range of intervals between the initial learning session and the second review session (3 minutes; one day; 2 days; 4 days; 7 days; 11 days; 14 days; 21 days; 35 days; 70 days; 105 days), and a range of intervals between the review and the test (7 days; 35 days; 70 days; 350 days). The information learned was 32 obscure facts. Testing included both a recall test and a recognition (multi-choice) test.

What was found? Well, first of all, the benefits of having a longer space before review were quite significant, much larger than had been seen in earlier research when shorter intervals had been used. For example, if you were being tested two or three months after your review, reviewing the material three weeks after learning it would more than *double* the amount you remember, compared to reviewing it immediately after learning (this is an average, of course, and individual performance will vary).

Secondly, at any given test delay, longer intervals between initial study session and review session first improved test performance, then gradually reduced it. In other words, there was an optimal interval between study and review.

In the tables below, you can see which review interval was best for each test delay period, and how much it improved performance (compared to a review interval of three minutes). The first table shows the situation for recall; the second for recognition.

Days until test	Optimal gap before review (days)	Improvement in recall
7	1	10%
35	11	59%
70	21	111%
350	21	77%

Days until test	Optimal gap before review (days)	Improvement in recognition
7	1	1%
35	7	10%
70	7	31%
350	21	60%

See how the optimal review gap increases as test delay increases, but plateaus at certain points (this simplifies the situation of course — if you're serious about study, you're going to review it more than once!).

Note, too, that the benefits are different for recognition than for recall. For a start, and unsurprisingly, the benefits are much greater for recall than for recognition (recognition being so much easier than recall, there's much less room for improvement, especially when the test is only a week after the review).

For recognition, the greatest impact was experienced when the test was 350 days after review: reviewing at the optimal gap of 21 days produced a 60% improvement in performance — meaning that performance on the multi-choice test rose from an average of around 44% to a very respectable 70%. But the greatest benefit was seen for recall at the 70-day test delay — a dramatic 111% for those who reviewed after 21 days (an increase from a test score of around 30% to over 60%!).

Overall, and given a fixed amount of study time, the optimal gap improved recall by an average of 64% and recognition by 26%. What this means in practical terms is that if you reviewed only once, at the end of your initial study session, and ended up getting 40% on your end-of-semester exam, then, by instead reviewing the material one week after your study session, you'd boost your exam score to a very creditable 65%! A significant difference indeed. (This figure is of course an average, and I must note again that individual experiences will vary.)

Having established which of the review intervals used in the experiment were best, the researchers then estimated what the ideal intervals would really be. They came up with these:

Days until test	Optimal review gap for recall (days)	Optimal review gap for recognition (days)
7	3	1.6
35	8	7
70	12	10
350	27	25

This suggests that, if your exam is in about three months, you should review the material about two weeks after your initial study; if you want to remember the material next year, you should review it after about a month.

One caveat: while the actual results fit very nicely on the imaginary lines used to produce the estimates for test delays of 7, 35, and 350 days, the results fit less well for the test delay of 70 days. This is due to one data point: performance on the 70-day test when the review had been at 14 days was unexpectedly low. As a consequence, the discrepancy between the optimal gap produced by the participants and the estimated optimal gap is much greater for the 70-day test than it is for the other test delays — 21 days vs 12. Other research (below) suggests that 12 days is indeed too short, and that 21 days is more accurate.

The need for review

Although it wasn't the focus of the study, let's take a moment to note how much recall falls after a year. In the situation where there's a 20-day gap between learning and review, those tested seven days later got pretty nearly everything right; those tested after 35 days got a very respectable average of around 80%; those tested after 70 days (about a school term) got about 60%; but those tested after a year were only hitting around 20%.

In other words, if you don't review, or only review once, you're not likely to remember the material by next year.

This may not matter to you, of course, if you're only concerned with passing an exam and have no intention of studying any further in the area. Equally, if the information is truly important, then you would expect it to keep being used and built on, being part of a 'natural review' process. Unfortunately, this is not always (or even mostly) the case. It depends on the structure of your curriculum and how extensive your reading is. In the absence of 'natural review', more direct measures are clearly called for.

What all this emphasizes is that the common educational practice of concentrating topics tightly into short periods of time is not a strategy that is likely to produce long-lasting learning. While it might look as if you've mastered the material when you take a section-end test, chances are that you won't hold on to a lot of this information (unless you review it).

Stretching the review interval

The research also makes clear that the cost of using a review interval that is longer than the optimal gap is decidedly less than the cost of using a shorter gap — in other words, it's better to space your learning out over a too-long interval than a too-short one.

This is supported in another, more typical, experiment. The first experiment in this set of experiments involved students learning 40 Swahili words, and varied the gap between the first study session and the review session from 5 minutes to two weeks (and included 1, 2, 4, and 7 days). The test was ten days after the review session.

The difference between a 5-minute review gap and a one-day gap was dramatic, with recall improving from around 55% to 74%. There was little difference in having review gaps greater than a day (bear in mind the final test took place only 10 days later).

This confirms the findings of the internet study — a one-day review gap is optimal when the time until test is around a week — but this study shows a much greater benefit to that review. The difference may have to do with the learning material, which is less meaningful (and thus more easily forgotten) than the facts that were used in the large internet study.

In the second experiment, the researchers used the same sort of obscure facts used in the internet study (e.g., "Who invented snow golf?") as well as names of unfamiliar objects. The gap between the two sessions was also extended, with gaps ranging from 20 minutes to six months (including 1, 7, 28, and 84 days), and the final test given six months after the review session.

With this longer period, the best performance was achieved with a review gap of 28 days, and the decline in performance from gaps longer than 28 days was relatively small.

Compare this result with those of the internet study, which estimated an optimal review gap of 27 days when the test was 350 days later, and 12 or 21 days (extrapolated vs actual) when the test was 70 days later. This finding suggests that the longer interval is the more accurate one. But you might like to take this uncertainty as a reminder that you shouldn't rigidly regard these numbers as absolute rules! The general guide is that, if your exam is several months away, then you should review the material 3-4 weeks after studying it.

What all these experiments make clear is two general principles:

- the optimal review interval is longer when testing is delayed longer

- the penalty of stretching the interval too far is much smaller than the penalty for not stretching it far enough.

Distributing your reviews

But it's not quite as simple as saying that you should spread out your revision or practice. While the studies I've been describing have only used a single review (in order to establish a baseline), we have already established that best learning practice is to review more than once. How, then, do you space subsequent reviews? Do you spread them evenly, or at increasing intervals, or at decreasing intervals?

Expanding intervals is now considered best practice, and this idea — of progressively stretching the length of time between review so that each interval is at the limits of your memory — fits in with another idea I will discuss later, the idea of desirable difficulties. To briefly anticipate, this idea is that learning is maximized when tests are as difficult as they can be while still achieving a high measure of accuracy (i.e., keeping your errors to a minimum).

Of course, your spacing depends entirely on how well you do on your revision session! If you do well, you'll want the next interval to be longer; if you don't do well, you'll need to shorten the interval before the next session.

In other words, the key to good spacing is monitoring your learning and responding appropriately.

How type of material & task may affect spacing's benefits

Although the evidence for the value of spaced practice is considerable, there are circumstances when it doesn't seem to be so effective. The benefits are smaller with:

- meaningless material (but while meaningless material is common in laboratory experiments, it is less common in the real world)

- simple material

- incidental learning (compared to intentional learning).

In other words, spacing your practice is most important in precisely those circumstances that generally apply in study! That is, the material is meaningful and complex, and you are intentionally trying to learn it.

It has also been suggested that the spacing effect doesn't apply to inductive learning (learning to generalize from a number of examples). Reasonably enough, spaced out examples would seem to make it more difficult to notice the features the examples share. This idea brings to the fore another important factor in spacing your practice: what you do in the spaces.

We will look at this question in the next chapter.

Points to remember

Spreading your learning out (spacing) is much more effective than 'binge' learning.

Although the benefits of spacing are very well-established, most students fail to appreciate them.

The best time to review your learning depends on how long you want to remember it for. Research looking at single reviews suggests that, for long-term learning, a review at around four weeks is optimal. For a semester-end exam, a week or two might be best.

Without any review (natural or deliberate), you are likely to forget almost all of the material (80%) within a year.

Best practice is to have three reviews, and these should be at increasingly longer intervals. I recommend a first review one day after your initial study session, with a second review 7-10 days later, and a third review 4 weeks after that.

These recommendations are guidelines only! The best spacing for you is an individual matter, and one that will also vary with subject matter. As a general principle, you should aim to review at the limits of your memory — you need to find that 'sweet spot' *just before* you would forget the information. Only trial and error will teach you that!

Remember that it's better to space your learning longer than too short — make your brain work for it.

Spacing your review is of most benefit when the material you are learning is meaningful and complex.

Review Questions

1. If you reviewed your material once right after learning it, and got 40% on the multi-choice test 35 days later, what score would you expect to get if you had reviewed the material again a week later

    a. 63%

    b. 44%

    c. 52%

    d. 36%

2. If you reviewed your material once right after learning it, and got 40% on the short-answer test 35 days later, what score would you expect to get if you had reviewed the material again 11 days later

    a. 63%

    b. 44%

    c. 52%

    d. 36%

3. If you reviewed your material once right after learning it, and got 40% on the multi-choice test 70 days later, what score would you expect to get if you had reviewed the material again a week later

    a. 64%

    b. 44%

    c. 52%

    d. 36%

4. If you reviewed your material once right after learning it, and got 30% on the short-answer test 70 days later, what score would you expect to get if you had reviewed the material again 3 weeks later

    a. 63%

    b. 44%

    c. 52%

    d. 36%

5. The best way of achieving long-lasting learning is to

    a. concentrate each topic tightly into a short period of time

    b. break each topic up into very short modules and scatter them among many other topics

    c. cover a topic intensively, but incorporate its material into later topics for natural review

    d. read through a topic lightly to start with, but reread it at optimal intervals afterward

6. It's better to have more reviews, close together, than to space out your reviews too far.   Y / N

7. The longer it is until your exam,

    a. the more reviews you need

    b. the later your reviews should be

    c. the closer-together and more frequent your reviews should be

    d. the further-apart your reviews should be

8. The length of time between reviews should

    a. get shorter

    b. get longer

    c. be equal

    d. stretch out, dependent on your review performance

9. Expanded spacing is the most effective way to review

    a. always

    b. particularly for complex, meaningful material

    c. particularly for simple material

    d. particularly when you're trying to work out what links items together

10. Without any review, how much of your study material are you likely to forget by the next year

   a. 50%

   b. 30%

   c. 60%

   d. 80%

Spacing within your study session

Timing is not only a matter of the intervals between study and review, or between reviews. It also comes into play in the distribution of items during a study session. This chapter looks at the spacing between repetitions, and in particular at what goes on in the spaces.

In the previous chapter, I talked about spacing as if the only issue was the intervals between your initial study and your reviews. However, spacing applies also to what goes on within a study session. That can be the source of some confusion. What, exactly, is meant by 'massed' or 'spaced' practice in this context?

A common procedure in experimental studies is for some words in a list to be repeated one or more times in succession, while others are repeated only after several other words have been presented. So, for example, if you're studying new vocabulary from a foreign language, you could

- test yourself on a word two or three times before moving on to the next, finishing your session when you come to the end of your words, or

- you could go through each word in the list, one by one, and then run through the list again, as many times as you think you need.

In the second case, each word is separated (spaced) from its own reoccurrence by all the other items in the list. The length of the list is therefore critical in determining spacing (this is a situation I'll discuss in more detail when I talk about practical strategies).

A third strategy, one which may reflect more common practice, is a schedule which is neither completely massed nor completely spaced. We may call it 'clustered'. For example:

● massed: a word is presented four times in succession

● clustered: a word is presented twice in succession and twice more in succession after eight other items had been presented

● spaced: a word is presented four times with four items between each presentation.

Comparison of these three strategies found learning was the same for words presented massed or clustered [6.1]. Only spaced words showed better learning.

Similarly, a comparison between very short learning sessions that were either spaced (three 2-minute sessions per day) or clustered (one 6-minute session per day) found that the spaced lessons produced much more learning than those who had received clustered lessons.

But how much spacing is optimal?

One factor that's important is how much information you're trying to learn [6.2]. If, for example, you're trying to memorize new words in another language, trying to cram in too many words at the same time may increase the space between repetitions beyond your ability to remember them. Additionally, the overall length of time needed to get through a long list, with the number of *correct* retrievals needed for each word, may be too long for you to maintain attention or interest.

But the study of individual words is a simple situation compared to that of studying complex information, such as the French Revolution, or photosynthesis. What does 'massed' and 'spaced' mean in that context?

Because such material is (or should be!) all connected, you need to think in terms of information-sets. Thus, spacing refers to the interval between one information-set and its review, not between your reading of each piece of information in the set. So, for example, one study used a web-based instruction module on the search for life on other planets, with one information-set describing the role of a planet's *mass* on the likelihood that a planet could be inhabited, and another information-set describing the impact of a planet's *distance* from the sun on its habitability (Richland et al. 2013).

When we talk about within-session spacing, the issue becomes *how* the material is spaced — what goes on in the spaces; how the items are ordered. Within-session spacing, then, inescapably brings us to **interleaving** — following an item or information-set (or problem or motor sequence) with a different item (set / problem / sequence).

The question of interleaving in cognitive practice (as opposed to skill practice) has focused on category learning, which is common in several areas of study, such as mathematics, medicine and biology. It's thought that interleaving is of special benefit to this type of learning, because category learning requires you to notice what members of a category have in common, that distinguishes them from non-members. In other words, what's important is the comparisons you can make easily. The comparisons available to you are governed by the order of items and their juxtaposition.

Note that in the context of this issue, 'massed' practice is generally referred to, for what will be obvious reasons, as 'blocked' practice.

The importance of interleaving for category and type learning

To demonstrate how interleaving works, let's look at a study that involved children being taught to solve four kinds of mathematics problems [6.3]. In each problem, they were given the number of sides of the prism base, and were required to find the total number of faces, corners, edges, or angles by using one of the four formulas supplied. They were tested one day after the practice session.

During practice, they were given the problems either in four blocks of each type (blocked condition), or in four blocks, each of which included all four kinds of problem presented in random order (interleaved condition). In the blocked condition, brief puzzles unrelated to this type of problem were interleaved with the math problems, in order to keep the same degree of spacing in the two conditions.

Interleaving always makes the task noticeably harder, which is why students resist using this strategy, and why it's particularly important to provide evidence for how well it works, to overcome that resistance. In this study (and in keeping with other such studies), performance during the practice session was notably worse in the interleaved condition (79% vs. 98% in the blocked condition). However, when tested on the following day, the interleaved group performed more than twice as well as the blocked group (77% vs. 38%).

This provides a very clear demonstration not only of the value of interleaving, but also of why your performance at the time of learning tells you little about how well you've really learned!

But the study went on to explore a very interesting question: what type of learning does interleaving benefit?

When students were told exactly what formula to use and only had to apply it (a common situation, unfortunately, in math instruction), the benefits of interleaving were very small. The value of interleaved practice lay entirely in the improved ability to choose the right formula to apply.

This is, of course, not surprising: interleaving enables you to practice choosing the right formula as well as putting it through its paces; blocked practice only rehearses using the formula. (A reminder of the general principle: practice the task you need to do.)

It's clear from this why interleaving is of particular benefit to mathematics, but the broader conclusion researchers have drawn is that interleaving improves discrimination and therefore interleaved practice is probably most helpful when items or tasks are similar.

So, for example, in another study, students practiced typing three different five-key sequences on the number pad of a computer keyboard [6.4]. Although, once again, those who practiced the sequences in separate blocks, working a sequence until they correctly completed it 30 times, learned to type the sequences faster and more accurately in the training session, on the following day, those who had practiced in the interleaved condition were dramatically better.

It's also worth noting that students in the blocked group were over-confident, expecting much better performance than they proved capable of, while the interleaved group were quite accurate in their predictions of how well they'd learned.

In a third study, the material to be learned was the painting style of 12 artists [6.5]. For six artists, paintings were shown in consecutive blocks, while the other six artists had their paintings displayed all mixed up, with participants never seeing two paintings by the same artist consecutively.

The artists whose paintings had been studied in the spaced condition were remembered markedly better than those whose work had been studied in the massed condition (61% vs 35%).

Interestingly, when another arrangement was tried, with cartoon drawing 'fillers' (which the participants were told to ignore) used to provide spacing between paintings by the same artist, there was no benefit to the interleaving. It only worked when paintings by the other artists provided the spacing.

This supports the idea that the crucial factor for category learning is seeing the differences between the categories, and therefore what matters are strategies that make it easier to notice such differences.

A further condition presented paintings by *different* artists simultaneously — a condition which maximizes your ability to notice the differences between artists. This did indeed produce the best performance, although it wasn't significantly better than the performance produced by the standard spaced condition. However, it may suggest that, in a more demanding task, such a format might produce significantly better learning.

As I said, category learning is common in study. In such cases, many students are inclined to study the examples of a category all together, rather than interleaving them with other categories. Textbooks, too, tend to clump examples all together, rather than showing examples from different categories on the same page. As with massed practice, the speed with which you become fluent in processing the material gives the illusion that you have learned it quickly.

Mathematics is the prime example of this. Typically, classes and textbooks devote themselves to different kinds of problem in turn. No surprise that when the final exam comes, and students are required to choose the right method for many different problems, they often fail. A vital part of math is being able to choose the appropriate method for different kinds of problem, and yet instruction all too often fails to provide the necessary practice in this.

One study that looked at the effect of interleaving on math learning found that interleaving *trebled* test scores (Rohrer & Taylor 2007).

The typing sequences, the math problems, and the artists' styles, are all examples of very similar items. It may well be that interleaving is of less benefit when categories are easy to tell apart. Some studies using very simple stimuli have found massing a better strategy — but it's unlikely that you will be studying such simple information! It is the nature of complex information and skills that they share some attributes with other information-sets and skill sequences, and learning is hampered when such similarities aren't noted.

Why should interleaved practice be more effective than massed practice?

Apart from helping you differentiate skills or information-sets in terms of their similarities and differences (which is very helpful for creating good memory codes), there is another reason interleaving might be of benefit. This goes back to the general principles discussed in chapter 1.

If you keep practicing the same thing over and over again, the set of neurons encoding this new information doesn't have to be repeatedly retrieved: it just stays at a higher level of activation, hovering in the outer circle of working memory. But it's repeated retrieval from long-term memory that really strengthens a path to a memory code. Interleaving brings in more information, pushing earlier information out of working memory, forcing you to retrieve it from long-term memory.

Remember the priming effect? A code is more easily found if linked codes have recently been retrieved. If you are studying just one information-set (a list of semantically-linked words; a specific topic), then, even if you have pushed an item out of working memory, it is likely to be linked to items that are in working memory. This means the item isn't completely gone. By pushing items into working memory that are completely unrelated, you clear working memory properly of those earlier items.

Interleaving also produces more changes in context.

I said in Chapter 1 that a memory code is more easily found if the encoding and retrieval contexts match (context effect), and that a code is more easily found the more closely the retrieval cue matches the code (matching effect). This would seem to suggest that having the same context is better for learning. And yet, spacing your items out produces better learning, despite the greater changes in context produced when items are spaced.

Here we have the same sort of paradox as before: putting confusingly similar items close together produces poorer learning in the beginning, but better learning in the long run.

How do we reconcile these findings?

Learning, as I mentioned in the first chapter, isn't only about building strong paths to your memory codes. It's also about providing more paths to the codes. Repetition in the same context makes the path stronger, but multiple contexts provide more paths — and this is of increasing importance the longer the time between encoding and recall.

Let's put it this way. You're at the edge of a jungle. From where you stand, you can see several paths into the dense undergrowth. Some of the paths are well beaten down; others are not. Some paths are closer to you;

others are not. So which path do you choose? The most heavily trodden? Or the closest?

If the closest *is* the most heavily trodden, then the choice is easy. But if it's not, you have to weigh up the quality of the paths against their distance from you. You may or may not choose correctly.

I hope the analogy is clear. The strength of the memory trace is the width and smoothness of the path. The distance from you reflects the degree to which the retrieval context (where you are now) matches the encoding context (where you were when you first input the information). If they match exactly, the path will be right there at your feet, and you won't even bother looking around at the other options. But the more time has passed since you encoded the information, the less chance there is that the contexts will match. However, if you have many different paths that lead to the same information, your chance of being close to one of them obviously increases.

In other words, yes, the closer the match between the encoding and retrieval contexts, the easier it will be to remember the information. And the more different contexts you have encoded with the information, the more likely it is that one of those contexts will match your current retrieval context.

Why people persist in believing massed practice is better

Unfortunately, even in the face of experience, people are remarkably resistant to changing their preference from massed to interleaved practice. Most of the blame for this lies in the fact that concentrated blocks seem to lead to much better learning at the time. The problem, that most of that learning will quickly fade, isn't obvious until later. Even when understood, this fading may well be dismissed as normal — if you don't have a comparison with more effective ways of learning, you've no reason to believe that any better learning is possible.

Sadly, the fact that blocked practice leads to better short-term performance but poorer long-term learning doesn't just fool the learners themselves, but also their teachers and instructors.

Researchers have devised a pithy term for the paradoxical effects of interleaving and spacing — **desirable difficulties**.

It seems that a certain level of difficulty during encoding leads to better learning.

On the other hand, too much difficulty can slow learning.

One of the reasons why effective studying is as much 'art' as 'science' is that it's hard to get the right level of difficulty — too simple and too hard are both, in their separate ways, potentially harmful to learning. Aptly, the benefits of getting the optimal difficulty level has been called the "Goldilocks Effect".

Interleaving is the trickiest of the strategies I mention in this book, because it does require good understanding and self-monitoring to get right. One reason is that interleaving can increase your cognitive load, giving you too much information to deal with. The trick, then, is to get the timing right. Interleaving is probably most useful when you've already achieved a certain level of competency with a skill or problem type or concept.

The other, bigger, reason why interleaving makes learning harder at the time is that it increases interference. We're all familiar with this — the way one task or piece of information can cause us to forget, or poorly remember, an earlier task or bit of information. Surely the interference between tasks or information-sets is beyond any 'desirable' difficulty?

Again, it's all about the detail.

Preventing interference

Research indicates that two skills / topics interfere with each other because the two information sets interact. This isn't simply a product of the two information sets sharing features (although the greater the similarity, the greater the interference); it's also a problem of timing.

The problem is that we're consolidating the first set of memories while encoding the second. While we *can* do both at the same time, as with any multitasking, one task is going to be done better than the other. Unsurprisingly, the brain seems to give encoding priority over consolidation (just as we so often give priority to incoming emails over the work we're in the middle of!).

Remember that new memories take several hours to stabilize. So, if you learned something a few hours ago and now you are learning something else, you are still consolidating that older learning while creating these new memory codes. What should be more reasonable than that your brain should look for commonalities between these two actions that are, as far as it's concerned, occurring at the same time? This is, after all, what we're programmed to do: we link things that occur together in space and time. Something's just happened, and now something else is happening, and chances are they're connected. So some mechanism in our brain works on that.

This can indeed be all to the good, if the two events/sets of information are connected. But if they're not, we get interference, and loss of data.

It's not only about whether or not two information-sets are consistent or not. If you think of the key problem being interference between Set 1 consolidation and Set 2 encoding, you'll see that the problem will be worse when these two processes are occurring in the same brain regions. But they don't have to. How much overlay there is will depend on what kind of material is being processed. If, for example, you learn a word list and then practice a motor sequence, the consolidation of the words will be occurring in the hippocampus while the encoding of the motor sequence will be occurring in the cerebellum. Two distinctly different (and physically very separate) brain regions.

However, if you learn the motor task first, followed by the word-list, then some interference might occur. For the motor task is being consolidated in the motor cortex, and this same region is also (somewhat surprisingly) involved in encoding words (words are tightly linked to their associated actions, faces, images, sounds, and so forth).

What all this means is that some tasks/information-sets are going to interfere with each other more than others, but it won't always be obvious why. Let experience help you determine which situations are okay and which are not, but the best general strategy is simply to provide a space for consolidation before embarking on new encoding.

There is another way you can protect against interference, but it's counterproductive because what it does is shift the interference rather than remove it. If you overlearn (that is, keep practicing for a while after you believe you can't get any better), then learning a second task won't interfere with your learning of that previous task (Shibata et al. 2017). However, it will interfere with your learning of the second task.

That doesn't make overlearning something to avoid! Overlearning helps lock in a skill. However, it does reinforce the idea that you should always allow time between new learnings.

Consolidation during rest

While consolidation occurs most notably during sleep, there's also evidence that a boost in skill learning can occur after rests that only last a few minutes (or even seconds). This phenomenon is distinguished from 'real' consolidation, because the gains in performance don't usually endure. However, while in some circumstances it may simply reflect recovery from mental or physical fatigue, in other circumstances it may have a more lasting effect.

One study that demonstrates this involved non-musicians learning a five-key sequence on a digital piano (Cash 2009). In the study, the participants repeated the sequence as fast and accurately as they could during twelve 30-second blocks interspersed with 30-s pauses. A third of the participants had a 5-minute rest between the third and fourth block, while another third had the rest between the ninth and tenth block, and the remaining third had no rest at all. Everyone was re-tested the next day, about 12 hours after training.

These brief rests had a significant effect on learning, but the timing of the rest was critical.

While participants showed large improvements during training after either 5-minute rest, it was only those who were given a rest early in the training that continued to show improvement throughout the training. This group also showed the greatest consolidation gain (that is, their performance 'jumped' more than that of the other two groups when tested on the following day).

What this indicates is that consolidation is affected by the timing of the rest. Typically, in motor learning, you improve quickly in the beginning, but this rate of learning soon slows down. This pattern was indeed seen in this study — among the late-rest and no-rest groups. For these groups, improvement during blocks 4-9 wasn't as rapid as it had been during the first three blocks. Those who rested after the third block, however, didn't show this slow-down. The faster rate of learning allowed more repetition of the sequence at a higher skill level, and this may have helped develop a more stabilized memory (short-term consolidation), and thus greater overnight (long-term) consolidation.

Although having a late rest didn't benefit participants as much as having an early rest did, and the immediate post-rest jump in performance after the late rest wasn't maintained, the size of that jump did affect how much the participant's performance improved after sleep. In other words, even if you don't get the timing exactly right, brief rests are still beneficial.

A couple of caveats though. There's evidence that consolidation and interference occur differently in pre-pubertal children, perhaps because their brains are still developing, perhaps because their lack of experience means they encode information in a more specific, less abstract, way than adults [6.6].

Age also makes a difference at the other end of life. The brain tends to change in several important ways as we age. One of these ways is that learning gets harder. Research now suggests that the reason for this is not that older adults find it harder to learn, but that they find it much harder to consolidate their learning [6.7]. This may be linked to interference — because they have more experience, and more connections, there is greater opportunity for interference. Another possible factor, one far less obvious, is that changes in time perception mean that older brains may regard more distant events as close in time.

Time perception is rooted in events. So one vital reason for two hours being such a long time for children is that there has been a great deal happening — a lot of new information — in that two-hour space. For an older adult, the two hours have probably been filled with the 'same old, same old' — no new information to process and encode.

In other words, interference may occur regardless of the length of time between events — what's important is what information has passed through the system in the time between.

All this suggests that interleaved practice may be even more important for older adults. And not only older adults. Although it slows down initial learning, interleaving (appropriately timed) may be especially helpful for all of those who have atrophy or impairment in specific brain regions (as often occurs with age, but also may happen as a consequence of injury, disease, or substance abuse).

Spacing & interleaving for complex material

Within-session spacing and interleaving are more complicated when it comes to more meaningful material [6.8]. Not surprising when you consider that the chief value of interleaving is that it helps you spot the differences in similar tasks or types. With complex information, learning it is primarily about understanding, not memorization. Studying meaningful material, such as the causes of the American Civil War, or the conditions needed for micro-organisms to reproduce, or the meaning of Milton's *Paradise Lost*, is about learning how the information fits together. As I discuss (in great detail!) in my book *Effective Notetaking*, it's about making connections, both between all the bits of information in the material-to-be-learned, and with information you already have in your head.

I've said that, for this sort of material, interleaving and spacing should be thought of as happening between information-sets, not bits of information. But what constitutes an information-set? For of course, just as memory is a network filled with sub-networks and sub-sub-networks, right down to the very smallest memory code which is itself a network, so meaningful information is itself all connected. Where do you draw the lines, and say that *this* particular collection of information is a 'set'?

Here's yet another reason why you can't learn how to learn 'by the numbers', why you need to understand the general principles and learn how to tune in to your own learning: *you* draw the lines. And the lines will, of course, move as you learn more. This harks back to cognitive load, to the limits of your working memory and the gradual building of bigger and bigger chunks.

An information-set is something you build.

Interleaving, then, with its focus on spotting differences, would seem to be inherently unhelpful when you are building an information-set, both because of the potential interference it brings and because it adds to your cognitive load. It may be more beneficial once you have solid information-sets, during review, for example. This is something you can try if you wish, but this is an advanced strategy for those who are skilled at self-monitoring. As a general rule, it's wisest to limit the use of interleaving to skill learning (where it is very useful) and the types of category learning I've discussed.

But if interleaving is a dubious strategy for complex information, the same can't be said for within-session spacing! Remember that while interleaving inevitably includes spacing, spacing doesn't have to include interleaving. Interleaving is about mixing up tasks or information to be learned, but you don't have to keep learning in the spaces. You can fill in the spaces with inactivity, and I talked before about the benefits of brief rests to allow new information to stabilize. You can also engage in activities that don't involve new information or skills, and that also provides the brain with some mental space to process the information it's recently acquired.

Points to remember

Spacing is also beneficial within a study session, as well as between sessions.

Within-session spacing obeys the same rules as between-session spacing:

longer spaces are better than shorter spaces, but the best spacing captures that moment just before you'd forget.

For individual items, within-session spacing is often entangled with interleaving, and in such a case spacing depends on the number of items.

Interleaving is a strategy in which you intersperse your learning of one type of task or information-set with another task or information-set.

Interleaving is of particular benefit in skill learning, math learning, and other types of category learning.

For complex material, within-session spacing can be fruitfully achieved by providing breaks.

Interleaving is probably most helpful when you need to notice differences between interleaved items.

Because interleaving makes initial learning more difficult, students usually believe that it produces poorer learning.

Interleaving and spacing help learning when they provide a level of useful difficulty (the 'desirable difficulty' effect). If the level of difficulty produced is too high, interleaving and spacing can harm learning.

One problem is that interleaving can increase interference.

Interference can be reduced by providing a brief rest to allow earlier learning to be stabilized.

Interference is much less of a problem for pre-pubertal children, and much more of a problem for older adults.

Interleaving may be most helpful when you've achieved a certain level of mastery of individual concepts or problem types using blocked practice.

Review Questions

1. If you're trying to memorize vocabulary, the most effective way is to

    a. test each word two or three times before moving on to the next, finishing your session when you come to the end of your words

    b. test each word in the list one by one, running through the list as often as you need

    c. test each word twice, and then again later in the list, finishing your session when you come to the end of your words

    d. test each word with enough spacing between each test of that word that you can just (but only just) remember it

2. The optimal list length

    a. is 10 items

    b. is 20 items

    c. depends on how long you can sustain your attention

    d. depends on how difficult (hard to remember) the words are

3. For complex, meaningful information, each 'item' is a

    a. fact

    b. topic

    c. tightly-connected information set

    d. word

4. Interleaving is most effective when

    a. each item is separated by a filler item (that doesn't need to be learned)

    b. items are arranged in alphabetical or numerical order

    c. items are arranged so as to make useful comparisons easily

    d. items are similar

    e. items are very different

5. Interleaving
    a. makes it easier to learn
    b. makes it harder to learn
    c. produces better long-term learning
    d. produces better short-term learning
    e. causes interference

6. Desirable difficulties
    a. slow learning
    b. refer to a level of difficulty that optimizes learning
    c. are problems that are useful
    d. are complications that increase your level of interest
    e. motivate you to do better

7. Interference can be caused by
    a. different items / actions being similar
    b. different items / actions occurring too close together
    c. multi-tasking
    d. the material / skill to be learned being too difficult
    e. contradictory information

8. Interference can be reduced by
    a. breaks between learning tasks
    b. a night's sleep
    c. interleaving
    d. attending to points of difference

9. Interleaving is most useful for
    a. older students
    b. mathematics

c. skill learning

d. beginners

e. complex material

10. Students don't like interleaving and don't believe it helps them learn, because interleaving makes initial learning more difficult.   Y / N

Putting it all together

Why is spaced retrieval practice so effective?

There are a number of ways in which retrieval practice may help learning:

- by matching the real testing situation, or normal-use situation

- by providing multiple routes to the memory code (by varying the contexts used in retrieval practice)

- by providing a degree of 'desirable difficulty'

- by providing opportunities to re-edit the memory code to make it easier to retrieve

- by raising your confidence in your ability to retrieve the target information.

Let's look briefly at each of these.

Matching the target situation

Remember the context principle: a code is more easily found if the encoding and retrieval contexts match.

Retrieval is always better than rehearsal, because retrieval is the task you should be practicing for, and because rehearsal gives you no feedback as to how well you've learned, while retrieval does. That's why testing is so valuable — more valuable as a learning tool than as an assessment tool. Testing *teaches*; even pre-testing (before you know the information to be learned) improves learning.

Providing multiple routes to the memory code

Every time you retrieve a memory, your starting point is a little different, and thus your path to that memory code is a little different. The more paths you have to a memory code, the greater the chance that you'll find one of those paths on any retrieval occasion. Moreover, by spacing out your retrieval practice, you increase the difference between the starting points, giving yourself a wider range of possible starting points that will work.

By providing a degree of 'desirable difficulty'

When a task or topic seems easy, you may not give it the attention it needs for good encoding. If you read a text and it all appears very obvious, your brain probably won't even tag it as 'new'. Why, then, should it bother to encode it at all? Only by trying to retrieve it will you determine whether you do need to encode it, and doing so also tells your brain that this is something you want to remember.

Moreover, by introducing a level of artificial difficulty, through spacing or interleaving, you give your brain a reason to apply more attention to the task, with the result that you will create a stronger memory code.

Providing opportunities to edit the memory code

In the experiment comparing keyword mnemonics and retrieval practice, keywords were remembered more often by the group that had retrieval practice, and providing the keywords on the final test significantly improved recall for the restudy-only group but didn't help the retrieval practice group. This suggests that forgetting the keyword was an important stumbling block for the restudy-only group, but the retrieval practice group forgot for different reasons. All of this indicates that the retrieval practice group remembered their keywords better. Why? A reasonable conclusion is that they had more memorable keywords — the experience of trying to recall the keywords showed them which keywords were hard to remember, motivating them to find better ones.

One of the most important benefits of retrieval practice is that it enables you to monitor your learning, and thus 'tweak' your learning strategy as needed.

Improving student confidence

When you're anxious, your worried thoughts and emotions take up valuable space in working memory, leaving less room for you to think and remember. No surprise, then, that test anxiety can significantly affect your performance on exams. By testing yourself repeatedly, you reduce that anxiety, freeing up that space in working memory for more useful thoughts.

The ten principles of effective practice

1. Practice the task you need to do.

When you are practicing or revising the skill/topic you want to learn, you should think about how you will be needing to remember this in future. For example, if you're learning foreign language words, you may wish to be able to:

- Remember the English meaning of the words when faced with them.

- Remember the foreign words when faced with their English counterparts.

- Spontaneously generate the foreign words when talking or writing.

What you practice depends on which of these tasks you want to be able to do.

Or perhaps you're learning about the French Revolution. Your aim may simply be to pass a multi-choice test at the end of the week, or it may be to get an A on an essay-type exam in two months time, or it may be that you actually want to remember most of these details for the long-term, and be able to talk intelligently about it as you incorporate it into your broader knowledge of history.

The first step in successful learning is always to think about what you want the learning *for*. Only then can you work out exactly how you should be learning it.

2. The single most effective learning strategy is retrieval practice.

Most 'real' learning is aimed at being able to retrieve memories from your long-term memory store. In line with the general principle 'Practice the task you need to do', you should be practicing your retrieval of the information you want to learn.

Retrieval practice is also an absolutely critical means of monitoring your learning, which is vital if you want to learn effectively. You cannot truly know how likely you are to remember something in future if you don't test your ability to remember it.

3. When you practice retrieval, only correct retrievals count.

Indeed, because of the risk you run in learning the mistake, you may even want to add extra correct retrievals to counteract the incorrect ones. But the important thing is not to give any weight to the mistakes — do not, whatever you do, think about (or tell people) about the stupid mistake you make. If you retrieve the wrong information, mentally toss it away, turning your mind instead to the correct answer, dwelling on why that answer is correct and any aspects of it that might help you remember it.

4. Aim to do at least two correct retrievals in your first study session.

How many correct retrievals you do depends on your learning abilities, level of expertise in the topic, and personal preferences. However, having two correct retrievals, rather than only one, produces the biggest difference. Three is recommended as a general rule of thumb.

5. Space your retrieval attempts out.

There is no point in simply retrieving something that is already in working memory. To benefit from your retrieval attempt, you need to be retrieving the information from long-term memory. This means you need to have retrieved several other items (to bump the earlier item out of working memory) before trying to retrieve a particular item again.

6. Review your learning on a separate occasion at least once.

Reviewing your material at least a day later makes a big difference to your chances of remembering it in future, compared to not reviewing it, or only reviewing it at the end of your study session.

7. Space your review out.

The general principal is that the longer you want to remember the material for, the longer the length of time you should put between your initial study and your review.

However, you don't want to stretch the review interval out too far. You should aim to review the material at the point where you still remember most of it, but will soon forget it.

As a guideline:

- Review after three days if you only want to remember for a week or two.

- Review after a week if you want to remember for a month.

- Review after two weeks if you want to remember for two months.

- Review after a month if you want to remember for a year.

Note that for simplicity, this guide refers only to a single review, but for long-term learning it's best if you review more than once.

8. Review at expanding intervals for long-term learning.

If you want to remember the material 'forever', you need to review it more than once. This may be taken care of if you use the material in the natural course of your work or study. If you don't, then you need to schedule some regular reviews.

The recommended number is three, and you should aim to have increasingly longer intervals between the reviews. If you find the interval is too long and you don't remember the material as well as you'd like, then I recommend not only shortening the next review interval, but increasing the number of reviews (i.e., don't count the poor review).

If you are serious about remembering it forever, I recommend you also review the material after a year.

9. Interleave your practice with similar material.

Interleaving is particularly helpful when you are learning a skill or are doing a category learning task, such as working on math problems or learning artists' styles or plant types.

Interleaving, like spacing, introduces a desirable difficulty which forces you to pay greater attention to features that you might otherwise not notice. It is therefore particularly useful whenever there are details that you *should* notice, but probably won't.

Interleaving is also useful for ensuring that earlier items are well cleared from working memory.

10. Allow time for consolidation.

New memories take up to six hours to be stabilized, and are vulnerable to interference until that happens. You can assist that stabilization process by providing brief rests — short periods of reflection, perhaps with your eyes closed — during which you give your brain mental space to focus on consolidating the new information.

This is particularly helpful for older adults, but less necessary for children.

Specific strategies to use for & with retrieval practice

Now that you understand why retrieval practice is so important and know the principles for practicing most effectively, let's look at some different techniques for practicing. In this section, I discuss different retrieval practice strategies and how to use them effectively for different subjects. The strategies include flashcards, mnemonics, linking differences, Q & A, and concept mapping.

Flashcards

> Using flashcards is a retrieval practice strategy. This brief chapter looks at how to use this well-known strategy most effectively.

The most obvious retrieval practice strategy — the one everyone knows — involves flashcards.

I'm sure all of you are familiar with flashcards, whether or not you've used them yourself. They are particularly popular for foreign language learning, but can also be used for simple facts as well as new technical words and their definitions.

You can buy ready-made flashcards for some languages and subjects, and I'm not advising against this, but it is more effective if you make them yourself. Not only will the cards be customized to your own use, but the activity of selecting words and writing them down provides an additional activity that helps you learn them.

On the other hand, some of the online flashcard programs now available for language learning are very good. One of their big advantages (when done well) is in having built-in spacing and interleaving. The downside is that the spacing is rarely customizable and may not be right for your individual needs.

To keep it simple, in this discussion I only talk about the traditional format of physical cards (which have, indeed, some advantages over a virtual program). The basic principles, however, can be applied to virtual cards.

A standard way of using flashcards is simply to go through a set number each day, separating out those you have trouble with, so you can review them more often. For example, if you keep troublesome ones handy, you can go through them at odd moments during the day when you're waiting for something.

Flashcards aren't simply useful as a means of testing yourself. For example, if they're word (as opposed to fact) cards, you can use them to group words in different ways, play a variety of card games with them, or make a bingo game with them. However, since our focus is practice, I'm going to restrict myself to discussing the best way to use them in their standard way: by going through a pile of cards, looking at one side, and trying to retrieve the matching response.

There are two main questions when it comes to using flashcards (ignoring the spacing and distribution questions, which I have already covered in earlier chapters):

- When should you 'drop' a card?

- How many cards should you have in a stack?

Let's start with dropping.

When to drop a card from the stack

Now, dropping cards from your stack that you have 'learned' does make sense, because it gives you more opportunity to practice the harder cards. The big problem is knowing when it's the right time to drop them. A study that looked at this found that people dropped cards for two reasons: the obvious one, that they thought they knew them and didn't want to waste time on them, and a less obvious one — that they considered these cards too hard to learn (Kornell & Bjork 2008).

There's nothing especially wrong with these principles, but in both these cases, the students' judgment tended to be awry. That is, they dropped easy cards too soon (remember how much difference that second correct retrieval makes), and they had insufficient faith in the power of retrieval practice, not realizing that if they had persevered with the harder cards, they would, for the most part, have found them learnable.

Aside from not realizing the power of retrieval practice, the students' major problem lay in not knowing this learning principle: **the value of studying is highest when items are closest to being learned**. Too often, students, fooled by the easy fluency that comes from repeating items in quick succession, believe they have learned something before they truly have, and stop practicing something just at the moment when studying is most valuable.

There's another problem with dropping — by doing so, you reduce the spacing of the cards you have left in the stack, which are presumably the more difficult cards. By having them come up more quickly, they will become more 'massed' than 'spaced', making you more likely to be fooled by the fluency effect into thinking you have learned them before you truly have.

Now, none of this is to say you shouldn't drop cards that you've learned. But you do need to be aware that it's not all benefit. The best strategy is to guard against dropping cards too soon. As a rule of thumb, I'd suggest that, when you get to the point where you think you can drop a card, give it one more turn. Most importantly, *don't* drop a card after only one correct retrieval!

Also, resist dropping too many too soon. If there are so many easy cards in your stack, consider adding more cards to the stack. Remember, to be effective, you don't want cards turning up again too quickly.

Relatedly, and more importantly, this dropping should not be carried over to the next time you run through the stack. Every time you review, all the cards should be returned to the stack, although you can drop the easy cards more quickly on these reviews.

How many cards in a stack

The question of how many cards there should be in a stack was explored in a study using GRE-type word pairs, such as *effulgent: brilliant* (Kornell 2009). Using digital flashcards, students studied two 20-word lists. For one list, the words were shown in a single stack of 20 flashcards, which were presented four times, always in the same order, and for the other list, the words were shown in four stacks of five cards, with each stack presented four times before going on to the next stack. With the single stack, then, each card only came around after 19 other cards, while with the smaller stacks, each card came around after only 4 cards.

Cards in the more spaced condition (i.e., the larger stack) were remembered significantly more when tested 24 hours later — 49% vs 36%.

As usual, after the learning sessions, students anticipated that they would do notably better with the smaller stacks than with the large stack. This is consistent with common student practice, which appears to be to divide larger amounts of cards into smaller stacks. Indeed, a leading GRE study guide apparently advises this (or did at the time this research came out, in 2009).

The next experiment employed a more realistic study situation, reflecting common student practice, and found the benefit of a large stack over smaller stacks became dramatic. In this scenario, the students spread their study over four days, with the single large stack being gone through twice on each day, and the small stacks each being reviewed eight times on one of the days. In other words, each card, regardless of condition, was experienced eight times.

In this situation, the large stack was recalled at an average rate of 54%, vs a mere 21% for the small stacks!

A further experiment had the students review all their cards on the fifth day, before being tested on the following day — again, a more realistic scenario. Although this improved performance on the test, the marked difference between the conditions was maintained, with an average correct for the large stack of 65% vs 34% for the small stacks.

In other words, having a larger stack nearly doubled test scores.

The researchers also analyzed individual differences, finding that spacing was more effective for 63 of the 70 students (90%), with three doing equally well in both conditions, and four doing better in the massed condition. Another reminder that general guidelines are only that, and even when a strategy is as strongly supported as this, a few individuals will always find a different approach more effective. You must work out what works best for you.

Best practice for flashcards

Don't drop a card before having at least two successful retrievals.

Use a reasonably large stack, in which cards are interspersed by a goodly number of other cards. Twenty cards is probably a good starting point — increase or decrease this in response to your performance.

Don't drop a card permanently — return it to the stack for the next review.

Flashcard variant

An easy variant for those who don't want to go to the trouble of making flashcards is simply to take a lined sheet of paper and fold it lengthwise down the center. Write the words or questions down one half, and write the meanings/English translation or answers down the other.

This is much easier (and cheaper) than writing a lot of flashcards, but does of course come with significant drawbacks. In particular:

- you can't change the order so readily (you can randomly skip all over the list, but this does make it harder to ensure that you've done them all)

- you can't group them in different ways

- you can't as easily drop items as you go (although you can make check marks beside the items and use these as a guide, which does have the advantage of providing a record of exactly how well you've done on previous occasions)

- you have to wait until the end of the page before you check any answer (or, if you do check an answer before you're finished, you'll see some of the other answers).

Nevertheless, using this technique may be sufficient in certain circumstances — for example, if you're cramming for a test, or if you want to do an initial cull and see which items are more resistant to learning.

Review questions

1. When using flashcards, the best practice is to
   a. drop each card when you correctly recall the answer
   b. exclude the cards you can't remember after 3 tries
   c. keep the stacks very small, so it's easy to get the right answers
   d. have a big enough stack that each card doesn't come around again until you've nearly forgotten it

2. If you have 20 words to learn, you're best to
   a. break them into 4 stacks
   b. break them into 2 stacks
   c. keep them as 1 stack

3. If you have 20 words to learn, which of these processes would produce better learning for your end-of-semester exam?
   a. break them into 4 stacks, but go through them many times
   b. break them into 4 stacks, but go through them many times over the course of a day
   c. break them into 4 stacks, but go through them many times over the course of a week
   d. go through them as a single stack as many times as you need to get them all right
   e. go through them as a single stack, dropping each card after you've got it right 3 times
   f. go through them as a single stack, dropping each card after you've got it right 2 times at least, but repeat the process the following day, and a week later

4. You get the greatest benefits from studying when you've very nearly mastered it.   Y / N

5. You can drop a card permanently from your review if you got it right 3 times and never got it wrong.   Y / N

Keyword mnemonic

The keyword mnemonic is a strategy you can use with practice, and is particularly useful for learning vocabulary and simple facts. This chapter looks at when and how to use this strategy, and provides many examples and opportunities for practice.

Like flashcards, the keyword mnemonic is especially popular as a means of memorizing new vocabulary, particularly for foreign languages. It has also proved its effectiveness for learning other associated pairs, such as authors and books, paintings and artists, countries and capitals, minerals and their attributes.

As I said earlier, this method involves choosing an intermediary word that binds what you need to remember to something you already know well. It's usually recommended that the word be something concrete that can easily form an image, although this isn't an absolute requirement. Sometimes it's very difficult to find an appropriate visualizable word and you must settle for a more abstract one. Some people, moreover, find it much easier to create verbal connections than visual ones.

Here's an example of how the keyword mnemonic can be used to remember a simple fact: that Canberra is the capital of Australia. You could create an image involving a *can* of *beer* (an obvious phrase for Canberra, particularly in light of the Australians' notorious enjoyment of beer!), and an Australian icon such as a kangaroo or a koala bear (to signal "Australia"). Thus, your image for remembering this fact could be a kangaroo swigging back a can of beer.

Canberra is the capital of Australia

"Can of Beer"

Kangaroo - icon for Australia

I discuss the keyword mnemonic in much more detail in my book *Mnemonics for Study*, but here are the basic principles for choosing a good keyword. Choose one that:

- sounds as much as possible like the to-be-learned word

- easily forms an interactive image with the word meaning

- is sufficiently unlike other keywords you're using to not be confused

- is a familiar word, easily recalled.

And here are the basic principles for constructing the image. An effective image:

- connects the keyword with its associated word (usually the target word's meaning) in a way that is *active* and personally *meaningful*

- is simple

- is clear and vivid.

Note that the really important principle is that the image be *interactive* — that is, a kangaroo *drinking* a can of beer, not a picture of a kangaroo *and* a beer can; a letter *in* a cart, not a letter *and* a cart.

The keyword mnemonic is an adjunct strategy in the context of practice. Flashcards are a retrieval practice strategy; mnemonics, on the other hand, are strategies for transforming hard-to-remember information into something more memorable. In other words, their role here is to provide a different content for practice. Accordingly, and given the power and ease of retrieval practice alone, I recommend that you limit your use of mnemonics to items that are not easy to learn without additional help.

The keyword mnemonic is one of the easier mnemonics to master, nevertheless, you may be put off because it requires a certain amount of creativity. Do be assured that coming up with words and images gets easier with practice.

The keyword method is undoubtedly an effective learning strategy, but it is mainly a strategy for recognition learning. You see the word *carta*, the keyword *cart* is triggered, and hopefully the image of the letter in the cart is then recalled and you realize the meaning of *carta* is *letter*. You see the word *Canberra*, you think of the kangaroo drinking the can of beer, you realize that the kangaroo indicates Australia. The method is not, unfortunately, as useful the other way around, that is, for remembering the Spanish for *letter*, or remembering the capital of Australia. But you can help with that by making sure you do your retrieval practice in both directions.

One way in which many users fall down is in focusing on the wrong aspect of the mnemonic. It's natural enough to concentrate on retrieving the word to be learned, but in fact it's better to focus (not exclusively!) on the link between the keyword and the image (or verbal counterpart), rather than the link between keyword and word-to-be-learned. The link between keyword and image is vital, because it's the image that holds the link to the target word. Don't assume you'll remember it without specific practice.

So, for example, you need to practice recalling the image of the letter in the cart in response to *carta*, and recalling the image of a letter in a cart in response to *letter*.

Remember the list of Italian words I used in chapter 2? I offered the keyword "sharp" for the word-pair "scarpa-shoe". So how do you practice these words?

In chapter 2, I said that, if you simply want to learn to read Italian, you want to practice retrieving "shoe" when you see "scarpa". But if you want to be able to read, write, speak, and understand Italian when spoken, then you need to practice both recalling "shoe" when you see "scarpa", and recalling "scarpa" when you see "shoe".

But more specifically, as I've discussed here, if you have a word or image linking the two words, you need to spend much of your time on the weak link, that between the keyword and the image (or verbal counterpart, such as a sentence or phrase). So in this case, you want to practice recalling the image of very sharp-pointed shoes, in response to the cues "scarpa" and "shoe", and having that image evoke the correct keyword: *sharp*.

So, imagine you have a flashcard:

You go through your deck first one way, using the Italian words as cues, and then the other way, using the English words as cues. In both cases, when you read the cue, your response should be first to recall the keyword image.

scarpa	shoe

I'd like to emphasize that the relationship between mnemonics and retrieval practice works both ways. It is not simply that the keyword mnemonic is a useful adjunct strategy to retrieval practice; retrieval practice is a critical adjunct to using mnemonics successfully.

shoe → [image] → sharp → scarpa

scarpa → sharp → [image] → shoe

This is something that often gets overlooked in mnemonics training programs. But the purpose of mnemonics is to make information more memorable, not to make it so memorable that you never need to practice it! Moreover, not only do novices tend to under-practice their mnemonics, but they often practice the wrong thing. Whatever the mnemonic (and there are several mnemonic strategies, which I cover in *Mnemonics for Study*; I have focused here on the keyword mnemonic because it has the broadest and clearest benefits), you need to practice all the links in the mnemonic chain.

Exercise 9.1

Remembering the principles for creating a good mnemonic, try to create keywords for the following Italian words:

angolo, corner —

campana, bell —

collo, neck —

mano, hand —

mare, sea —

Rate each keyword 0 or 1 for each of these criteria (best score=4):

1. sounds as much as possible like the to-be-learned word

2. easily forms an interactive image with the word meaning

3. is sufficiently unlike other keywords you're using to not be confused

4. is a familiar word, easily recalled.

Exercise 9.2

Try to come up with keywords for these Latvian words (if you have difficulty, just move onto the next — don't give up on the whole exercise in a fit of despair! as with any strategy, you can't really understand this strategy until you've properly practiced it, and my discussion afterward will make more sense if you've tried your best):

ezis, hedgehog —

kas, who —

nams, house —

uguns, fire —

zirnis, pea —

Rate each keyword you've come up with.

Exercise 9.3

Now try these Italian words:

ancora, yet, still —

dopo, after —

fiume, river —

strofinare, to rub —

sviluppare, to develop —

Rate each keyword you've come up with.

Choosing when to use the keyword mnemonic

You probably found the first list easier than the second, and both much easier than the third. Do you know why?

Words vary along several dimensions, in particular,

- the extent to which they're easily visualizable (obviously concrete nouns are the best, and prepositions among the worst)

- the extent to which they are naturally connected to words you already know

- how many syllables they have.

The extent to which they're visualizable is not, however, as important as you might think — otherwise the keyword mnemonic would be very limited! I've emphasized the image step of the process, but it isn't necessary to restrict yourself to things that can be visualized. If you fall back to purely verbal connections, that's okay. So, for example, an obvious keyword for *ancora* is *anchor*, but how do we display *yet*, or *still*? That's difficult in an image, but easy in a phrase: *still anchored!*

Similarly, you may have had trouble coming up with a visualizable keyword for *ezis*, but there's a very *easy* one if you're not worried about creating an image.

Regarding the length of the word, you may have found the last two words, each four syllables, trickier than the shorter ones, simply because it's much harder to come up with a similar-sounding word. You can either choose to go with a two or three word phrase, or focus on what you regard as the key part of the word, that will cue you to the rest. That's a matter of judgment, and will depend on the word. Both can work well, if you've chosen appropriately.

But the factor that I want to emphasize is the second — the extent to which the word you're learning is naturally connected to words you already know. This is important, because you don't want to be trying to create keywords for every word you need to learn! For one thing, it's not the easiest thing to do (as you probably found), and for another, you're adding to your cognitive load. If there are real, meaningful connections between words, they'll be much easier to learn (require less practice; be more resistant to forgetting) than arbitrary ones you have to force. There's also the risk of setting up interference if you use keywords for everything, since the number of potential keywords (words that come easily to your mind), is much smaller than your total vocabulary, and you'll find it hard to avoid doubling up if you're overusing the mnemonic.

These are the critical principles: **only use a mnemonic when the material cannot be meaningfully linked**, and **limit your use of mnemonics to material that you need extra help to remember**. In other words, a mnemonic should be your *last* resort, not your first!

With these principles in mind, let's return to the list of Italian words I used in chapter 2:

acqua, water —

denti, teeth —

fratello, brother —

giorno, day —

libro, book —

nave, ship —

pneumatico, tire —

risposta, answer —

scarpa, shoe — *sharp*

sole, sun —

You see the keyword *sharp* is already written in. Now think about the other words. How many of these Italian-English pairs are meaningfully connected? For example, *acqua* is related to, and sounds like, aqua / aquarium / aquatic, which are all meaningfully related to *water*. Picking one of those, therefore, would be a good connector to help tie *acqua* and *water* together. Which one you choose depends on your own experience — select the one that comes most easily to mind, and will reliably make the connection to 'water' (*aqua*, for example, might make you think of the color, rather than water; *aquarium* might evoke fish more reliably than water).

What do you do with this connector word? You need to incorporate it into your retrievals, in the same way that you incorporated the mnemonic keyword *sharp* into your retrieval process. However, because it's a meaningful (and easy) connection, you won't need to focus on it so much.

So, you look at your flashcard saying "acqua", and you think "aquatic — water". Or you look at the word "water", and say "aquatic — acqua".

It should be immediately apparent that, even with this very easy connection, thinking of "aquatic" when faced with "water" is harder than thinking of "aquatic" when faced with "acqua ". That's because the number of potential connections we could make to "water" is so much greater. So you will have to focus a bit harder on that connection — which means not only paying greater attention, but also increasing the number of successful retrievals.

Exercise 9.4

Find connector words for each of the other words in this list. They are all cognate pairs, but some connections may be more obscure than others (*scarpa* and *shoe* are also cognate, in fact!).

I provide my own suggested link-words in the Answers section, but don't worry if they're very different from your own! Keywords and connections are very much an individual thing. What's important is how meaningful the connection is *to you*, and how easy it is for you to make that connection. If your word works better for you than mine, then that's what matters.

Exercise 9.5

Now do the same for the words from Exercises 9.1 and 9.2, all of which also have cognates in the English language (well, except for one which has a Latin cognate you might know):

angolo, corner —

campana, bell —

collo, neck —

mano, hand —

mare, sea —

ezis, hedgehog —

kas, who —

nams, house —

uguns, fire —

zirnis, pea —

Do remember that you are not restricted to English! If you happen to know words in other related languages that provide a meaningful connection, it's absolutely fine to use that. Just remember that it needs to be well-known to you.

You'll probably find that in some cases, the connector word you choose may be the same as the keyword you chose in the earlier exercise. That's fine. You can look at them now and see that they are actually meaningful connections. Knowing that is important, as it naturally provides a stronger connection, which usually won't need to be practiced as much.

Exercise 9.6

Using the information from Exercise 9.5, transform each word pair into the steps you would use in practicing them. For example:

angolo [cue] — angle — corner; **corner** [cue] — angle — angolo

campana —

collo —

mano —

mare —

ezis —

kas —

nams —

uguns —

zirnis —

Using mnemonics for simple facts and definitions

So far, we have just looked at the task of learning new words in a language other than your native one. Let's now consider other situations.

Studying a subject, be it physics or art history, invariably involves learning new words. Sometimes they are completely new terms, other times they are familiar terms with new (or more precise) meanings. Learning this sort of new word is more akin to learning a simple fact than to learning a new word in another language, because rather than a single matching word, you have a (possibly quite lengthy) definition. If the term contains a new concept, a different strategy is most effective for learning, which I will discuss shortly. But sometimes the definition is quite simple, not in any way a new idea, and all you need is something to help you remember the word itself.

For example, consider the following technical terms (from geography, geology, and medicine):

peneplain, a low, nearly featureless tract of land of gently undulating relief

littoral, pertaining to the shore

glossalgia, pain in the tongue

Let's take the first term, **peneplain**. You could use a keyword such as *pen in a plane*, and that's nicely vivid — you could perhaps imagine a giant pen stabbing a plane. But what precisely would you be linking this to? There isn't a simple word you can connect it to.

On the other hand, you could re-interpret "a

pen in plane

peneplain

low, nearly featureless tract of land" as "a plain", and realize pene- means *almost, nearly*, as in pen-insula (almost an island), and pen-ultimate (nearly the last); thus peneplain is an almost-plain — which fits perfectly with the "gently undulating relief". So now you understand it, and to practice it you would lean heavily on the pene- as in peninsula / penultimate (depending on which is more familiar to you):

> **peneplain** [cue] — pene-, as in peninsula, meaning almost an island — almost a plain — a low, bare tract of land that's not flat but gently undulating

On the other hand, a term like **littoral**, defined as pertaining to the shore, has a very simple definition and is as arbitrary as any other-language word might be. Here a keyword mnemonic might well be helpful.

You see how in this case we can easily link the word to the definition, because the definition is so simple, and can be easily expressed in an image or a verbal phrase.

The next term, **glossalgia**, has a simple definition, but there are meaningful connections to be made. The -algia ending is found in a number of medical terms, of which the best known is probably *neuralgia*. It's also found in the more familiar word, *nostalgia*. In all cases, the meaning is the same: pain. If you know the word *neuralgia*, or any of the other medical words, then the meaning will be easy to remember. If the only word you know is *nostalgia*, then it will help if you dwell on its stronger meaning — not the gentle pleasure in things that remind us of a happier past, that it has come to mean, but a more urgent homesickness (the first part of this word means *returning home*). If you know several words with the -algia ending, it will be easier for you to make that connection to pain.

What about the first part of the word? The gloss- prefix signals that this word has to do with the tongue or language. Hence words like epiglottis, glossary, glossolalia, glottal, polyglot.

All this may seem more complicated than using a keyword, especially if you're only familiar with the words *nostalgia* and *glossary*, which don't, on their own, immediately evoke *pain* and *tongue*! But if you use this information to make and practice these connections, you will have knowledge that is much more resistant to forgetting. Moreover, building these connections will pay off in the long run, as you grow your knowledge of your language, making it easier to make and other connections and strengthen your networks.

So, how would you practice this term, given this information?

If you're looking at the side of the flashcard that says "glossalgia", then your first action should be to break it into its elements: gloss- and -algia. You remind yourself that the gloss- prefix indicates *tongue* (I've used *glottal*, but it all depends what words are most familiar and useful to you); then you remind yourself the -algia ending indicates *pain*. Then you put those two ideas together, getting "tongue pain". If you're going through the cards the other way, so your cue is "pain in the tongue", then you once again break it down into its two parts, pain and tongue, and follow through the steps in reverse.

You will notice that, as with the keyword mnemonic, going from the definition [English word, in the other-language examples] to the term to be learned is more difficult than going from the term to the definition. Again, as with the mnemonic, that means you have to expend a bit more time and effort on that direction, focusing on the weak link (in this example, pain — neuralgia; tongue — glottal). That's why it's much better if this cue word is familiar to you.

glossalgia		pain in the tongue
gloss → glottal → tongue		pain →neuralgia → algia
algia →neuralgia → pain		tongue → glottal → gloss
tongue pain		**glossalgia**

Making some of these connection may seem beyond you, but you don't need to have a deep knowledge of prefixes, suffixes and roots to make these connections! A good dictionary will help you with this. I find the Oxford English Dictionary particularly useful (many public libraries offer online access to their members). To use this to find meaningful connections, look up the target word and note what it says under etymology. That may direct you immediately to a prefix component or related word, but if it doesn't, copy the root word and go to Advanced Search to find other words that derive from the same word. Like any skill, this will become easier with practice.

Exercise 9.7

Consider the following terms and their definitions. How would you go about learning them? Remember to look for meaningful connections before falling back on mnemonics.

bioturbation, disturbance of sediment by burrowing or other activity of living organisms —

clastic, consisting of broken pieces of older rocks —

cryofracture, technique in which an object is rapidly and drastically cooled in order to break it down for internal study or disassembly —

euphony, language which sounds pleasing to the ear, quality of having a pleasant sound —

geophagy, practice of eating earth —

hermeneutics, theory and methodology of the interpretation of texts —

orexigenic, something that stimulates appetite for food —

myelin, white fatty substance that coats nerve axons in the brain —

paleogeography, the study of the physical landscapes in the past —

tectogenesis, the formation of the highly distorted rock structures characteristic of mountain ranges —

Using mnemonics for associated pairs

I said that the keyword mnemonic is especially popular as a means of memorizing new vocabulary, but has also proved its effectiveness for learning other associated pairs, such as authors and books, paintings and artists, countries and capitals, minerals and their attributes.

For example, to remember that the capital of Maryland is Annapolis, you could use the keywords "marry" and "apple", as in this image:

The capital of Maryland is Annapolis

Notice that in this type of task, you need two keywords. Also, although only one statement is on the image above, there are two ways of expressing this information, both of which are important:

The capital of Maryland is Annapolis.

Annapolis is the capital of Maryland.

And these are matched by the two possible situations in which you would need this information, in response to either of these questions:

What is the capital of Maryland?

Annapolis is the capital of which U.S. state?

To be in the position to answer either of these satisfactorily, you would need the following process in your retrieval practice:

But this mnemonic was originally devised for children. Probably most adults, in the U.S. at least, won't need help to remember these two names, although they may need help to tie the two together. In which case, retrieval practice on its own is probably sufficient — that is, you look at your flashcard that says *Maryland*, and you retrieve the capital city *Annapolis*; you go through them

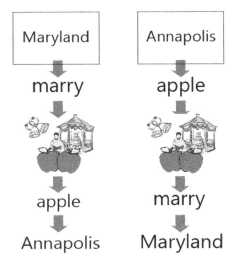

the other way, responding *Maryland* when you see *Annapolis*.

On the other hand, if you were trying to remember that Porto-Novo is the capital of Benin, you might require the help a mnemonic can give you.

What about a slightly more complex set of associations? For example, in a study I discuss in my book on mnemonics, students were given mnemonics for taxonomic information about fish, e.g., "The order Scorpaeniformes includes the family Triglidae, which in turn includes the two fish species, Gurnard and Robin."

The mnemonic instruction given was "Imagine that a scorpion has a hold of a tiger. The tiger leaps down toward a guard who is guarding a robin." There was also a picture illustrating this. I've provided my own:

The order **Scorpaeniformes** includes the family **Triglidae**, which in turn includes the two fish species, **Gurnard** and **Robin**

How would you practice that? Let's begin by considering the keywords.

Scorpion for Scorpaeniformes is a very obvious keyword, as is bird *robin* standing in for fish *robin*. *Guard* for *gurnard* is pretty good (not as good as the others, because Scorpaeniformes actually means shaped like a scorpion, and the connection screams out at you). The hardest one is *tiger* for Triglidae. *Troglodyte* would be a better keyword, in that it has greater similarity to the sound of the word. However, it is a much less familiar word than *tiger*, and much harder to visualize. Compromise like this is often necessary. It just means you have to work the connection a bit harder.

So, you visualize the scorpion holding the tiger attacking the guard guarding the robin, and as you hold the picture in your mind, you connect the scorpion to Scorpaeniformes, the tiger to Triglidae, the guard to gurnard, and the robin to the robin fish. Because the *Triglidae—tiger* link needs extra work, you'll want to pay particular attention to that.

But it's important that you make sure you pay attention to each link, even the obvious ones. The more tightly connected each item is, the more likely it is that you will retrieve the whole image, and the more opportunities you will have to get at it.

In the beginning, you want to very explicitly verbalize each link in the chain (while simultaneously trying to visualize the images as vividly as you can), and you might be put off by what seems a relatively lengthy process. Don't worry, it gets quicker each time you retrieve the image, and eventually, if you have given it sufficient practice, the mnemonic itself won't need to be explicitly called at all. As with a skill, which starts off being explicitly verbalized, and later becomes a memory that you seem to have encoded in your body, the mnemonic becomes unnecessary once it has served its purpose, and you should just 'know' that Scorpaeniformes include Triglidae which include gurnard and robin fish.

Let's think about the possible starting points (i.e., retrieval cues) that would require you to retrieve this information. I can think of quite a few:

- What species belong to the order Scorpaeniformes?

- What families belong to the order Scorpaeniformes?

- What order does the family Triglidae belong to?

- What order do Gurnard belong to?

- What order does the fish species Robin belong to?

- What family do Gurnard belong to?

- What family does the fish species Robin belong to?

That means you want to practice all these links (in both directions):

- Scorpaeniformes — Gurnard

- Scorpaeniformes — Robin

- Scorpaeniformes — Triglidae

- Triglidae — Gurnard

- Triglidae — Robin

Flashcards don't seem the most appropriate way to do this, because each term has multiple possible responses.

If you're using the keyword image, you need to practice bringing to mind the keyword image in the face of any of these four potential cues — Scorpaeniformes, Triglidae, gurnard, robin — and making sure you retrieve each target word as you cast your mental eye over each element in the image. A list with these items is all you need to practice that.

Of course, if those four words, all connected, were all that was on your list, it wouldn't really work! But it's not likely that, if you're learning taxonomies, you'd only be learning one. Let's imagine you also have the following taxonomies to memorize:

Perciformes — Latridae — tarakihi, moki, silver trumpeter

Lophiiformes — Lophiidae — goosefish, monkfish

Scombriformes — Centrolophidae — blue warehou, rudderfish

Zeiformes — Cyttidae — King dory

That would give you a total of five images, and 20 items / cues. Which is a good size for a list. So you write down all these items, *in jumbled order*, and then you can practice going through the list. Because each image is going to call forth at least three items, you don't need to go through the list more than once, assuming you get everything correct.

You don't have to use a mnemonic, of course. If you don't believe you need any extra help to remember these names, you can use retrieval practice on its own to practice these links. If so, it makes more sense to limit your responses. To see why, let's consider how it would work if you practiced retrieving all the words connected with each cue as you run down the list:

Latridae [cue] — Order Perciformes, species tarakihi, moki, silver trumpeter

Goosefish [cue] — Family Lophiidae, Order Lophiiformes, other species monkfish

Scombriformes [cue] — Centrolophidae, blue warehou, rudderfish

The last of these is the only one that works well. The problem with the Family as cue is that you have to go in two directions, up to the Order and down to the species. With a species name, the problem is the other species that belong in the same Family. You can do this, of course, it just doesn't flow very well. My own feeling is that you'd be best to go in just one direction. So, if the cue is an Order, you can respond with the full set; if it's a Family, just go with the species; if it's a species, go up to Family, then Order.

This does mean that some links will be practiced more than others, but then, some links need to be practiced more than others, so there's always that inherent inequality. It's more important to be responsive to your learning than to rigidly follow some hard-and-fast rule. You practice what needs to be practiced, and as much as you need to practice it, and then you leave them for another day. Having practice sessions on other days is more important than getting the number of retrievals 'right' in any one session.

Do note that, if you're using a keyword mnemonic to learn this sort of multi-word associations, you want to make sure the image has all its elements integrated. To see what I mean, compare the following two images, the first an integrated keyword mnemonic, the second one that is not integrated (example taken from Carney & Levin, 2003):

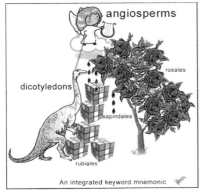

These show that the plant classification *Angiosperms* contains the class *dicotyledons*, which in turn contains the three orders *rubiales*, *sapindales*, and *rosales*. The keyword 'angel' represents *angiosperms*; the keyword 'dinosaur' represents *dicotyledons*, 'roses' for *rosales*, sap for *sapindales*, and 'Rubik's cubes' for *rubiales*. The picture shows the **angel** overseeing its pet **dinosaur** (note the leash), that is climbing the pile of **Rubik's cubes** so that it can lick the **sap** dripping down from the **rose** tree.

The second example is an extreme version of what not to do! What people are more likely to do is have several simple mnemonics, each showing one or maybe two associations. For example:

There are two problems with this, the main one being that there's nothing to connect the image bringing together Angiosperms, rubiales, and rosales, with the other necessary part, bringing together dicotyledons and sapindales. The lesser problem is that 'like' isn't the strongest verb for tying them together. I mean, you can imagine angels rolling around among roses and rubies in ecstasy, while dinosaurs are happily consuming sap, but it's not as active as, say, crushing and pouring — e.g., angels crushing roses and rubies under their feet while dinosaurs pour sap over them.

But better still would be angels riding dinosaurs as they crush roses and rubies under their big feet, then slide on the sap (or you could use *sapphires* for sapindales, which would be in keeping with the rubies).

The big advantage of a truly integrated mnemonic is that it tells a story. The human brain loves stories, and finds them much easier to remember than isolated facts. So a complex mnemonic, with lots of information, can be much easier to remember than a simple one, as long as it tells a coherent story. Also, note that this final story follows the appropriate hierarchy, the angiosperms above the dicotelydons, the dicotyledons above the rubiales, sapindales, and rosales.

I've described various options for keywords and actions because I want to emphasize that there is no one 'correct' answer. The proper answer is the one that works best for you, bearing in mind the general principles.

Exercise 9.8

Construct interactive and integrated mnemonics for the fish taxonomies:

Perciformes — Latridae — tarakihi, moki, silver trumpeter

Lophiiformes — Lophiidae — goosefish, monkfish

Scombriformes — Centrolophidae — blue warehou, rudderfish

Zeiformes — Cyttidae — King dory

You don't have to draw them! Come up with keywords for each, and an image / story that you can describe.

Exercise 9.9

Write down all the possible questions you might get in an exam, for which these various items would be the appropriate answers.

Using mnemonics for complex information

Mnemonics are not usually the appropriate strategy for complex information. However, there is a situation in which they can be useful. If you want some help to remember information that you might need for an essay in a closed-book exam, or for an oral presentation you need to give without notes. In such a situation you want to chain your cues, so that each one recalls the next one in the sequence. Each cue also needs to elicit all of its associated information. So first you need to practice recalling the information associated with each cue, and then you need to practice recalling each link in the chain.

This is not quite as straightforward as it may seem.

Here, for example, are the main points you might want to cover if giving a speech on the genesis of suicide terrorism (based on an article by Scott Atran, published in *Science*, and reproduced in *The Best American Science and Nature Writing 2004*):

- Definition (freedom fighters; French Resistance; Nicaraguan Contras; US Congress, act; two official definitions; restriction to suicide terrorism)

- History (Zealots; hashashin; French Revolution; 20th century revolutions; kamikaze; Middle East – 1981 Beirut; Hezbollah; Hamas; PIJ; Al-Qaida - Soviet-Afghan War; fundamentalism error)

- Difficulties of defending against (many targets, many attackers, low cost, detection difficulty; prevention)

- Explaining why (insults; attribution error; Milgram; perceived contexts; interpretation)

- Poverty link (crime – property vs violent; education; loss of advantage)

- Institutions (unattached young males, normal, personal identity – Palestinians, Bosnians; peer loyalty; emotional manipulation)

- Benefits (to individuals, to leaders, to organizations; effect of retaliation)

- Prevention strategies (searches; moles; education; community pressure; need for research)

Now, if you simply learn this chain of cues, perhaps through a story/ sentence mnemonic, such as "**Definitions** of **history fail** when they don't **explain why poverty** is dangerous, how **institutions benefit**, and how to **prevent** this", then you're going to have to mentally recite this each time you come to the end of a section and need to move on to the next one. You'll also have to recall which cue belongs to the section you've just finished before you know which one is next.

Rather than rehearsing your chain of cues, then, it's better to practice finishing each section with a sentence that recalls the cue (for example, at the end of your section on history, you say "Well, that's the history."), and practice each link as an associated pair. Thus, **history** is linked to **difficulties** — you practice retrieving "difficulties" when you hear "history".

Practicing this in variants may help you not get fixated on reproducing your text verbatim, and protect you from being knocked off course by some slight difference in your words. So you could practice: "Well, that's the history. Let's talk about the difficulties of defending against this type of terrorism."; "So much for history. Let's talk about the difficulties of defending against suicide bombers." ; "I hope this recounting of the history of suicide terrorism gives you some idea of the difficulties of defending against this type of terrorism. Let's talk about that next."; and so on.

In the case of writing an essay in an exam situation, however, it's fine to simply practice the complete chain, because you can look back over what you've written. You can even jot down the whole chain at the beginning.

Using a mnemonic effectively

- only use a mnemonic when the material cannot be meaningfully linked, or must be remembered in a specific order

- limit your use of mnemonics to material that you need extra help to remember

- always think about how you'll be trying to remember the material

- focus on every link in the mnemonic chain.

Review Questions

1. Which of these are important factors to look for in choosing a good keyword

    a. familiarity

    b. concreteness / visualizability

    c. how closely it sounds like the to-be-learned word

    d. unusualness

    e. distinctiveness

2. Which of these are important factors to look for in constructing an image for a keyword

    a. complexity

    b. simplicity

    c. interactivity

    d. vividness

    e. meaningfulness

3. What is the most important thing to consider when you're faced with a new word to learn

    a. how many syllables it has

    b. how unusual it is

    c. how difficult it is for you to learn

    d. how hard it is to pronounce

    e. whether you can connect it meaningfully to other words you know

4. The main purpose of the keyword mnemonic is to

    a. help you remember the meaning when you see the target word (recognition learning)

    b. help you recall the target word when you see the meaning

    c. provide a hook to help you remember when you can't meaningfully connect the new information to information you already know

    d. add interest, helping you engage with the information to be learned

5. Because the keyword mnemonic is such an effective means of memorizing words, you should always use it for learning vocabulary. Y / N

Linking differences & asking questions

This chapter goes into some detail as to how to frame your questions for Q & A practice, but it begins with a brief look at a strategy for learning new concepts that are easily confused with similar concepts. This is a very common situation in academic subjects, since a crucial aspect of expertise is learning to see the differences between similar ideas.

Linking differences

I said earlier that if a term you're learning contains a new concept, a mnemonic is not the best strategy, but that I'd discuss the most effective strategy a little later. The strategy I want to discuss is one which is particularly designed for learning concepts that are easily confused with similar concepts. This is a very common situation — in fact, a study found that in Introductory Psychology exams at a U.S. university 94% of multiple-choice questions involved highly-similar concepts (Hannon et al. 2009).

Differential-associative Processing (as Hannon called it, but I'm going to call it the linking differences strategy) has two components:

- identifying differences between highly similar concepts

- associating each part of the identified difference.

Let's see that in action (example taken from Hannon et al. 2009).

Here are the definitions provided for the highly similar concepts fluid and crystallized intelligence:

Fluid intelligence: The natural ability to solve problems, reason, and remember. Fluid intelligence is thought to be relatively uninfluenced by experience. It's the type of intelligence that is probably determined by biological or genetic factors. It tends to decrease in late adulthood.

Crystallized intelligence: Knowledge and facts acquired from schooling, culture and life in general. It is knowledge and facts acquired through experiences and consequently, is not determined by genetic factors. It increases with age.

The first step in the strategy is to identify differences, for instance:

- fluid intelligence is not influenced by experience whereas crystallized intelligence is influenced by experience

- fluid intelligence decreases with age while crystallized intelligence increases with age.

The next step (less obvious) is to form the link with the concept. This is done by using half the difference as a cue to practice recalling the associated concept. So, for example, you could practice the following cue-response pairs:

- this type of intelligence decreases with age — fluid intelligence

- this type of intelligence increases with age — crystallized intelligence

- this type of intelligence is influenced by experience — crystallized intelligence

- this type of intelligence is not influenced by experience — fluid intelligence

The trick to this is to make sure you identify the differences that you might be tested on, so, once again, it's important to think about the situations in which you'll want to retrieve the information (that is, the retrieval cues you'll be responding to).

Exercise 10.1

Given the following pairs of related terms, (a) identify the distinctive features, then (b) write out the cue-response pairs you would use in practice.

(a)

Genotype: You cannot see a person's genotype. It is the actual genetic information inherited from one's parents. A genotype will tell you what type of genes someone has. For example, although a woman may not have breast cancer, she could potentially develop breast cancer because she carries the genotype for breast cancer that she inherited from her mother.

Phenotype: It is the expression or behavioral manifestation of the genotype. It results from the interaction between a person's genotype (nature) and the environment (nurture). You can see a person's phenotype. For example, a child may have brown eyes that he inherited from his father or he may demonstrate artistic qualities that he has inherited from his mother.

(b)

Morpheme: A morpheme is the smallest unit of language that carries meaning. Some morphemes such as word stems like DOG and RUN can standalone as words, while other morphemes such as the prefixes PRE- and UN- and the suffixes - ED and -S cannot standalone. The English language has more than 40 morphemes.

Phoneme: A phoneme is the smallest unit of speech that distinguishes one word or word element from another in a specified language. For example, /p/ and /b/ are phonemes distinguishing pond from bond. The English language has 44 phonemes.

(c)

Proactive interference: This type of interference occurs when material previously learned interferes with the material you are currently trying to learn. For example, if you were trying to remember a new phone number, the older number usually interferes, making it harder to learn.

Retroactive interference: This type of interference occurs when material you're learning interferes with material you learned earlier. For example, if you started learning Italian, that might interfere with your previous learning of Spanish.

(d)

Mitosis: A type of cell division in which chromosomes in the nucleus are duplicated and separated into two distinct nuclei. Mitosis is generally preceded by the "S" stage of interphase, when the cell's DNA is replicated, and followed by cytokinesis, when the cytoplasm and cell membrane are divided into two new daughter cells.

Meiosis: A type of cell division in which a dividing parent cell proceeds through two consecutive divisions, ultimately producing four genetically unique daughter cells in each of which the chromosome number is half of that in the original parent cell. This process is exclusive to cells of the sex organs in sexually reproducing eukaryotes, where it serves the purpose of generating gametes such as eggs, sperm, or spores.

(e)

Balance of payments: A record or summary of all economic transactions between the residents of a country and the rest of the world in a particular period of time (e.g. over a quarter of a year or, more commonly, over a year). These transactions are made by individuals, firms and government bodies. Thus the balance of payments includes all external visible and non-visible transactions of a country.

Balance of trade: The difference between the monetary value of a nation's exports and imports over a certain period. Sometimes a distinction is made between a balance of trade for goods versus one for services. "Balance of trade" can be a misleading term because trade measures a flow of exports and imports over a given period of time, rather than a balance of exports and imports at a given point in time. Also, balance of trade does not necessarily imply that exports and imports are "in balance" with each other or anything else.

(f) Sometimes there are more than two highly similar concepts!

Momentum: is the product of the mass and velocity of an object. It is a vector quantity, possessing a magnitude and a direction

Velocity: The velocity of an object is the rate of change of its position with respect to a frame of reference, and is a function of time. Velocity is equivalent to a specification of an object's speed and direction of motion (e.g. 60 km/h to the north). It is thus a vector quality.

Speed: the speed of an object is the magnitude of its velocity (the rate of change of its position); it is thus a scalar quantity. The average speed of an object in an interval of time is the distance travelled by the object divided by the duration of the interval; the instantaneous speed is the limit of the average speed as the duration of the time interval approaches zero.

Questioning

Flashcards and mnemonics are tools for learning words and simple facts. Although these are valuable details that can anchor more complex material, your study of meaningful material requires another approach. Earlier, I discussed how you need to produce a set of learnable points from such texts (or lecture notes), and talked blithely about turning these into a 'Q & A' format. While this should be a relatively straightforward task (by far the trickier part is selecting the important points in the text), here are some pointers to the process.

Let's use the set of learnable points from the ozone text to demonstrate the process in action. This is a more complete learnable set, including information omitted earlier, when I assumed some background knowledge.

1. Ozone is important because it shields the surface from harmful ultraviolet radiation.

2. The stratosphere holds 90% of the ozone in our atmosphere (the ozone layer).

3. The troposphere holds 10%.

4. The troposphere is the lowest part of our atmosphere, where all of our weather takes place.

5. The ozone layer protects us; tropospheric ozone is a pollutant found in high concentrations in smog.

6. Wavelength is a measure of how energetic is the radiation.

7. The visible part of the electromagnetic spectrum ranges from 400 nanometers to 700 nm. Red light has a wavelength of about 630 nm; violet light about 410 nm.

8. Radiation with wavelengths shorter than those of violet light (at the short end of the visible spectrum) is called ultraviolet radiation. UV waves are dangerous because they're energetic enough to break the bonds of DNA molecules.

9. Of the three different types of ultraviolet (UV) radiation, the shortest (UV-c) is entirely screened out by the ozone layer, while the longest (UV-a) is not so damaging, so the main problem is UV-b.

10. The high reactivity of ozone results in damage to the living tissue of plants and animals, and is often felt as eye and lung irritation.

11. While our bodies can repair the damage done by UV waves most of the time, sometimes damaged DNA molecules are not repaired, and can replicate, leading to skin cancer.

12. The strong absorption of UV radiation in the ozone layer reduces the intensity of solar energy at lower altitudes. More energetic photons (ones with shorter wavelengths) are also less common.

13. Because ozone is most protective on the most dangerous wavelengths, a 10% decrease in ozone would increase the amount of DNA-damaging UV by about 22%.

14. Time and season affect how much UV radiation is absorbed by ozone because the angle of the sun affects how long the radiation takes to pass through the atmosphere (the path is shorter when the sun is directly overhead, so the radiation meets fewer ozone molecules).

15. Measurement:

    a. Solar flux = the amount of solar energy in watts falling perpendicularly on a surface one square centimeter; units are watts per cm2 per nm.

    b. The action spectrum measures the relative effectiveness of radiation in generating a certain biological response (such as sunburn) over a range of wavelengths.

You will learn more from this if you try turning these into questions before looking below at my suggestions.

Some of the learnable points are very simple and readily break down into a Q & A set. It's useful to include alternate ways of expressing the questions.

1. Ozone is important because it shields the surface from harmful ultraviolet radiation.

    Q: Why is ozone important?

    A: Because it shields the surface from harmful ultraviolet radiation.

    Q: What shields Earth's surface from harmful ultraviolet radiation?

    A: Ozone

2. The stratosphere holds 90% of the ozone in our atmosphere (the ozone layer).

    Q: What proportion of the atmosphere's ozone is in the stratosphere?

    A: 90%

Q: Where does 90% of atmospheric ozone lie?

A: The stratosphere.

3. The troposphere holds 10%.

Q: What proportion of the atmosphere's ozone is in the troposphere?

A: 10%

Q: Where is ozone found in the atmosphere, and in what quantities? (This merges both Q2 and Q3.)

A: 90% in the stratosphere and 10% in the troposphere.

4. The troposphere is the lowest part of our atmosphere, where all of our weather takes place.

Q: What part of the atmosphere is the troposphere?

A: The lowest part, where weather happens.

Q: Where in the atmosphere does weather occur, and what is this region called?

A: In the lowest part, the troposphere.

6. Wavelength is a measure of how energetic is the radiation.

Q: What does wavelength tell us?

A: How energetic the radiation is.

Q: What property of matter shows how energetic its radiation is?

A: Wavelengths.

Note that even simple learnable points can sometimes break down into several questions:

7. The visible part of the electromagnetic spectrum ranges from 400

nanometers to 700 nm. Red light has a wavelength of about 630 nm; violet light about 410 nm.

Q: What is the range of the visible part of the electromagnetic spectrum?

A: 400 nanometers to 700 nm

Q: What is the wavelength of red light?

A: About 630 nm.

Q: What is the wavelength of violet light?

A: About 410 nm.

Sometimes you have to pull out what is 'between the lines' (i.e., not explicit), to seek out the important message. For example, from the following learnable point you could offer a series of straightforward questions:

5. The ozone layer protects us; tropospheric ozone is a pollutant found in high concentrations in smog.

Q: What does the ozone layer do?

A: The ozone layer protects us.

Q: What does tropospheric ozone do?

A: Tropospheric ozone is a pollutant.

Q: Where is this pollutant found?

A: In smog.

These might, in fact, be what you need, if you are coming to the topic with no relevant knowledge at all. But if you know well enough that the ozone layer protects us, it's probably better to go with the following question (note that your aim should not be to make up easy questions for yourself! Your learnable points should encompass the important information that you don't know, or don't know well enough, and your questions should reflect that):

Q: Is ozone always protective?

A: No. The ozone layer protects us, but tropospheric ozone is a pollutant found in high concentrations in smog.

So, with the following learnable point, you might feel the need to include three questions:

8. Radiation with wavelengths shorter than those of violet light (at the short end of the visible spectrum) is called ultraviolet radiation. UV waves are dangerous because they're energetic enough to break the bonds of DNA molecules.

Q: Where is violet light in the spectrum?

A: At the short end (i.e., the end with the shorter wavelengths).

Q: What is ultraviolet radiation?

A: Radiation with wavelengths shorter than those of violet light.

Q: Why is ultraviolet radiation dangerous?

A: Because it's energetic enough to break the bonds of DNA molecules.

When you break points down to questions in this way, you might also become aware of additional questions not answered in your learnable points. So, for example, you may not know what "break the bonds of DNA molecules" means. You may need to return to the text, or perhaps even have to seek further to answer your questions. Whether or not you do so depends on your motivation and goals.

The next two sets of questions may similarly make you realize there's some confusion in your mind.

9. Of the three different types of ultraviolet (UV) radiation, the shortest

(UV-c) is entirely screened out by the ozone layer, while the longest (UV-a) is not so damaging, so the main problem is UV-b.

Q: How many types of ultraviolet radiation are there and what are they?

A: Three. UV-a, UV-b, and UV-c.

Q: Which of the three different types of ultraviolet radiation is most dangerous and why?

A: UV-b. Because the shortest (UV-c) is entirely screened out by the ozone layer, and the longest (UV-a) is not so damaging.

Again, you may want to pursue the question of why the shortest wavelengths can't get past the ozone layer, and why the longest wavelengths aren't as damaging.

10. The high reactivity of ozone results in damage to the living tissue of plants and animals, and is often felt as eye and lung irritation.

Q: How does ozone damage us?

A: Because ozone is a highly reactive form of oxygen, it can irritate the eyes and lungs.

This begs the question of what "highly reactive" means. Again, you may understand what it means, or you may not care.

Some statements are less readily turned into questions. The following, for example, requires a little thought. Your first off-the-cuff idea may be something like "How do UV waves damage us?", but is this really the best question? Sometimes it helps to think of the answer first, and work back. In this case, the "While" is making the Q & A format less obvious. Try ignoring that to start with.

11. While our bodies can repair the damage done by UV waves most of the time, sometimes damaged DNA molecules are not repaired, and can replicate, leading to skin cancer.

A: Skin cancer occurs when damaged DNA is not repaired.

Having created this answer, the question is more obvious.

Q: Why does UV damage sometimes cause skin cancer?

And now, in response to that question, you may want to expand on the answer, incorporating what was alluded to in that "While ...".

A: Skin cancer occurs when DNA damaged by UV radiation is not repaired, as it usually is.

The following question is in a format that is misleadingly easy to transform into a Q & A:

12. The strong absorption of UV radiation in the ozone layer reduces the intensity of solar energy at lower altitudes. More energetic photons (ones with shorter wavelengths) are also less common.

Q: What does the strong absorption of UV radiation in the ozone layer do?

A: Reduce the intensity of solar energy at lower altitudes.

When framing questions from a text, you know what the answer is meant to be. That's fine as long as the text is fresh in your mind, but if you're seeking longer-lasting memories you want questions that are phrased in such a way that someone knowing the topic but not the specific text would answer it 'correctly' (i.e., how you meant it to be answered). The following version makes it clearer what information you're seeking:

Q: What effect does the ozone layer's absorption of UV radiation have on energy levels at lower altitudes?

An alternate question that gets to the heart of the learnable point without being so 'leading' would be:

Q: Why is it safer for living things at lower altitudes?

A: Because the ozone layer absorbs a lot of the UV waves, reducing the sun's intensity, and because the more energetic photons are less common.

Sometimes you need to refer back to earlier points to properly answer the question. In the next learnable point, the "most dangerous wavelengths" are not explicitly identified, but adding it to your answer does reinforce an important point (that UV-b are the most dangerous wavelengths).

13. Because ozone is most protective on the most dangerous wavelengths, a 10% decrease in ozone would increase the amount of DNA-damaging UV by about 22%.

Q: Which wavelengths does ozone protect us from most?

A: The most dangerous wavelengths: UV-b

Q: How much would a 10% decrease in ozone increase the amount of DNA-damaging UV?

A: By about 22%.

A "because" in a learnable point makes the Q & A pretty obvious:

14. Time and season affect how much UV radiation is absorbed by ozone because the angle of the sun affects how long the radiation takes to pass through the atmosphere (the path is shorter when the sun is directly overhead, so the radiation meets fewer ozone molecules).

Q: Why does time of day and season affect how much UV radiation is absorbed by ozone?

A: Because the angle of the sun affects how long the radiation takes to pass through the atmosphere (the path is shorter when the sun is directly overhead, so the radiation meets fewer ozone molecules).

Note that this could have been broken into two questions, rather than adding that explanatory note in brackets in the answer. The issue of how many questions you use is reminiscent of the issue of how many steps you break a process into — it depends on your 'chunks', that is, on your existing knowledge and your grasp of the material.

Definitions, as in the last two points, would seem to be readily transformed into a Q & A (What is a ....? What does .... measure?), but there are two aspects you might like to note. One is whether you need an additional question relating to the unit of measurement, and the other is whether you want to pursue further explanations of any unclear concepts. For example, what does "the relative effectiveness of radiation in generating a certain biological response over a range of wavelengths" really mean?

15a. Solar flux = the amount of solar energy in watts falling perpendicularly on a surface one square centimeter; units are watts per cm2 per nm.

Q: What is solar flux?

A: The amount of solar energy in watts falling perpendicularly on a surface one square centimeter.

Q: What unit is solar flux measured in?

A: watts per cm2 per nm

or:

Q: How is solar energy measured?

A: In watts falling perpendicularly on a surface one square centimeter.

15b. The action spectrum measures the relative effectiveness of radiation in generating a certain biological response (such as sunburn) over a range of wavelengths.

Q: What does the action spectrum measure?

A: The relative effectiveness of radiation in generating a certain biological response (such as sunburn) over a range of wavelengths.

Q: What is used to measure the capacity of ultraviolet radiation to damage living tissue?

A: The action spectrum

___

One important aspect of using a Q & A format for retrieval practice is the issue of organization and order. I have said that practicing in different ways is best because it provides opportunities for different retrieval cues to be used, new paths to be forged. However, in the case of meaningful information, this strategy should be tempered. Remember that your priority is to create and strengthen good memory codes — ones where the various bits of information are tightly clustered and strongly connected. The human brain loves stories. Stories form just about the best links there are, and one of the reasons for this is that stories ('proper' stories!) are based on a narrative chain — a cause-&-effect chain.

You don't need narrative to have a chain of linked events. A lot of science, and history (of course), is explained in such a way. You want to take advantage of this, which means you don't want to mess with the order too much, when studying or revising the material.

This is particularly true in your early reviews. Initially, you do want to concentrate on getting that integrated story/network firmly into your head, so it's best to practice the facts in logical order. Once you've got that, you can jumble up the questions as thoroughly as you like, to build up different paths and strong retrieval cues. What you can do, however, to provide some useful variety is to have alternative questions, such as I provided for some of the above examples.

Do note that 'logical order' doesn't necessarily mean the exact order of points in the text. Move them around to whatever makes sense to you. For example, below I provide a comparison of the questions in the original order of the text and in an order that's logical for me (to keep this list from becoming too long, I haven't included alternative questions).

Note that, when you re-organize them, and when you only focus on the questions, you may realize that a particular question only made sense as a follow-up to the answer of its original predecessor (as with Question 11). This suggests a re-phrasing of the question, perhaps even of both questions.

Original order

1. Why is ozone important?

2. What proportion of the atmosphere's ozone is in the stratosphere?

3. What proportion of the atmosphere's ozone is in the troposphere?

4. What part of the atmosphere is the troposphere?

5. What does wavelength tell us?

6. What is the range of the visible part of the electromagnetic spectrum?

7. What is the wavelength of red light?

8. What is the wavelength of violet light?

9. What does the ozone layer do?

10. What does tropospheric ozone do?

11. Where is this pollutant found?

12. Is ozone always protective?

13. Where is violet light in the spectrum?

14. What is ultraviolet radiation?

Practice order

1. Why is ozone important?

9. What does the ozone layer do?

2. What proportion of the atmosphere's ozone is in the stratosphere?

3. What proportion of the atmosphere's ozone is in the troposphere?

4. What part of the atmosphere is the troposphere?

12. Is ozone always protective?

10. What does tropospheric ozone do?

11. Where is this pollutant found?

17. How does ozone damage us?

5. What does wavelength tell us?

6. What is the range of the visible part of the electromagnetic spectrum?

7. What is the wavelength of red light?

8. What is the wavelength of violet light?

13. Where is violet light in the spectrum?

15. Why is it dangerous?

16. Which of the three different types of ultraviolet radiation is most dangerous and why?

17. How does ozone damage us?

18. Why does UV damage sometimes cause skin cancer?

19. What does the strong absorption of UV radiation in the ozone layer do?

20. Why is it safer for living things at lower altitudes?

21. Which wavelengths does ozone protect us from most?

22. How much would a 10% decrease in ozone increase the amount of DNA-damaging UV?

23. Why does time of day and season affect how much UV radiation is absorbed by ozone?

24. What is solar flux?

25. What unit is solar flux measured in?

26. What does the action spectrum measure?

14. What is ultraviolet radiation?

15. Why is it dangerous?

16. Which of the three different types of ultraviolet radiation is most dangerous and why?

21. Which wavelengths does ozone protect us from most?

18. Why does UV damage sometimes cause skin cancer?

26. What does the action spectrum measure?

19. What does the strong absorption of UV radiation in the ozone layer do?

20. Why is it safer for living things at lower altitudes?

22. How much would a 10% decrease in ozone increase the amount of DNA-damaging UV?

23. Why does time of day and season affect how much UV radiation is absorbed by ozone?

24. What is solar flux?

25. What unit is solar flux measured in?

How to display your questions

You can write your questions on cards if you like, and if you anticipate needing a lot of review to master this material, this may be a good option. However, most learners can probably settle for the much easier strategy of writing the questions down in one or (preferably) two lists (the second list is for your alternative questions), with the answers on the back of the sheet.

You may be tempted to omit the answers, on the grounds that you have your set of learnable points to refer to, but I do recommend actually physically writing out the answers — not only because the process will help reinforce the answers, but also because you will find it easier to check your answers. It's easy to omit this step when you are sure of your knowledge, but, especially in the early reviews, it really does pay to check!

Exercise 10.2

Practice transforming information into Q & A format using these simple facts.

1. The Hundred Years War between England and France began in 1337.

2. The first steam engine was created by Thomas Savery in 1698.

3. The second most common element in the Earth's crust is silicon.

4. The earliest cockroach fossil is about 280 million years old, 80 million years older than the first dinosaurs.

5. Mafic rocks are igneous rocks that are high in magnesium and iron.

6. Cassius Dio was a famous Roman historian of the 2nd century.

7. The Orkhon River is the longest river in Mongolia.

8. The tuatara is the only surviving member of the Rhynchocephalia.

9. Disko Island is in Greenland.

10. Euskara is the name of the Basque language.

Exercise 10.3

Take the learnable points you collected in Exercise 2.1 and transform them into a Q & A format

Exercise 10.4

Take the learnable points you collected in Exercise 2.2 and transform them into a Q & A format

Points to remember

There is no one-to-one correspondence between learning points and questions — one learning point may generate several questions.

How much you break the learning point down depends on your background knowledge and understanding of the material.

Your questions should be neither too easy (if you already know the answer perfectly well, it's pointless to test it) nor too difficult (if you don't understand the material sufficiently well to answer the question, then you need to work on that more first).

Take care to frame questions so that they 'stand alone' and don't rely on your memory of the original sentence.

Include variants of your questions, to enable you to review with different questions.

Put your questions in an order that makes sense to you, and keep that order for the initial reviews, only mixing it up when you are confident of your understanding.

Review Questions

1. When you transform a complex text into a set of learnable points

   a. only the first sentence in each paragraph needs to be transformed into a learnable point

   b. only the final sentence in each paragraph needs to be transformed into a learnable point

   c. every sentence in the text should be transformed into a learnable point

   d. every fact in the text should be transformed into a learnable point

   e. you only need to consider what's important that you don't already know

2. When you transform a complex text into a set of learnable points and then a set of questions and answers

   a. every learnable point should be turned into a question

   b. every learnable point should be turned into two questions, so you have an alternate set for review

   c. every learnable point should be turned into at least one question

   d. not every learnable point needs an associated question

3. Your questions should

   a. always follow the same order as the text

   b. keep to the same order as the text for the first two reviews, then randomly mix them up

   c. follow an order that is most meaningful to you

   d. follow an order that is most meaningful to you, then rearrange them when you're more confident of the material

4. If a question only makes sense as a follow-up to another question, you should

   a. always keep them together

    b.   combine them to form a single question

    c.   rewrite the question so it makes sense on its own

    d.   discard the question

5. If a question is too difficult, you should

    a.   break it down into several questions

    b.   discard it

    c.   return to the text and work out what you don't understand

    d.   keep practicing its retrieval until you get it right

Concept maps

This brief chapter discusses how to use concept mapping and mind mapping as a retrieval practice strategy for learning complex material.

The second strategy for practicing complex text that I want to discuss is concept mapping. Earlier in the book, I mentioned research showing that concept maps, when used in the presence of the text, were no more effective than re-reading. I am actually a big fan of concept maps, so this shouldn't be taken as a slur. The point is how to use them effectively.

Concept maps are great for organizing your knowledge, and thus especially useful for understanding complex topics and forming those strong, meaningful connections. Concept maps are also a good strategy for 'priming' your mind — getting yourself into the right head-space for studying a topic, attending a lecture, doing a test.

Most importantly in this context, concept maps are also a good strategy to use with retrieval practice.

When I discussed them earlier I kept making the point that in the study the concept maps were drawn in the presence of the texts. Actual retrieval wasn't required. But if you *don't* have the text in front of you, if you draw a concept map as a means of retrieval practice, then this is a completely different story.

Concept maps are a good strategy for retrieval practice because:

- many people find them more enjoyable than, say, writing down a list of points, or answering a list of questions.

- they can be a little different each time, giving you the opportunity to make new connections.

- they provide a spatial visualization — and spatial information tends to be more easily remembered.

Concept maps are not as widely known as they should be, not as well-known as mind maps are. I'm sure you're familiar with mind maps, even if you haven't used them yourself. Here are some of the important ways the two differ:

- In a concept map, lines connecting the concepts are labeled to show the relationships between concepts.

- In a mind map, the main themes are connected only to a single central image, not to each other, and the connections between concepts are not labeled.

- Mind maps are usually more visual, and concept maps more verbal.

The fact that the links are all labeled is a crucial factor in what makes concept maps such an effective tool for developing understanding, and why I prefer them over mind maps as a means of taking notes. It's one thing to realize that two concepts are connected; it's quite another to be able to articulate the nature of that connection. However, when it comes to retrieval practice, you may find the simpler mind map easier to use.

My own recommendation would be to use a concept map for initial review, when you're still consolidating your grasp of the material, and then perhaps using a mind map or simplified concept map (without labeling the links) for later reviews.

Drawing concept maps for understanding is something I cover in considerable depth in *Effective note-taking*, but for retrieval practice we can keep it simple. Here are the basic steps:

1. Articulate the question that is your main focus.

2. List the key concepts.

3. Describe the attributes of these concepts.

4. Articulate the relationships between the concepts.

5. Order the concepts in a rough hierarchy from most general to most specific, in this context.

Let's see that process in action:

1. Focal question: Why is ozone important?

2 & 3. Key concepts, with attributes:

- **ozone**: a type of oxygen molecule found in small concentrations in the atmosphere

- **ozone layer:** holds 90% of atmospheric ozone; in stratosphere; protects against UV-radiation; entirely blocks UV-c, partially blocks UV-b

- **tropospheric ozone**: holds 10% of atmospheric ozone; pollutant; large component of smog

- **wavelengths**: shorter wavelengths are more energetic than longer ones; very energetic wavelengths can damage DNA by breaking their bonds

- **visible spectrum**: wavelengths humans can see; range 400nm to 700nm; red at long end (630nm); violet at short end (410nm)

- **ultraviolet waves**: wavelengths shorter than violet; range 1-400nm; three types: UV-a, UV-b, UV-c (longest to shortest)

- **DNA**: the instructions in biological cells

- **solar flux**: a measure of solar energy; varies depending on time of day and season; measured in watts per square centimeter

- **action spectrum**: a measure of radiation damage

4. Relationships between concepts:

- **visible spectrum** contains a subset of **wavelengths**

- **ultraviolet waves** are beyond the **visible spectrum**

- **ultraviolet waves** can damage **DNA**

- **ozone layer** blocks most of the **ultraviolet waves**

- **ozone layer** contains 90% of atmospheric **ozone**

- **tropospheric ozone** is 10% of atmospheric **ozone**

- **solar flux** measures **ultraviolet radiation**

- **action spectrum** measures **ultraviolet radiation** damage to **DNA**

5. Concept order (most general to most specific):

- **ozone**

  - **ozone layer**

  - **tropospheric ozone**

- **wavelengths**

  - **visible spectrum**

  - **ultraviolet waves**

    - **solar flux**

  - **DNA damage**

    - **action spectrum**

On the next page you can see an example of a concept map produced from this.

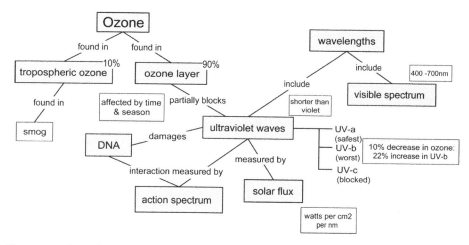

Do note that there's no 'right' answer! When using concept maps for retrieval practice, the important thing is simply to make sure that you get all the key concepts. You don't have to write down all the details — but do say them (preferably aloud) to yourself.

You can, of course, add as much detail as you wish to your concept maps. However, your review maps don't need to be as complete as those you make when mastering the material. Think of it as a progressive series. A concept map for understanding will be quite detailed; your first practice map will be less so, and subsequent maps simpler still, culminating with a quickly sketched mind map, such as this one (the original used various appropriate colors, but here, sadly, we must use our imagination):

But remember, the idea is that these labels are representing a larger body of knowledge that you have safely stored in your memory. If all you can remember is a few different words, with none of that meaningful knowledge behind them, then it's not going to do much good!

Do remember, too, that you don't need to choose between questioning and concept maps for your review strategies. My own recommendation for revising complex texts would be to use both Q & A and concept maps, on different review occasions.

Exercise 11.1

Transform the text from Exercise 2.1 into a concept map

Exercise 11.2

Transform the text from Exercise 2.2 into a concept map

Exercise 11.3

The following text begins with some learning goals. With these as your focus, build your set of learnable points, a Q & A set, and a concept map.

Microeconomics and Macroeconomics

By the end of this section, you will be able to:

- Describe microeconomics

- Describe macroeconomics

- Contrast monetary policy and fiscal policy

Economics is concerned with the well-being of *all* people, including those with jobs and those without jobs, as well as those with high incomes and those with low incomes. Economics acknowledges that production of useful goods and services can create problems of environmental pollution. It explores the question of how investing in education helps to develop workers' skills. It probes questions like how to tell when big businesses or big labor unions are operating in a way that benefits society as a whole and when they are operating in a way that benefits their owners or members at the expense of others. It looks at how government spending, taxes, and regulations affect decisions about production and consumption.

It should be clear by now that economics covers considerable ground. We can divide that ground into two parts: Microeconomics focuses on the actions of individual agents within the economy, like households, workers, and businesses. Macroeconomics looks at the economy as a whole. It focuses on broad issues such as growth of production, the number of unemployed people, the inflationary increase in prices, government deficits, and levels of exports and imports. Microeconomics and macroeconomics are not separate subjects, but rather complementary perspectives on the overall subject of the economy.

To understand why both microeconomic and macroeconomic perspectives are useful, consider the problem of studying a biological ecosystem like a lake. One person who sets out to study the lake might focus on specific topics: certain kinds of algae or plant life; the characteristics of particular fish or snails; or the trees surrounding the lake. Another person might take an overall view and instead consider the lake's ecosystem from top to bottom; what eats what, how the system stays in a rough balance, and what environmental stresses affect this balance. Both approaches are useful, and both examine the same lake, but the viewpoints are different. In a similar way, both microeconomics and macroeconomics study the same economy, but each has a different viewpoint.

Whether you are scrutinizing lakes or economics, the micro and the macro insights should blend with each other. In studying a lake, the micro insights about particular plants and animals help to understand the overall food chain, while the macro insights about the overall food chain help to explain the environment in which individual plants and animals live.

In economics, the micro decisions of individual businesses are influenced by whether the macroeconomy is healthy. For example, firms will be more likely to hire workers if the overall economy is growing. In turn, macroeconomy's performance ultimately depends on the microeconomic decisions that individual households and businesses make.

Microeconomics

What determines how households and individuals spend their budgets? What combination of goods and services will best fit their needs and wants, given the budget they have to spend? How do people decide whether to work, and if so, whether to work full time or part time? How do people decide how much to save for the future, or whether they should borrow to spend beyond their current means?

What determines the products, and how many of each, a firm will produce and sell? What determines the prices a firm will charge? What determines how a firm will produce its products?

What determines how many workers it will hire? How will a firm finance its business? When will a firm decide to expand, downsize, or even close? In the microeconomics part of this book, we will learn about the theory of consumer behavior, the theory of the firm, how markets for labor and other resources work, and how markets sometimes fail to work properly.

Macroeconomics

What determines the level of economic activity in a society? In other words, what determines how many goods and services a nation actually produces? What determines how many jobs are available in an economy? What determines a nation's standard of living? What causes the economy to speed up or slow down? What causes firms to hire more workers or to lay them off? Finally, what causes the economy to grow over the long term?

We can determine an economy's macroeconomic health by examining a number of goals: growth in the standard of living, low unemployment, and low inflation, to name the most important. How can we use government macroeconomic policy to pursue these goals? A nation's central bank conducts monetary policy, which involves policies that affect bank lending, interest rates, and financial capital markets. For the United States, this is the Federal Reserve. A nation's legislative body determines fiscal policy, which involves government spending and taxes. For the United States, this is the Congress and the executive branch, which originates the federal budget. These are the government's main tools. Americans tend to expect that government can fix whatever economic problems we encounter, but to what extent is that expectation realistic? These are just some of the issues that we will explore in the macroeconomic chapters of this book.

(excerpted from the OpenStax textbook, Principles of Economics 2e, figures excluded. Download for free at https://cnx.org/contents/vEmOH-_p@7.7:1wsl_jdK@8/1-2-Microeconomics-and-Macroeconomics)

Review Questions

1. Concept maps are a good strategy for

    a. making connections

    b. organizing your knowledge

    c. understanding difficult subjects

    d. getting your mind into the right head-space for a particular topic

    e. testing your recall

2. Select the true statements:

    a. Retrieval practice only works if you're retrieving the to-be-learned information from long-term memory.

    b. Drawing a concept map for retrieval practice is more effective when you have the text to refer to.

    c. Drawing a concept map for retrieval practice is less effective when you have the text to refer to.

    d. Drawing a concept map for retrieval practice is only effective if you don't refer to the text.

3. A mind map

    a. is the same thing as a concept map

    b.   differs from a concept map in that it connects all the main ideas to a central image

    c.   differs from a concept map in that it doesn't label the connections

    d.   is much more colorful than a concept map

4.   Concept maps are a good strategy for retrieval practice because

    a.   you can do them many times and vary it each time

    b.   they're more fun than drilling on a set of facts

    c.   they're easier than answering questions

    d.   they provide a spatial layout that helps make the information more memorable

    e.   they can be really detailed

5.   Mind maps can also be used for retrieval practice. Y / N

Section Points to remember

Flashcards (or flashcard software) are very good for learning foreign or technical words, and can also be used for simple facts (e.g., What is the capital of Australia?).

The keyword mnemonic is an effective strategy for making difficult words or facts more memorable, and can be used in conjunction with a flashcard strategy.

Linked differences is a good strategy for learning closely related concepts.

Complex information can be practiced by transforming the learnable points you have generated from the text into sets of questions.

Concept maps can also be used to practice your retrieval of these learnable points, and you can improve your learning by using both concept maps and questions on different review sessions.

Skill practice

Some of you may have been a little bewildered by the use of the word "practice" in the context of study, where the more usual term is "revision". The reason for using it is of course to emphasize that the most effective way of revising is to use retrieval practice. But the word "practice" is more usually used in connection with skills, which have a greater role in study than you might think. In the next two chapters, we will look at how skill learning is different from other learning, the effectiveness of deliberate practice for skill learning, and how cognitive skills in particular are crucial to many subjects.

Learning a skill

Learning a skill, whether a motor skill like playing golf or a musical instrument, or a cognitive skill like chess, is a different process than learning information. Accordingly, some changes must be made to our list of effective principles. In particular, while retrieval practice is the focus of effective information learning, deliberate practice is the central element in effective skill learning.

When you think of skill learning, you probably think of learning a sport, learning to play a musical instrument, to type, to ride a bike or drive a car. These are typical examples of skill learning, and the common element is that these are all motor skills. But there is another type of skill which is more relevant to study, and that is cognitive skills.

A typical example of a cognitive skill is chess, but of course reading and study skills are also cognitive skills. Moreover, many study topics are not only informational, but also contain cognitive skills. Mathematics, chemistry, medicine, and foreign languages are prime examples of these.

We are all well aware that skills are learned and remembered differently than information. You probably think that motor skills and cognitive skills are equally different from each other. Well, that's true in a sense, but all three of these share similarities. Cognitive skills are more similar to information memory than motor skills are, but most motor tasks have an information component, to a greater or lesser extent (something which significantly affects some aspects of practice).

In other words, while these three domains have important differences, they can be thought of as all belonging to a continuum of memory and learning, with information at one end and physical actions at the other, rather than as completely separate domains. This is despite the fact that information and physical actions are encoded and processed quite differently.

Because it's the "purer" example of skill learning, the following description of how skill learning works focuses largely on motor skills. After that I'll talk about cognitive skills specifically.

Skill learning begins with instruction

Skill learning is thought to go through three stages. It begins with instruction, which usually involves both verbal instruction and a physical demonstration of the skill. The quality of that instruction is one factor affecting how quickly you learn a skill.

We've all had experience of good instructions and bad instructions, even if we can't articulate exactly why the instructions are good or bad. In regard to physical skills, one factor has to do with the direction of focus. Instructions that tell you what to do with your body ("The right index finger and thumb continue to grasp the short end ...") are often not particularly effective. Instead, instructions are usually better to direct your attention to the *effects* of those movements (Wulf et al. 2010). So, for example, it's often better for golfers to be told to focus on the swing of the club rather than the swing of their arms.

It seems that directing attention to an external rather than internal focus (the tool being manipulated or the thing in the environment being interacted with, rather than any part of your body) helps shorten the first stage of skill learning, speeding up the progression to a less conscious, automatic process.

Having said that, this advice depends on the specific skill being learned, and also on the degree of expertise you have. At certain stages of skill learning, instructions specifying precisely what you do with your body may well be more effective. The point to bear in mind, then, is simply that this distinction exists — that instructions may direct your attention to your body or to something outside your body, and if one type of instruction isn't working well for you, to try the other.

Explicit instruction, however, is not the only means of teaching a skill, and for motor skills verbal instruction is almost invariably accompanied by a physical demonstration of the skill.

Modeling

We now know that neurons in our brains activate in response to other people's actions in the same way (although at a lower level of activation) that they respond to our own actions. We experience this echo effect every day, when we wince or clutch at our body on seeing someone else being hurt, when we observe someone dancing and feel an answering impulse in our body, when we yawn on seeing another person yawn.

This imitative behavior is not simply the key to how children learn, but enables all of us to benefit from observation as a form of practice. That observation doesn't have to be of an expert.

One useful practice method for physical skills is collaboration in pairs. Research has found that, when paired individuals alternate between performing the skill themselves and observing the other, both individuals learn at least as much, and sometimes more, as they would if they'd spent the same amount of time practicing the skill (Wulf et al. 2010).

There are two main advantages that paired practice might give. The first relates to the greater variability of the practice, since people are likely to perform differently, despite being instructed in the same way and provided with the same demonstrations. Consistent with this, paired practice has been found to encourage more flexible performance. The second advantage relates to motivation. Paired practice is often more enjoyable than solo practice, and also can provide the spur of competition.

Of course, if your partner makes you feel inadequate, or performs poorly, such practice may do more harm than good! As always, the general principle must bow to the specifics of a situation, and your own personality.

Video demonstrations, done well, can also provide excellent models. One of the big advantages of observation is that it provides an opportunity to focus on specific aspects in a way that might not be possible when you're performing the action yourself. A video, which you can stop and freeze and replay, as often as you like, is great for this.

Observing others, then, is a useful strategy that may help you short-cut your learning of physical skills. Just be aware that you can equally easily pick up bad habits by observing poor performances!

Automating action sequences is the heart of motor skill learning

The initial instruction phase is followed by a period during which you learn to coordinate the various physical actions and strengthen the connections between successive actions. During this stage, you still need verbal reminders to tell you what to do. In the final stage, however, you lose the verbalization entirely.

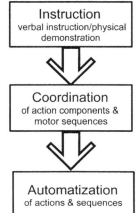

This is the great difference between learning a skill or motor sequence, and learning information. Once the sequence has become automatic (through repetition, that is, practice), you can do it faster and without putting much load on your working memory (thus freeing up working memory for 'higher-level' strategic thinking). The downside is that, once it reaches this stage, if you do 'engage your brain' and start to actually think about what you're doing, your performance of it will almost certainly deteriorate. We're all familiar with this!

How 'muscle memory' is different from information memory

I said that we all know that learning and remembering skills is different from learning and remembering information. This is reflected in the way we talk about 'muscle memory'. Despite its name, the memory is held in the brain rather than in the muscles themselves (although of course the muscles will also be changed by the practice of the movement). But the term 'muscle memory' isn't, I don't think, so much a sign that people really believe memory is held in the muscles, as it is simply an acknowledgement that this type of memory is noticeably different from other types of memory. In particular, it seems to be far more durable, more resistant to the effects of disuse. There are several reasons for this.

Motor skill learning takes place in a different region of the brain than information learning (known more formally as **declarative memory**), and this region is in one of the oldest parts of the brain (the **hindbrain**). Motor learning transfers from short-term to long-term storage much more quickly than declarative memories: within a few hours in some cases, within a few days at most (in contrast to the weeks before declarative memories are completely transferred).

This difference in timing has important consequences for effective practice.

Additionally, the transfer process tends to drop what it regards as unimportant details to an even greater extent than occurs with declarative memory. In other words, only a small part of the information you have encoded in your short-term memory will be passed on to your long-term memory. Thus, while sophisticated subtleties of motion and action are easily noted and encoded in short-term memory (enabling, for example, a baseball batter to adjust to the pitches), such subtleties are usually lost — within some 10-15 minutes, once the event is over. Quickly in and quickly out, seems to be the motto!

What this means is that only the broad outlines of a procedure get locked into long-term memory. Muscle memories are easily acquired and the details are just as readily lost. On the plus side, they are also quickly picked up again with a little practice. All this is reflected in the way we talk of motor skills getting 'rusty', our knowledge that we have to constantly use skills to keep them honed, and our confidence that, if we have neglected them, nonetheless we will get them back with a little work. It's also why even experts don't just walk into a situation of using their skills (a concert; a ball game) without some warm-up.

Because muscle memory is so strong once properly consolidated, and perhaps also because distinguishing details are likely to be lost, interference is even more of a potential problem than it is for declarative memory. This means you need to watch out for steps within the new skill that are antagonistic to steps contained in an already mastered skill — for example, if you decide to move from using a standard QWERTY keyboard to a Dvorak one (where the letters are arranged differently), this is much more difficult than if you start off with a Dvorak keyboard from the beginning, and your difficulties will be directly linked to how well you typed on the QWERTY keyboard.

As a general principle, the better your learning of the first skill, the harder it will be for you to learn an antagonistic skill. However, if a new skill is *compatible* with an old skill — if it has action sequences in common — then the better you are at the old skill, the faster you will learn the new.

Because skills are encoded differently than information, because they are so quickly consolidated yet so vulnerable to interference, the way you practice them is even more crucial to your success. In particular, spacing and interleaving are even more important, and so is the content and quality of your focus.

Deliberate practice

All of this is tied up with the concept of 'deliberate practice' (Ericsson et al. 1993). Ericsson makes a very convincing case for the absolutely critical importance of this type of practice, and the minimal role of what is commonly termed 'talent' (you will no doubt have heard of his '10,000 hours' theory, which was popularized by Malcolm Gladwell). His research shows that experts only achieve their expertise after several years (typically ten or more) of maintaining high levels of regular deliberate practice. But most people, he suggests, spend very little (if any) time engaging in deliberate practice even in those areas in which they wish to achieve some level of expertise.

So what distinguishes deliberate practice from less productive practice?

Ericsson (1996) suggests 6 factors are of importance in deliberate practice:

- The acquisition of expert performance needs to be broken down into a sequence of attainable training tasks.

- Each of these tasks requires a well-defined goal.

- Feedback for each step must be provided.

- Repetition is needed — but that repetition is not simple; rather the student should be provided with opportunities that gradually refine his performance.

- Attention is absolutely necessary — it is not enough to simply mechanically 'go through the motions'.

- The aspiring expert must constantly and attentively monitor her progress, adjusting and correcting her performance as required.

Breaking down a skill

Knowing where to divide a skill is something that develops with practice. For a musician, it might mean practicing a piece in appropriate sections that are only a few bars long (maybe only one!), with special focus on those that are difficult. For a sportsperson, it means breaking actions into self-contained components with a special focus on one specific aspect of performance.

For example, one long-time professional golfer (Moe Norman), renowned for being a great ball-striker, attributes his success to the systematic practice he began at 16 (Starkes et al. 1996). For well over ten years, he hit 800 balls a day five days a week (on the weekends he played golf). During this practice, he always had a specific focus, such as hitting to a bucket, hitting to an image of a specific hole, controlling a particular aspect of his swing. As a result, he swings at the ball with incredible consistency, always straight, the ball always going precisely where he wants it to go.

This focus on segments (musical sections; action components) harks back to the 'chunks' I mentioned in regard to working memory and information learning. Regardless of whether you're trying to master an academic subject or a physical skill or even a visual task (such as learning to recognize the works of different artists), you always need to break it down into manageable chunks (which may be very small at the beginning, because working memory is very small), and you always need to be able to judge (through feedback and self-monitoring) the relative difficulty of those chunks, so that you can apportion your time and effort appropriately.

'Appropriately' means spending more time and effort on difficult bits and less time on easy ones. This may seem obvious, but many a student has done it the other way around, on the grounds that one is hard and the other is easy! That's all very well if your aim is simply to 'get through' a specified practice/study time, without any wish to achieve much, but if you do actually want to improve, you need to focus on the hard stuff.

But you don't get points for making it more difficult! If something is too hard for you, keep breaking it down until you have a piece you can handle. Remember that working memory is very small, and the key to increasing its capacity is to increase the size of your chunks. You do that bit by bit, not by trying to leap to where you want to be. It is not, therefore, an admission of weakness or failure to begin with very small chunks (sections, elements, movements); the size of the chunk merely reflects your previous relevant experience. Appropriately directed experience will grow your chunks.

Varied repetition

As Ericsson says, while repetition is vital, that repetition shouldn't be 'simple'. To refine your performance, you need variation. You can't work out the best way of performing an action without trying out subtle variations, such as varying the force of your pitch, the distance you are throwing, the angle of your arm, etc. But 'refining' your performance is about more than that — it's about making it more flexible.

A distinguishing difference between novices and experts is that novices are less adaptive. They find it harder to adjust their performance in response to changes in conditions (such as weather changes, for drivers; a different acoustic environment, for musicians; a change in pitch, for cricketers). This isn't surprising — experts develop abstract ideas of what they're doing; they know what's 'core' and what (and how) other details might change. Novices are still performing by rote. To develop the necessary abstraction, a mental **schema**, you need to experience variations.

This is similar to the way we develop concepts in semantic memory: we build the concept of 'dog' by experiencing a variety of dogs and non-dogs (such as cats), working out what features the dogs share, how they're different from non-dogs. It would be very hard to build a good 'dog' concept if you only knew corgis!

In a similar way, as you build a skill, you build an abstract idea of the skill — which features are important, which are not, what goes together and how, what leads to what. To learn all this, to build the abstract schema that will guide your performance across a range of contexts, you need to vary your experiences and actions.

Variation isn't, then, solely a matter of subtle changes in your movements, such as changing the angle of your arm or the force of your throw. It's also about context. Thus, a study in which baseball players learned three different kinds of pitches found that those who practiced the pitches in separate blocks learned significantly more poorly than those who practiced them in blocks in which different pitches occurred randomly, with no one type of pitch occurring more than twice in a row [12.1].

Interleaving is therefore of particular value in skill learning. There are two aspects to this. In the previous example, interleaving different pitches mimics what happens in a real game, providing the opportunity to practice the necessary skill of recognizing the type of pitch and responding appropriately. This is hardly specific to baseball pitches! In almost all real-world scenarios, we're required to make such judgments and adapt our performance accordingly.

The second aspect is that benefit of interleaving that I discussed earlier: the way it helps you see vital similarities and differences. If your new skill contains components (action sequences, movements, musical sections, etc) that are similar but not identical, interleaving them, although it will slow your initial learning, will pay off in the long run.

Do remember that interleaving involves *repeated* mixing of tasks! Simply following one task (set, sequence, skill) with another is very bad for learning, since it promotes interference without any mitigating factors. Thus, in one study, music students learned to play a short melody (a 13-note sequence) on the piano in the evening, before being tested on it the following morning (Allen 2012). Some students learned only one melody, while others learned this melody and then another. A further group also learned both melodies, but briefly practiced the first melody again at the end of the training session. Only the first melody was tested in the morning.

Those who learned only one melody showed the usual post-sleep consolidation jump that I discussed earlier. Those who learned another melody after the first one showed no such improvement, demonstrating how such interference blocks consolidation. But those who played the first melody again, after training on the second melody, did show the usual post-sleep improvement.

Feedback

Feedback has two main roles in practice: monitoring, and motivation. Let's talk about motivation first.

Do I need to say that motivation is important? Sometimes we dismiss motivation as if it's a luxury, a non-vital factor that only comes into play when the individual lacks the self-discipline to do what they know they should do. But 'motivation' has to do with having a 'motive', and a 'motive force' is a force that makes things move. It is motives that drive our actions, and motivation is vital to actions and to practice. It's not simply about giving someone money, or a treat, or a gold star.

Motivation is about having a goal, and being able to maintain that goal.

Feedback is a factor in providing motivation because it can help you stay committed to your goal. It can also cause you to discard your goal, to give up. It's crucial, therefore, to get feedback right.

In the context of motor skill learning, feedback is generally concerned either with the outcome of the action or the quality of the action. It may be explicit (such as your coach or teacher telling you exactly what you did wrong) or implicit, inherent in the action itself (if you're aiming at a target, or if you're trying to sink a putt, it's obvious how well you've done).

Implicit feedback is less potentially dangerous than explicit feedback. You may decide to give up because you're not doing as well as you think you should, but that's a problem of your expectations and goal-setting, rather than a problem inherent in the feedback. Implicit feedback is vital for good self-monitoring. Explicit feedback, on the other hand, is more problematic. When we think of feedback as a de-motivator, it's generally external feedback that's the problem.

Research indicates that, in the context of skill learning, negative feedback — feedback about errors, or feedback telling you that you're not doing as well as your fellow students — can worsen performance. However, feedback telling you that you're doing well (regardless of its accuracy), improves performance.

It's suggested that one reason why negative feedback might hamper skill learning is that it increases thoughts of 'self'. This comes back to the third phase of skill learning — the aim is to remove consciousness from the process. When you're thinking about your self, when you're fretting over your performance and thinking about exactly what your body is doing, you're standing in the way of the proper performance of the skill.

If your coach, teacher, or fellow-students are overly critical, therefore, you might find it helpful to either:

- change them for more supportive people!

- try to convince them that negative feedback is counterproductive, or
- find some occasions to practice without them.

But of course feedback has another, entirely positive (indeed crucial) role: monitoring.

Accurate self-monitoring is critical to successful practice. You can't do it right if you don't know when you're doing it wrong! While coaches and teachers (and more experienced peers) can certainly provide explicit feedback that helps you monitor how you're doing, it's still a good idea to learn to do it yourself even when you do have such resources. Sure, when you start with a new skill, some sort of guide is extremely helpful, if not critical. However, once you've grasped the basics of the skill, your aim should be to regard mentors as additional resources rather than primary. No one can be at your shoulder at every minute of your practice, and in any case, learning is always individual— only you know how your body feels on the inside, what your mind thinks and feels.

This is probably why external feedback seems to be most effective when it's only given on some occasions, rather than all. If you know you're going to get feedback every time you do something, you have less incentive to pay attention to what you're doing, less incentive to learn how to assess and monitor your own performance.

Timing is another issue with explicit feedback. Implicit feedback occurs naturally in the course of performance, but explicit feedback, of course, can be given at any time. Previously, in the context of information learning, I said that feedback can be effective even when a little delayed. However, with motor skills, because of the speed with which muscle memories are consolidated, it's more important that feedback occurs quickly. Another opportunity for explicit feedback to get things wrong!

Self-monitoring and goal-setting

The point of monitoring is to help you work out when you're doing things right and when you're doing them wrong. That's not simply about recognizing errors, although error recognition is an important part of self-monitoring. You can, after all, want to improve your performance from "not bad" to "good", or from "good" to "better". Self-monitoring

— watching and assessing your performance — helps you adjust and adapt your performance appropriately.

So how do you improve your monitoring skills?

One factor that helps considerably is explicitly articulating your immediate goal. Science, it's said, has to be testable; if you can't test the theory, it's not scientific. In the same way, a goal isn't really a goal if you can't tell when you've met it. A clearly specified goal should give you the information you need to assess your performance (and by 'should', I mean that, if it doesn't give this information, you need to specify it better!).

A vital part of deliberate practice, therefore (as it is with all learning!), is to clearly articulate your goal.

A useful distinction here is that between process and outcome goals. Process goals relate to fundamental techniques, to mastering specific procedures. Outcome goals relate to the outcome or product. So, for example, in learning to throw a dart, the outcome goal might be to hit the bull's eye or to achieve a specific score, but the process goals might relate to the proper execution of a specific forearm throwing motion, or extension of the fingers.

A study in which 90 school-girls were taught to throw darts compared several types of goals:

- no set goal

- outcome goal ("try to attain the highest possible score")

- process goal ("concentrate on properly executing the final two steps in every throw")

- transformed goal (depending on where the dart strikes, concentrate on one of these steps on the next attempt)

- shifting goal (students were given the process goal, before shifting to the outcome goal after 12 minutes of practice).

Those given the shifting goal learned best and became most interested. The worst (excluding those not given any goals at all) were those who were only given outcome goals [12.2].

It's worth noting that one of the advantages of process goals seems to be that it encourages the learner to attribute any failures to strategy rather than lack of ability. In this study, the girls who were given process goals were more likely to attribute their deficient performance to a strategy than were those girls given an outcome goal or no goal. This in turn led to having a greater belief in their ability to learn, and more enjoyment in the task.

Self-monitoring and goal-setting are both examples of what is called **metacognition**, which includes both your understanding of cognitive processing in general and your understanding of your own cognitive processing.

Metacognition and self-monitoring

Research exploring how practice differs between experts in a skill and beginners has found that, while there are certain tendencies in specific strategies used (tendencies only, not hard and fast differences!), the fundamental difference between experts and novices lies in metacognition. Experts understand their own strengths and weaknesses, understand the different tasks involved in their skill, recognize when approaching a task which parts of it will be more difficult for them.

Experts, you could say, approach learning strategically.

This is why, although expertise is specific to a domain or topic, if you're an expert in one thing, you have a head start in mastering another subject. You know *how* to be an expert; you know how an expert approaches learning.

Another consistent factor in developing expertise lies in the response to errors — also a metacognitive act. Novices tend not to recognize when they have made errors, and when they do, often ignore them (not necessarily deliberately). The vast majority of novices practice by repeatedly performing an activity. One of the problems with this is that they are far less likely to remember any errors they made, and when they repeat the activity, the chances are that they'll repeat the errors too, and cement them into the action.

One of the reasons why there isn't a clear distinction between experts and novices in the specific strategies used is that some strategies, that are generally regarded as poor strategies, might well be appropriate in the early stages of acquiring the skill. Other strategies, generally regarded as effective, may be less appropriate at higher levels of expertise.

The successful learner changes strategies over time and with experience. With a motor skill, you need a basic foundation in place before getting 'strategic', but early adoption of a metacognitive approach — one in which you are attentive to your performance and aware of different strategies for improving it — will speed your progress considerably. Bear in mind that, while no specific strategies can be unequivocally pointed to as critical, the adoption of *systematic* practice strategies is significantly associated with expertise (accounting, in one study, for around 11% of the difference between individuals, which is more than any other single factor).

In other words, finding effective strategies is important, but effective strategies are specific to the individual. You can't assume that because something is the best strategy for your best friend, that it's going to work equally well for you. What's important is that you find *your* effective strategies, and practice them regularly (that's the 'systematic' aspect).

How do you develop metacognitive skill? One part of it is what you're doing now — learning about learning and how your brain works; learning about different strategies that may be effective for your specific task. The second part is learning to monitor.

I said before that one way to improve your monitoring skills is to get in the habit of explicitly articulating your immediate goal. Another helpful strategy is explicitly verbalizing what you're doing and why. You don't have to do this every time you perform! But if you make the point of doing it periodically, you'll develop your monitoring skills, and also find it very useful for your specific practice. Note that you don't have to do it either completely or not at all — having verbalized the whole action sequence, you should have some idea what the difficult elements are; you can therefore make a point of verbalizing at those points only.

You also should consciously think about your performance and your learning process — not in a "oh it was so awful" way, but in an analytical "mistakes are there to learn from" way — and discuss it with others (learning to listen to others' criticism, and to give helpful criticism to others, is itself a skill that gets better with practice!).

Self-monitoring can be an annoyance if you're new to it — you may be inclined to see it just as something that slows down your practice. But keep in mind that monitoring is a skill, and will get faster and less hampering as you become more practiced at it. It really is worth forcing yourself through the initial pains, because self-monitoring is a crucial skill if you're serious about practicing and learning effectively.

The importance of self-monitoring is part of the reason why the core attribute of deliberate practice is constant and intense focus. This need for a high level of concentration is why deliberate practice is limited in duration. Whatever the particular field of endeavor, there's a remarkable consistency in the habits of elite performers that suggests 4 to 5 hours of deliberate practice per day is the maximum that can be maintained.

This, of course, can't all be done at one time without resting! As I discussed earlier, you may find it helpful to concentrate your activity in short 15-minute bursts, followed by brief periods of rest. Five minutes 'quiet time', during which the skill will consolidate in your brain, is worth a great deal, and, as I mentioned, is better earlier in practice than later. This may be of greater benefit for novices — as you gain experience, you should be able to increase those activity periods. Even for experts, however, an hour seems to be long enough, and day-time napping is common among elite performers operating at these high levels of concentration.

Not all practice is, or should be, deliberate practice

Deliberate practice is hard work. While it's critical for improvement, those engaging in physical pursuits also need other activities that are aimed at general fitness. Additionally, there may be tactical or theoretical issues to master. And, of course, the role of 'fun' activities shouldn't be overlooked either. You aren't going to persevere with a skill if you never enjoy exercising it (going back to the importance of motivation).

In general, experts reduce the amount of time they spend on deliberate practice as they get older. It seems that, once a certain level of expertise has been achieved, it isn't necessary to force yourself to continue the practice at the same level in order to maintain your skill. However, as long as you wish to improve, a high level of deliberate practice is required.

But you shouldn't take the '10,000 hours' too literally. It's now clear that there is considerable variability between individuals. While Ericsson was certainly right, and groundbreaking, when he propounded the virtues of practice and a diminished value for 'natural talent', talent is still a factor. There's no doubt that some people need far less practice to achieve the same (or higher) levels of performance compared to others. Having said that, it's not yet clear to what extent this is a matter of individual talent, or simply a product of using the practice time better. That is, for whatever reason (natural ability; a wise mentor; dumb luck), some people practice effective strategies from an early stage.

None of this is to assume that your aim is, or should be, to become expert at whatever skill you're learning! I discuss how experts differ from novices in order to show the path; you can stop at any point on the path to expertise. We learn, or want to learn, many skills, and all of these at different levels of expertise. How skilled you want to become is part of your outcome goal.

Mental practice

Another type of practice I should touch on is 'mental practice', that is, of imagining yourself practicing a skill. This idea has become popular, and deservedly so in some domains — but not perhaps in all those domains in which it has become popular! While it seems clear from the research that mental practice is of significant benefit to cognitive skills, its value to motor skills is not so certain. It's likely that a motor skill only benefits from mental rehearsal to the extent that it has cognitive elements. So, for example, it's useful to mentally practice solving a Rubik's cube, but less useful to imagine yourself typing.

The benefits of mental practice also depend on your imagery abilities. But don't rule yourself out if your visualization skills are poor! While the ability to visualize does vary markedly between individuals, the skill does respond to practice.

In any case, visual imagery isn't the only type of imagery there is. One you may not have thought of, that is particularly relevant to the learning of motor skills, is kinesthetic imagery. This refers to your ability to sense your own body and imagine how a movement feels during a task. This strikes me very much as a skill that would improve with deliberate practice.

A study involving skilled golfers found that those who had greater kinaesthetic imagery ability benefited more from mental practice [12.3].

Given that a skill is high in cognitive elements, will mental practice always be helpful? Research indicates that it is most effective when you already have some experience with the skill (Feltz & Landers 1983). For beginners who are unclear about what they should be doing and how they should be doing it, it's only too easy for them to practice the wrong thing — for mental practice doesn't, of course, allow for much in the way of feedback, to tell you how accurately you're performing.

Research also suggests that mental practice is of particular benefit when the task is complex — that is, when it contains many elements, when it puts high demands on working memory (Feltz & Landers 1983).

In the chapter looking at specific subjects, I discuss music. Even if you have no interest in learning music, or a musical instrument, it's worth reading the section to see the very specific breakdown of how a pianist could mentally practice

You can see in this description the process of breaking the task down that I talked about as so critical for deliberate practice. One step, however, is specific to mental practice — the recommendation to swap between mental and physical practice. I think this is probably an important strategy in building your visualization skills, and that the timing of it may also be important — not right at the beginning, and not leaving it too late. Finding the right time is, like so many other aspects of successful learning, a matter of becoming attuned to your abilities and performance.

There is one benefit from mental practice that probably occurs across all types of skills, and for both newbies and experts: mental rehearsal for priming. By engaging in some mental rehearsal before performing the skill, you prepare the mind and body for the task ahead, helping you direct your attention to the aspects that matter.

Mental priming

Getting into the right frame of mind is something all sportspeople know about. It applies to other domains too, and it's not simply a matter of emotional state. It's about activating the parts of your brain that are involved in this skill. In music, this might be achieved by listening to a recording of a piece before starting to work on it. In study, by reading the Table of Contents, advance organizers and summaries (in the case of textbooks), or doing any required reading before a lecture, and (in both cases) thinking about what you expect to learn from the book or lecture.

Many people would probably find it surprising how well priming works, even with tasks that would seem very dependent on actual physical practice. One study, for example, found that you could markedly reduce your training time for a visual search task if you began your training trials simply imagining yourself searching for the target object (Reinhart et al. 2015).

In the study, such imagining improved the focusing of visual attention better than actual practice did. It's suggested that, because such a task involves you finding a specific target object in a group of irrelevant objects, these distractions linger in your visual system, providing a certain amount of interference. When you *imagine* searching, however, you are free to minimize the number of distractions, enabling you to apply greater focus.

Of course, you can only go so far with such imaginings! But as a starting point, before beginning 'real' training, it seems to have some value.

Similarly, in a study in which participants practiced a simple reach-to-grasp task, those who spent the initial practice trials imagining themselves doing the task did at least as well as those who spent those trials physically performing the task [12.4].

Recordings of brain activity revealed that the mental practice primed the brain for learning when physical practice occurred. That is, changes in brain activity associated with learning didn't occur during the mental practice itself, but occurred rapidly once physical practice began.

Apart from working on your ability to mentally visualize objects and actions, you might improve your mental practice skills by practicing meditation-type exercises, such as breathing exercises and exercises in which you focus on one specific part of your body or internal sensation.

Points to remember

The essence of a skill — the key factor distinguishing it from information learning — is its potential for automatization, which is only achieved through practice.

Motor skills, perceptual learning, and information learning are all processed in different brain regions, and processed differently.

The 'gist' of actions is transferred very quickly to long-term memory, and remembered for a very long time even if not used. However, details are quickly lost, meaning that, if you want to keep a motor skill 'sharp', you need to keep using it.

Learning a new skill will be helped or hindered by the extent to which it shares elements with existing skills, or contains antagonistic elements.

Spacing and interleaving are critical factors in effective skill learning.

A necessary, though not sufficient, requirement for effective skill learning is regular deliberate practice.

Deliberate practice is focused and goal-oriented. In deliberate practice, you select a manageable chunk, specify a goal, monitor your performance and adjust it accordingly.

Goals should be responsive to your performance and needs, aimed either at specific steps/techniques, or at outcomes, as appropriate.

Variation, in your performance and in the environment, helps you develop good mental schemata that enable you to adapt to changing demands.

Deliberate practice is intensive and thus you're limited in how much you can do (effectively) at one time and over the course of a day.

Motor skill learning can benefit from observing others perform, not simply as a demonstration of how to do something, but as a form of practice.

Feedback is most useful when it's an integral part of the action. The best explicit feedback is occasional and positive.

Mental practice is useful for cognitive skills, or for the cognitive elements in motor skills, but less so for motor skills themselves.

Mental practice is particularly useful for complex tasks, and for practitioners with some experience.

How you approach learning is more important than any specific strategy for working on your skill — you need to think analytically about your performance, monitor it, and respond constructively to errors.

Review Questions

1. The best instructions for learning a motor skill

   a. spell out every step

   b. tell you exactly what to do with your body

   c. direct your attention to the effects of your movements

   d. depend on the skill and your present level of expertise

   e. involves both verbal instruction and a physical demonstration

2. Paired practice

   a. only works if one person is an expert

   b. is a strategy in which paired individuals alternate between performing the action and observing the other

   c. encourages more flexible performance, probably because there's more variability in the practice

   d. can be more motivating than practicing alone

   e. can harm your learning, if the other performs poorly or too well

3. The main difference between skill learning and information learning is that

   a. skill learning is learned by your muscles, and information learning is learned in your brain

   b. skill learning relies on physical observation, while information learning is learned by reading or hearing

   c. skill learning becomes automatic with sufficient practice

   d. you can't verbalize a skill, but information learning is all about verbalization

4. Compared to information learning, motor skill learning is

   a. more easily forgotten

   b. less easily forgotten

   c. transfers to long-term memory more quickly

    d.   transfers to long-term memory more slowly

    e.   better at holding onto details / subtleties of movement

    f.   worse at holding onto details / subtleties of movement

5.   Interference is a more important issue when learning new information compared to learning new skills.   Y / N

6.   Spacing and interleaving are more important when learning new information compared to learning new skills.   Y / N

7.   Deliberate practice is characterized by which of the following factors?

    a.   constant monitoring

    b.   well-defined goals

    c.   variable repetition

    d.   appropriate feedback

    e.   focused attention

    f.   small well-chosen steps

8.   Variable practice helps you

    a.   stay interested

    b.   build an abstract model

    c.   adapt to changes in conditions and contexts

    d.   build different muscles

9.   Feedback is important in skill learning because

    a.   it keeps you motivated

    b.   it can help you maintain your goals

    c.   it's crucial for monitoring your learning

    d.   it stops you repeating the wrong action

10. Feedback is best when it's

    a.   explicit

b. implicit

c. negative

d. positive

e. immediate

f. a little delayed

11. The most effective goals are

    a. broad

    b. very specific

    c. focused on outcome

    d. focused on the process of what to do

    e. flexible, changing from process to outcome as expertise develops

12. Which of these statements are true:

    a. There are specific strategies that are critical for acquiring expertise that you need to learn.

    b. Effective strategies are specific to the individual.

    c. Effective strategies are specific to a particular skill.

    d. The use of systematic practice strategies is important for acquiring expertise.

    e. A strategy you find effective for learning a particular skill will always be effective for that skill.

13. To improve your self-monitoring skills,

    a. notice all your mistakes and beat yourself up about them

    b. consciously think about what you're doing and analyze any mistakes to establish why you made them and how you can avoid making them again

    c. get in the habit of explicitly articulating your immediate goal

    d. as often as needed, explicitly verbalize what you're doing and why

   e. limit your deliberate practice to short periods of intense, closely monitored activity, lengthening the periods as you build expertise

14. All your practice should be deliberate practice.   Y / N

15. Mental practice is a good strategy for

   a. motor skill learning

   b. learning cognitive skills

   c. motor skill learning to the extent that it has cognitive elements

   d. people who are naturally good at visualization

   e. people who have good visualization skills

   f. learners with some level of expertise

   g. beginners

16. Effective mental practice

   a. requires solitude and a quiet mind

   b. focuses on what you can see

   c. is interleaved with actual physical practice

   d. is best done at the beginning of your physical practice session

   e. is best done at the right times, depending on the progression of your physical practice

Cognitive skills

In this brief chapter, I look at the importance of pattern recognition in learning cognitive skills, and the usefulness of worked examples.

I said earlier that cognitive and motor skills represent two ends of a continuum. The main factor determining where a skill is placed on that continuum is information content. To the extent that information underlies the skill, that skill is 'cognitive'. Wrestling requires little in the way of knowledge; playing a musical instrument involves knowledge of music pieces and music theory, although its focus is on the physical action of playing; playing chess makes no significant demands on the body. Thus, wrestling is a motor skill, playing an instrument is a motor skill with a significant cognitive component, and playing chess is a cognitive skill.

Research has found that the most important predictor of chess rating is cumulative serious practice, of which the most important element is practice alone — that is, analysis of positions from chess books and other written resources (Charness et al. 1996). Note the power of serious study alone over other activities such as tournament play and analysis with others. Researchers suggest that this activity allows the most control over what is being practiced and for how long (it also gives the player the freedom to safely try out approaches they wouldn't risk in play with others).

What this deliberate practice of chess positions and movements does is grow a databank of patterns in the mind of a chess master. Research has shown that chess masters can look at a chess board in the middle of a game and easily remember exactly where each piece is (an ability which helps a great deal when performing the amazing feat of playing many games simultaneously!) — but this skill deserts them as soon as the pieces are randomly scattered about the board (Richman et al. 1996). Their impressive memory derives solely from the stored patterns, the chunks, in their long-term memory. Expert netball, basketball, and field hockey players similarly have been shown to have stored defensive player patterns that give them not only a better memory for play in their own sport, but in other sports as well.

Eye-tracking research has also found that chess experts concentrate their attention on the main chess pieces that are crucial for the game, in that specific situation, but novices show eye gaze patterns that are much less focused, jumping all over the board [13.1].

In other words, their databank of patterns helps experts focus on what matters.

To a large extent you can say that, while motor skills revolve around learning action sequences, the heart of cognitive skills (or the cognitive component of motor skills) is learning patterns. Learning the patterns important for your cognitive skill is essentially a type of perceptual learning. In reading, for example, some of the patterns are letter-combinations and words and their associated sounds and meaning, but the more sophisticated patterns that underlie reading *skill* are the patterns of words and phrases that allow you to anticipate what comes next. Indeed, prediction is central to skill, because it is the ability to anticipate what comes next, to prepare for the next neural activations, that enables the faster processing that is the hallmark of skilled performance.

In mathematics, patterns can be seen in the format of different types of problems ("The profit in dollars for the manufacture and sale of x soft toys is given by $P(x) = 50x - 0.002x2$; Find the number of soft toys to be sold to maximize profits." "Find the derivative of $y = \operatorname{cosec} x$"). In medicine, it's the recognition of certain symptoms ("I've seen that rash before; it looks like measles"), and the recognition of the grouping of certain symptoms ("Wheezes and crackles in his lower lungs; no fever; white blood count stable — I think it's chemical pneumonitis").

While cognitive skills require just as much practice as motor skills, that practice is aimed at building and recognizing patterns rather than automating action sequences. To recognize a pattern, you must extract from the mass of real-world data the bits that matter. This is not something that's readily taught. You can (and should) be guided (by a coach or mentor, or other resources), but at the end of the day, what's critical is varied experience.

Having said that, a guide can substantially reduce the amount of experience you need. While motor skills generally require a coach or teacher to provide that guide, for many cognitive skills this role can be taken by written resources. In chess that may be books analyzing chess movements and positions; in other cognitive skills, other types of models, such as worked examples, can be useful.

Worked examples provide models for cognitive skills

Worked examples — the cognitive equivalent of physical demonstrations — are particularly common, and valuable, in mathematics. However, they're not necessarily of equal value to everyone, or in all circumstances. Worked examples seem to be most useful to novices. Unsurprising, you may think, but the important point is that worked examples give the most help when you don't have a schema, a mental model, for the task. Once you have your own schema, worked examples can actually hurt your learning if they're not worked out in a way consistent with your schema.

In other words, not all worked examples will work for *you*.

One benefit of worked examples is to help reduce cognitive load, and for that reason it seems likely that they offer most benefit to students with a low working memory capacity. This is consistent with their greater benefit for novices — working memory capacity is much less of an issue for experts, who have:

- schemata that reduce the load on their working memory

- strategies to off-load some of the information onto other people or artifacts

- the hard-learned skill of knowing what to pay attention to and what to ignore.

Like any model, the effectiveness of worked examples does depend on their design. Consistent with the fact that a principal benefit is to reduce the load on working memory, effective examples need to:

- avoid splitting the student's attention (as happens when text and images are physically separated)

- avoid redundancy

- make subgoals (if any) explicit through labeling or by visually isolating sets of steps.

So, for example, here's a step-by-step instruction without labels (examples taken from Margulieux & Catrambone 2016):

1. From the basic palette drag out a *Button*.

2. Set the image source to "gypsy.jpg".

3. Clear the default text.

4. Set the width to fill the parent's width and the height to 300 pixels.

5. From the basic palette drag out a label.

6. Place the label underneath the image.

7. Set the text to *Click button to see your fortune.*

8. Rename it to *FortuneLabel.*

Compare this to the same example with labeled steps:

Create Component

1. From the basic palette drag out a *Button*.

Set Properties

2. Set the image source to "gypsy.jpg".

3. Clear the default text.

4. Set the width to fill the parent's width and the height to 300 pixels.

Create Component

5. From the basic palette drag out a label.

6. Place the label underneath the image.

Set Properties

7. Set the text to *Click button to see your fortune.*

8. Rename it to *FortuneLabel.*

Even this very simple set of labels is enough to help the reader grasp what's going on more quickly, and remember the process more easily.

These three attributes can be summed up in a sentence: worked examples should be focused and explicit.

If you don't find an example useful, it's probably because:

a. there's more information than you need,

b. it's missing information you need, or

c. it puts too much load on your working memory by separating related information.

If (a), you can go through the example and draw a line through information that seems irrelevant. If (b), you should try and work out exactly what information is missing (usually steps that are obvious to the instructor), at which point you can seek help (finding an answer is much easier when you have a specific question!). If (c), you can try re-working the example so that related information is closer together.

Research also indicates that more experienced students can get the most out of worked examples if they explain each step to themselves as they go (van Gog & Rummel 2010). However, beginners should be wary of this, as it's only helpful if they're capable of providing good explanations. Similarly, students with prior knowledge can benefit from seeing both correct and incorrect solutions (that is, good and bad examples), but newbies are better off seeing only correct solutions — unless the incorrect examples include good explanations of why they are incorrect.

Although I've talked about when worked examples may not work well, that's merely by way of warning. Worked examples are valuable tools when it comes to learning cognitive skills. In mathematics, simple practice of modeled problems has been shown to be the highest predictor of performance on the type of problem modeled, even in the absence of feedback.

Exercise 13.1

1. Compare these two very simple worked examples (taken from Mwangi & Sweller 1998). Which is better?

   Example 1:

   Julie is 7 years old (OOOOOOO)

   She is 2 years older than Kate (OOOOOOO — Kate)

   Alice is 4 years older than Kate (OOOOO + OOOO — Alice)

   How old is Alice?

   Answer: Alice is 9

Example 2:

Julie is 7 years old

She is 2 years older than Kate

Alice is 4 years older than Kate

How old is Alice?

Julie	Kate	Alice
(OOOOOOO)	(OOOOOOO)	(OOOOO + OOOO)

Answer: Alice is 9

2. Compare the following worked examples (adapted from Tarmizi 1998). Which one is better?

Example 1:

Students were instructed to follow the numerically ordered steps (1 & 2), and advised that the angle values in bold were those calculated, the other values being those given.

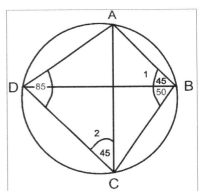

Example 2:

(i) ABD = 180 - ADC — CBD (opposite angles of a cyclic quadrilateral sum to 180)
(ii) ABD = 180 - 85 - 50 = 45 degrees
(iii) ABD - ACD = 45 degrees (angles in the same segment of a circle are equal)

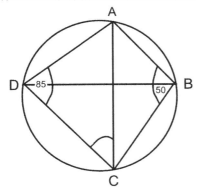

3. Compare the following worked examples (adapted from Ward & Sweller 1990). Which one is better?

Example 1:

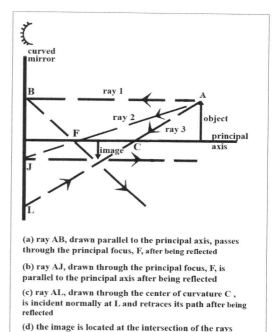

(a) ray AB, drawn parallel to the principal axis, passes through the principal focus, F, after being reflected

(b) ray AJ, drawn through the principal focus, F, is parallel to the principal axis after being reflected

(c) ray AL, drawn through the center of curvature C, is incident normally at L and retraces its path after being reflected

(d) the image is located at the intersection of the rays

Example 2:

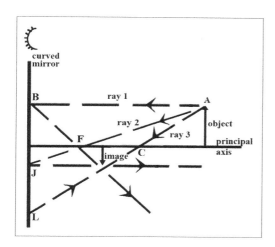

Exercise 13.2

Identify which of the following problems are missing necessary information and which contain redundant information:

a. Rhoda invested one-half of her money at 5.75% interest and one-quarter of her money at 5.5%. If her total interest at the end of one year was $136, find her original sum of money.

b. David invested $750 at a compound interest rate of 5% per annum. After three years he received bonus interest of 1%. What amount was in his account at the end of two years?

c. Alba invested a certain amount of money at 6% annual interest and another amount at 8% annual interest. Last year she received $580 in interest. How much did she invest at each rate?

d. The length of the sides of a blackboard are in the ratio 2:3. What is the perimeter (in m) of the blackboard?

e. The length of a rectangular park is 6 m more than its width. A walkway 3 m wide surrounds the park. Find the dimensions of the park if the park has an area of 432 m2.

f. A rectangular lawn is 12 m long and 6 rn wide. Calculate the area of a path 1.75 m wide around the lawn.

Automatization is the core attribute of all skills

Like motor skills, cognitive skills also become 'automated' in the sense that, with practice, many subprocesses no longer need conscious attention. This has the effect of reducing the load on working memory, and also reducing the number of steps that the expert is aware of — indeed, in familiar scenarios they'll often just 'know' the answer, and are at a loss to explain how they know. This explains why experts are often not the best teachers!

Similarly, the pattern recognition that is central to expertise in cognitive skills is a perceptual process that has become automatic — like instantly recognizing that a shoe is a shoe, or that *that* face belongs to Albert

Einstein. Perceptual learning, which is encoded and processed in different brain regions compared to both motor sequences and information, is also, like motor skills, remarkably durable. One study, for example, found that complex stimuli, practiced over two days, were still recognized a year later (Hussain et al. 2011).

Reading is a cognitive skill that displays both these attributes very clearly. Reading is a process that encompasses a whole hierarchy of subprocesses, including the recognition of individual letters, the association of letters and letter combinations with particular sounds, the recognition of whole words, the knowledge of words and their meanings (semantic memory). A skilled reader has automatized all of these subprocesses, and can concentrate on the meaning of the text. The recognition of letters and words is, of course, a matter of pattern recognition.

Like reading, learning another language is a prime example of a study topic that combines both informational and skill learning. The information component is self-evident: all those new words and grammar points. The skill component is perhaps less obvious, depending on your (or your teacher's) approach.

Today, there's far more emphasis on conversation (nothing wrong with that! 'Practice the task you need to do.') But back when I learned Japanese at university, the prevailing theory encouraged something called pattern drills. These seemed to have fallen somewhat into disrepute nowadays, which I think is a shame, because they seem to me to be great examples of deliberate practice. The idea was that you'd be given a 'pattern sentence', such as this:

Sore o misete kudasai. (Please show me that one)

The pattern lies in only some elements: in this case, the *te* at the end of *misete* (show) and *kudasai* (please). In the drills, you would practice substituting different verbs and objects into the pattern. Thus:

Kore o tabete kudasai. (Please eat this)

Chotto matte kudasai. (Please wait a moment)

Language is made up of patterns. Think of how often certain phrases, even whole sentences and more, trip from your tongue, without any need for you to think about what you're going to say. Think of how often you 'know' what someone's going to say before they do. Knowing the patterns of a language, practicing them until they can be produced automatically, is a fundamental element in fluency.

Fluency, in other words, reflects automatization, and is therefore a skill, and can only be achieved through practice.

Approach skill learning like an expert

I talked before about the path to expertise, which is simply another way of saying 'skill'. You don't have to become an expert to learn a skill, but becoming skilled is what it means to become an expert. So the journey is the same; it's just a matter of where you stop.

I also talked about how an expert approaches learning.

Wherever you plan to stop, that is, however skilled you want to become, you can benefit from approaching skill learning as an expert does. What does that mean?

First of all, you need to understand yourself — how you think, what you're good at, what you're poor at, what things are easy for you and what things are difficult. Remember that the point of this is not to avoid things that are difficult, but to help you recognize what's difficult for you so that you can focus on it.

You need to understand the whole before getting bogged down in details. Spend time observing; don't rush in to try things out yourself. Get the big picture first.

Work out the different tasks involved in the skill, so that you can practice individual tasks separately before putting them together.

Consider different strategies for performing the tasks.

Motor skills and cognitive skills share the fundamental attributes of skills: goal-directed actions that achieve speed and fluency through automatization. But cognitive skills in particular benefit from taking a metacognitive approach — thinking like an expert.

Exercise 13.3

Identify the following as examples of motor skills, cognitive skills, or declarative (information) learning (which may have a skill element):

1. riding a bike

2. reading in your native language

3. using the keyword mnemonic

4. dart throwing

5. drawing a concept map

6. playing Go

7. playing the piano

8. playing bridge

9. doing arithmetic

10. speaking another language

11. diagnosing illnesses

12. performing surgery

13. categorizing galaxies

14. doing chemistry experiments

15. writing history essays

Exercise 13.4

Identify the cognitive element(s) in the following activities:

1. playing the violin

2. driving a car

3. gardening

4. speaking your native language

5. cooking

Exercise 13.5

Identify the skill element(s) in those same activities

The 10 principles of effective skill practice

Here again are the 10 principles of effective practice I gave earlier:

1. **Practice the task you need to do.**

2. **The single most effective learning strategy is retrieval practice.**

3. **When you practice retrieval, only correct retrievals count.**

4. **Aim to do at least two correct retrievals in your first study session.**

5. **Space your retrieval attempts out.**

6. **Review your learning on a separate occasion at least once.**

7. **Space your review out.**

8. **Review at expanding intervals for long-term learning.**

9. **Interleave your practice with similar material.**

10. **Allow time for consolidation.**

How well do these principles apply to skill practice?

The first principle is self-evidently applicable to skill learning, but clearly so integral to the process of learning a skill that it doesn't need to be explicitly named. Obviously, when you practice a skill you are practicing the task you need to do.

The main difference between information learning and skill learning, in terms of effective principles of practice, is that retrieval is not the focus in skill learning. Automatization is. For motor skills, it's all about automating sequences. For cognitive skills, it's about learning to automatically recognize certain patterns, and automating subprocesses. Practice, then, is far more important for skills (since automatization only occurs through repeated practice), but *retrieval* practice is not — automatization means that the actions will occur automatically in response to actions or environmental cues, rather than requiring a database search.

What this means is that, whereas the central element in effective practice for information learning is retrieval practice, the central element in effective practice for motor skill learning is deliberate practice. For this reason, most of the above principles are not applicable to motor skill learning (I'm specifying motor skills here, because cognitive skills by their nature contain an information component for which retrieval is still relevant). However, those that remain are even more critical — those principles that relate to spacing, interleaving, and reducing interference.

1. **Skill level is directly related to the amount of deliberate practice you do.**

2. **Break the skill down into self-contained sequences or sections that can be practiced separately.**

3. **Practice difficult sections more than easy ones.**

4. **Respond to errors by repeating the section/sequence more slowly and carefully, building up speed on successive repetitions.**

5. **Focus on only one aspect of the skill at a time.**

6. Systematically vary the way in which you perform the skill, and the circumstances in which you do it.

7. Monitor and reflect on your performance.

8. Practice regularly but space it out — be aware of how long you can focus before your concentration fades, and allow time for consolidation.

9. Interleave your practice of sequences or problems with similar, but non-identical, sequences or problems.

10. Use observation of those who are better than you as a means of practice, and of learning new ways.

Points to remember

Deliberate practice of cognitive skills is focused on learning patterns, and automatizing subprocesses.

Because pattern recognition requires you to extract what matters from a mass of data, repeated experience is crucial, and a guide of some kind is extremely helpful.

Worked examples are most helpful when focused and explicit, and can help reduce the load on your working memory.

Review Questions

1. Cognitive skills require

    a. just as much practice as motor skills

    b. less practice than motor skills

    c. practice in learning patterns

    d. practice in automating action sequences

2. Worked examples are most useful

    a. to students with some expertise

    b. to beginners

    c. when you have a mental model for the task

    d. when you don't have a mental model for the task

    e. to students with low working memory capacity

    f. to students with high working memory capacity

3. Effective worked examples

    a. physically separate text and images

    b. integrate text and images into a coherent whole

    c. have lots of redundancy, to ensure clarity

    d. avoid redundancy, to keep it focused

    e. highlight subgoals in some way

4. If a worked example doesn't work for you, it may be that it:

    a. is too hard for you

    b. omits information you need

    c. includes unnecessary information

    d. separates information that needs to be together

    e. puts information together that should be kept apart

5. Motor skills and cognitive skills are alike in that they

    a. involve action sequences

    b. involve pattern recognition

    c. involve sequences of movements that can become automated

    d. involve processes that can become automated

    e. involve the same parts of the brain

Putting it all into practice

In the final two chapters, I offer some general advice on applying these strategies to certain subject areas, and briefly discuss how false beliefs, anxiety, and poor habits, can all stand in the way of your successfully implementing the effective strategies I've discussed.

Specific subjects

In this chapter, I look in more specific detail at how to learn languages, mathematics, science, and music.

This is not in any way put forward as an exhaustive discussion of how to study these subjects! Think of these discussions as case studies, provided because it always helps to anchor principles in specific cases. They provide pointers, that's all.

Languages

A language has many components, including:

- sounds

- written letters / characters

- words

- phrases

- sentences

Notice I don't mention grammar (or any other of the 'technical' terms, such as semantics, phonetics, etc). That's because we're looking at it from the point of view of learning — and not simply learning a language, but learning *another* language. Acquiring language in the first place is a different matter (not completely different, but by no means the same), because you approach subsequent languages with that understanding of language that you've built up learning your native language.

So, for example, if the language you're learning uses the same alphabet as your native language, then you've automatically skipped one and a half steps — the half step is because any language you learn, no matter how closely related, is likely to have at least one or two sounds that are not found in your native language, plus of course there's the whole matter of accent, which will often change the precise sound of vowels especially.

'Grammar' is a fancy way of saying the ways in which words are put together, which is why I talk about phrases and sentences.

Let's go through each of these aspects.

Sounds

The main reason why most people feel you have to learn a language at a young age in order to speak it like a native is because of sounds. We learn which sounds are used in our language in infancy, and our brains focus on those sounds, allowing other potential language sounds to fade away. It's true that it's much harder to re-acquire those long-forgotten sounds in adulthood, but few language learners really throw their heart into doing so. Accepting that it's not going to happen, they settle for a rough approximation to sounds that are not part of their own language.

But how well you learn to speak depends very much on how much effort you want to put into it — as long as that effort is well-directed! Deliberate practice is the means to acquiring this skill. The internet can provide resources for hearing the requisite sounds.

Musicians have a head start, because they are used to listening for just detectable differences in sound. But that doesn't mean that non-musicians should concede the fight! It does suggest that, if you're having trouble hearing the differences in words, you could try training your ear with music (there are apps for that). The most important thing is not to be put off by its initial difficulty.

Remember that this is a skill, which means it responds to practice. In the beginning, if you have no experience in listening for small differences, it may seem impossibly hard, but remember the principles of deliberate practice. Start with the easiest differences to discern, take it in small steps, build up your ability to hear the differences.

Hearing is not the only aspect, of course. Hearing is in fact the feedback mechanism (if you can't hear the difference, you certainly can't replicate it). The important thing is being able to produce the sounds accurately. It's useful here to find descriptions of the mechanical aspects — what to do with your tongue and lips. It really does help to use these! (Being able to follow these instructions and move your tongue and lips in the ways described is a motor skill, so it also will be very responsive to practice.)

So you begin with these attempts to move your mouth in the appropriate ways, and you use your hearing skills to compare your example (that's why audio clips on the internet are such a boon to language learners) with your own attempts at the sound, gradually refining your mouth movements until the sound you're producing matches the example. Don't expect to achieve this in a single session! But having achieved it with one sound, you will find it easier to follow the process for other sounds, because (a) you believe it can be done, and (b) you'll have a better understanding of the instructions for moving your tongue and lips.

If you're having trouble with that, start by looking for instructions on how to produce the sounds of your native language. As you produce the sound yourself, focus on how you're instinctively moving your tongue and lips. Compare different sounds, and see the different ways your tongue and lips move. Once you understand that properly, it will be easier to understand the instructions for unfamiliar sounds.

Learning a new alphabet

Some languages will use a completely different writing system from your own. How should you go about learning a new writing system, if that's necessary?

You need to learn the shapes of the letters — some of these may be the same or very similar to ones in the alphabet English uses, so the first step is to identify the ones that are new to you. Physically tracing and/or drawing the letters, will allow your more durable 'body memory' to enhance your learning.

You need to learn the names/sounds of the letters — some of the letters that appear similar to ones in the alphabet English uses may have different sounds. You need to identify the ones that are unexpectedly different. Flashcards (or equivalent) for each of the new letters and those that are misleadingly similar will allow you to practice recognition of these letters. Simple retrieval practice, on an effective schedule, is all you need here, but because this is a skill, for which over-practice is greatly recommended (to achieve automatization), you should increase the levels of practice, both within each session and across more sessions, until you achieve the necessary level of instant, automatic recognition.

Practice with recognizing the letters in the context of words ('reading'!), will build up your knowledge of common letter combinations. For example, think of how, in English, q is almost always followed by u, of the common verb endings of -ed and -ing, of the letter-combinations of -ght, -tch, -ff. Those who do crosswords or play scrabble will know how useful it is to know about common letter combinations, but it's not only in such activities that such knowledge is useful. Reading is about prediction — the better your knowledge of common combinations, the better your ability to predict what's coming next, which makes you a faster reader.

Learning vocabulary

If your language belongs to the Indo-European family of languages (as English does), identify cognate words that are easy to learn, and put them in 'easy' lists for retrieval practice. Look for words that you can meaningfully connect to words in your native language, and remember to explicitly make those connections during your retrieval practice. Create keyword mnemonics for those words which are difficult to learn, and incorporate those into your retrieval practice. For words whose meaning is contextual, such as prepositions and conjunctions, you need plenty of reading practice (i.e., reading passages of text), as well as retrieval practice (plus, if you can make any meaningful or mnemonic tags that will help you remember them, do so — these are the hardest words to remember, so they need all the help they can get).

Remember that reading practice is the best way of keeping your vocabulary strong, as well as expanding it — but you need to achieve a certain level of expertise before you can read well enough to make this a useful practice. Once you do, though, you should try to read every day, even if it's only a very small amount.

Don't restrict yourself to single words either. A surprisingly large amount of language are what linguists call collocations — multi-word phrases. Apart from the fact that many of these phrases won't mean exactly what the individual words seem to mean, remember that I said that reading is about prediction. Learning the words that go together makes an immense difference to your fluency, and also moves you from obviously-foreign to sounding much more native to the language.

Some of these collocations are called idioms, and you'll find common idioms for your language on the internet and in books. Others are simply phrases, but again, you'll find some of them in good textbooks. The important thing is to give them just as much attention and effort as you do individual words. Group them with the words they're connected to, so you build up a strong network of related words and phrases. This will help build your ability to predict what's coming next, in conversation or written texts.

Learning grammar

Adults have several advantages over children in learning a language, despite all that's said about the amazing abilities children have in acquiring language (children do have advantages, of course, but they have disadvantages too). One big advantage adults have is the ability to understand abstract rules. Children learn grammar implicitly, by practicing and hearing sentences. That's not a bad way of acquiring grammar — in fact, I recommend it — but children require a great deal of repetition and trial-&-error to achieve mastery, which adults can short-cut by guiding and supporting that practice with some academic learning. In other words, the 'rules' are important! But not as rules to memorize. Instead, you want to use the rules to explain and reinforce the practical stuff.

This example will show you what I mean.

In German, 'a' and 'the' are the main carriers of the information about a noun's gender and place in the sentence. Because German word order is very different from our own, this information can be vital to the meaning. Let's see this at work:

Der Bruder hast das Buch. The brother has the book.

Der Bruder hast den Hund. The brother has the dog.

Der Bruder hast die Klasse. The brother has the class.

Die Schwester hast das Buch. The sister has the book.

Das Baby hast das Essen. The baby has the food.

So far, so simple. We have four different versions of 'the': *der, das, den, die*.

Der is masculine. Das is neuter. Die is feminine. Den is also masculine, but it denotes that the noun is the object of the sentence, not the subject.

What can we conclude from these examples? Look at the objects (in these examples, the word order is the same as in the English translations).

Yes, for both feminine and neuter, 'the' (die and das) is the same whether the nouns are the subject (nominative) or the object (accusative) of the sentence. It is only the masculine *der* that changes to *den*.

But here is the reason that you must learn the gender of the noun when you learn the noun:

Der Hund der Schwester hast das Buch.

What's going on here? There's two 'der's in this sentence. But we know that Schwester is a 'die' word (feminine), so (if we know how *die* varies), we know that *der* indicates either the genitive (possessive) tense or the dative. In this case, it's clear that it's the genitive: The dog of the sister, or as we would more likely say, The sister's dog has the book.

Here's the table. Study it and draw your own conclusions about the patterns before reading on.

	masculine	neuter	feminine	plural
nominative	der	das	die	die
accusative	den	das	die	die
genitive	des	des	der	der
dative	dem	dem	der	den

From this we can see that *der* and *den* are the tricky ones. *Die* must be feminine (nominative or accusative) or plural. *Das* can only be neuter (nominative or accusative). *Des* can only be genitive (masculine or neuter). But *der* can be

- masculine nominative

- feminine or plural genitive

- feminine dative.

And *den* might be masculine accusative or plural dative.

Thus, to distinguish what part the noun is playing when *der* is with it, you must know the gender of the noun.

You do have some additional help in determining whether a noun is plural or not, because many nouns are changed in the plural (in the same way that English words add an -s or otherwise change in the plural). However, some words do not change (in the same way that in English we say 'sheep' for both an individual and many sheep). So you do still need that gender information even if plurals are involved.

So what do you need to memorize from all this?

It's not a bad idea to try and memorize the table itself. The visual layout of it helps make it more memorable (in general, humans have a good visual memory). So do study it as a table. But as you do, you want to pay particular attention to the patterns that we've talked about, and you want to articulate those patterns. That means, that you look at the table and you look at different patterns and actually say them out loud to yourself. So, for example:

Masculine changes every time. Neuter's the same in nominative and accusative, but changes for genitive and dative like masculine does. Feminine is only ever die or der. Plural is the same as feminine for everything but dative.

Das always means neuter. Dem always means dative. Des always means genitive. Die always means feminine or plural. But der might be nominative or genitive or dative, and to know which I need to know if it's masculine or feminine, singular or plural. Den might be nominative or dative, and to know which I need to know if it's singular or plural.

Don't try to learn this by repeating it over and over to yourself!

Write out the empty table and try and fill it in from memory. Try and visualize it, and also use what you remember of the patterns. Say what you're thinking out loud as you go.

Every now and then, over days and weeks, repeat this exercise, until you're confident you have it down cold.

Additionally, and crucially, pay attention to this every time you read a sentence, and spell it out. So, for example, on reading or hearing

Der Hund des Bruder

you say to yourself: 'des' can only be genitive, therefore the 'der' must indicate nominative, and 'hund' is masculine singular, so that fits. Therefore this translates as 'The dog of the brother' / 'The brother's dog'.

All this no doubt seems laborious, but once you've become practiced at this, it will become automatic and you will just 'know' it, rather than needing to spell it out. Spell everything out in the beginning, then let the easy ones go once they become obvious to you. Eventually, you'll be able to automatically recognize even complex constructions. But don't try to rush ahead too quickly. This really needs to be embedded very firmly.

And there's a bonus, to emphasize that building expertise the right way has benefits beyond rote-learning specific details. It isn't only the 'the's that change like this. Other words with a similar usage follow similar patterns. So now you've also mastered the endings of:

- dieser (this)

- jener (that)

- jeder (each, every)

- mancher (some, many a)

- solcher (such)

- welcher (what, which).

Achieving fluency

I do want to emphasize that grammar should be learned as a skill, not as you would acquire vocabulary. Remember that declarative knowledge is where you begin learning a skill such as driving, but only stands in your way if you keep relying on it. Your instructor might initially tell you: "This is the brake. This is the pedal you press when you want to stop or slow down. The brake is on the left of the accelerator." and so on; they might give you the mnemonic A B C, to remember the order of the pedals. This is all useful information, but if you keep repeating that information as you try to drive the car, you're going to make very slow progress! Indeed, you'll never attain mastery as long as you're relying on your declarative knowledge.

In the same way, while it helps to begin with the abstract rules, you don't want to lean on them too heavily.

An interesting study found that, when it comes to a language's morphology, it's better not to over-think it [14.1].

Morphology refers to the internal structure of a word. Words that can be broken down into separate parts — for example, re-collect-ed, cheer-ful-ly, sing-ing — contain internal structure. Regular endings such as -ed and -ing are simple enough, but languages tend to have many much more complicated tenses and irregularities, which adult learners usually stumble over. Research has found that children are particularly good at learning these sort of tricky structures. Indeed, this is one of the big reasons (the other is accent of course) why children can more readily sound like a native speaker.

It has been theorized that children are more successful because they don't over-analyze the structures.

The study used nonsense words that belonged to categories defined by the order of sounds. Participants listened to a continuous stream of these nonsense words, repeated in three-word sequences where there was one word from each category, in a specific category order. Later, they were tested on their ability to judge whether new words were in the 'right' place in the sequence.

So this is a test of how well they've picked up the unsaid grammar of this artificial language.

The group who was told not to over-analyze what they were hearing (and who were offered a simple activity to do while they were listening), did much better on that test than the group who had been told to try to identify the words as they listened.

As with math, learning a language is about balancing theory and practice. The abstract knowledge of grammar helps connect your practice of pattern sentences, but humans are highly skilled at recognizing patterns (to the extent that we'll see patterns that don't exist — hence superstitious behavior). Abstract knowledge helps you organize and understand information faster, but you should give your brain space and time to absorb patterns in its own way as well.

Fluency is achieved in the body as well as the mind. That isn't only a matter of what the body does (speak, write), but also a matter of the senses. Even in our own language, there are many occasions when we don't really hear what was said — we don't realize how often that occurs, because we can predict so well, from what we do hear, what the rest is. Similarly, a skilled reader doesn't read every word — they speed through on prediction, on expectation.

To achieve fluency, you need to provide as much practice as it takes to enable you to grasp in your gut the *flow* of the language — what words go with other words, how words change, what those changes mean.

So, let your mind loose to listen to the language. But also, anchor those learnings in abstract rules and patterns of grammar.

Look for cognates, and use them and mnemonics to anchor your vocabulary, which can be practiced both as stand-alone words, and within the context of pattern sentences. Use the principles of effective retrieval practice to minimize the amount of practice you need to achieve long-lasting learning.

Fluency is achieved through over-practice. But simply practicing things over and over again is not an efficient use of your time — remember the principles of deliberate practice. Focus on what's hard. Break things down where necessary — achieve a certain level of fluency with one element before moving on to more complex situations.

Exercise 14.1

A common grammatical mistake in English involves when to use **its** vs **it's**. The rule is very simple. **Its** (no apostrophe) is possessive. **It's** is shorthand for *it is*. Yet people confuse the two over and over again. Why?

The problem is that apostrophes are used in both circumstances — to indicate possession (e.g., Susan's book; the dog's bone; the book's cover), and to show that something has been omitted (e.g., hasn't = has not; that's = that is; I'd = I would). Those examples are typical, which is why we don't usually have much grounds for confusion. People, animals, things, they can all possess something. A 'that', or a 'has', cannot. But 'it' can be used both as a stand-in for an animal or thing, and in a hundred other ways (it is necessary; it has been; it is said; it is no use ...).

As specifically as you can, lay out how you could cement the correct usage in your head (or another person's).

Exercise 14.2

Pick a language (other than your native one) that you have some familiarity with and interest in. Identify the elements of the language that need different types of practice, and say how you would go about learning them. Be as specific as possible.

Summary of strategy choice

Pronunciation:

- Find audio resources that you can replay endlessly, to hear the sounds of the language.

- Find information on how to move your tongue and lips to reproduce the sounds.

- Use deliberate practice to build your skill at hearing and reproducing these sounds, starting with differences you can clearly hear and progressing to differences that are much harder to distinguish.

Alphabet (if necessary):

- If the alphabet shares elements with an alphabet you know, identify characters that are new to you.

- Physically trace and / or draw the letters (even if you only want to learn to read, not write).

- Use flashcards as a retrieval practice strategy to learn the names / sounds of the letters and practice letter recognition.

- Use higher levels of practice, in order to achieve the necessary level of instant, automatic recognition.

- Build up your knowledge of common letter combinations by practicing letter recognition using written text.

Vocabulary:

- Use flashcards as a retrieval practice strategy (when I say this, I hope it is understood that you are applying the principles of retrieval practice!)

- If the language is related to a language you know, search for cognates (related words), and group them in lists that need less practice.

- Look for meaningful connections between words-to-be-learned and words you already know (in whatever language).

- Use the keyword mnemonic only where there are no meaningful connections to be made.

- Multi-word (even just two word) phrases are just as important as single words — practice them too.

Grammar:

- Use grammar rules to add meaning to the ways in which words are arranged.

- Practice sentence patterns, both by remarking on them as you read, and by writing them, while holding an awareness of the relevant grammar rule.

Fluency:

- Use the principles of deliberate practice to improve your skill at understanding and producing sentences.

Mathematics

Mathematics involves several kinds of thinking and knowledge, including:

- symbolic understanding / knowledge

- number sense (includes a feeling for quantity as well as magnitude)

- pattern recognition

- spatial visualization

- embodied thinking

Symbolic knowledge & number sense

Mathematics can be done by rote or with understanding.

When you're given an example problem and shown step-by-step how to solve it, and then given problems to which you are expected to apply the same steps, then you are doing it by rote. You don't need to understand what you're doing; you simply need to be able to apply the steps to a problem that is very similar to the example.

If, on the other hand, the problems are expressed in different ways from the original example, you need to have some understanding of what you're doing, in order to apply the right steps to the right bits of the problem.

Your ability to apply learning to a situation that is not exactly the same as the one you've been instructed in reflects your depth of understanding of the problem.

So, for example, a student might be taught that to divide fractions, they should turn the second fraction upside-down and multiply it by the first fraction, as in:

$$\frac{a}{b} \div \frac{c}{d} = \frac{a}{b} \times \frac{d}{c}$$

To show this in action, they're given this worked example:

$$\frac{1}{4} \div \frac{1}{8} = \frac{1}{4} \times \frac{8}{1} = \frac{8}{4} = 2$$

Which would be followed by a number of practice problems of the same kind, such as:

$$\frac{1}{3} \div \frac{1}{6} =$$

$$\frac{1}{2} \div \frac{1}{4} =$$

$$\frac{1}{5} \div \frac{1}{10} =$$

Other problems could extend this a little:

$$\frac{2}{3} \div \frac{3}{4} =$$

$$5/7 \div 2/6 =$$

And further:

$$2 \div 3/4 =$$

$$5 \div 2/9 =$$

And further still:

> Jane has $2/3$ of a pound of butter. How many portions can she make if she divides it into portions that are each $1/9$ of a pound?
>
> Charlie has $3/4$ of a cake left. He wants to divide it equally among his 12 children. How much will each one get?
>
> Kate has $1\frac{3}{4}$ yards of fabric with which to make cushions. Each cushion needs $1/3$ yard. How many cushions can she make?

You can solve all these problems using the method described, but the greater the difference between the problem and the worked example, the more likely it is that a student will fail.

So how could their instruction have been improved?

The understanding that enables you to generalize to a wider set of problems is hugely helped if you're actually instructed in the general principles. If you are encouraged to work them out for yourself, that's great, but if you can't work them out, you should be given them. You then need to work with those general principles, applying them to a variety of different problems, until you do understand them.

A study that bears on this asked 55 college students the following three questions:

1. Which of these two values ($a/5$ or $a/9$) is larger? How do you know?

2. Which of these two values ($a/0.1$ or $a/0.05$) is larger? How do you know?

3. Which of these two values (a/n or $a/n-1$) is larger? How do you know?

Students were told that *a* was a positive number and *n* was a positive number greater than one.

Unsurprisingly, the first question was correctly answered the most (42/55). The hardest question was the second, involving decimals (29 correct, vs 34 correct for the third question).

But the important thing was that the weakest students explained their answers in terms of concrete aspects, while stronger students explained them in terms of concepts — but the best students tended to use general rules that weren't necessarily conceptual.

Examples of the first type of answer (concrete) are:

> "If a is 1, $\frac{1}{5}$ is bigger than $\frac{1}{9}$."
>
> " $\frac{a}{5}$ is larger because if a is a positive number it would take less for the fraction to become a whole."
>
> " $\frac{a}{5}$ is bigger because 9a is bigger than 5a."
>
> " $\frac{a}{9}$ is larger than $\frac{a}{5}$. 9 being greater than 5. Because 9 is larger."

Examples of the second (conceptual but limited) are:

> " $\frac{a}{5}$ is larger because it is cut into less pieces."
>
> " $\frac{a}{5}$ is larger because a out of 5 is more than a out of 9."
>
> "Drew two circles, one divided into 5 pieces, the other into 9."

Examples of the third (general rule) are:

> " $\frac{a}{5}$ is larger than $\frac{a}{9}$ because in fractions when the denominator is larger the amount is smaller." (non-conceptual; rule-based)
>
> " $\frac{a}{5}$ is larger because a is being divided by a smaller number, the smaller the divider the larger the answer." (conceptual)

The last example is both conceptual and general. Those who gave this sort of answer were least likely to answer incorrectly.

The difficulty of the question was, of course, also a factor — just because a student could give a conceptual answer for the first question didn't mean that they could do the same for the second. Indeed, this failure to extend the conceptual understanding to the more difficult questions is a signal that the math hasn't been deeply understood.

What practical lessons can we draw from all this?

First, that your understanding will develop (as long as you encourage it to do so!) as you build a wider experience of problems. Students who have only experienced fraction problems involving denominators that are whole numbers, for example, will probably not have the same depth of understanding as students who have experienced problems where the denominators can also be variables or decimals.

Second, that, although your initial understanding may rest on concrete features, you do want to move away from that as fast as you can. You want to achieve a level of understanding of the general principles involved, which enables you to tackle the range of potential problems, not simply ones that precisely follow the examples you have been taught. Remember: that is the aim of the instruction. Not to simply follow a rote set of steps when you come across a problem that is exactly like the ones you've practiced on, but to know what to do when you come across problems that are expressed in different ways.

Understanding the conceptual underpinnings may or may not help with that — on the other hand, your conceptual understanding will expand with each type of problem you understand the conceptual foundations of, so even if it doesn't directly help with that particular type of problem, it will indirectly help with your math learning, as it builds expertise.

So, aim for the conceptual and the general, with the general being of special importance for the task at hand, and the conceptual particularly important for generally building your ability to learn math.

How does that work?

Explicit instruction in the concepts and principles of a mathematical task helps you gain the general understanding you need to use their knowledge in a wider context. However, understanding on its own isn't enough. Without repeated practice, you can easily come away from the instruction with the illusion that you have 'learned' the task. But you won't remember it. Practice is vital for cementing the principles in your brain.

Explaining matters to yourself is an excellent strategy for building conceptual understanding. This applies not only to explaining problems and your solutions, but also any errors you make. Indeed, comparing erroneous solutions to correct ones and explaining where you went wrong seems to be more effective than restricting yourself to correct solutions.

Research also suggests that, rather than simply following a worked example for numerous problems of the same type, you can gain a better conceptual understanding if you explore different ways of solving the problem. By coming at the problem from different directions, and being forced to really think about what you're trying to do, you'll gain an understanding that will pass you by if you're simply copying a formulaic path. Once you've explored the problem, it's time enough to study a worked example, which you can then compare with your own attempts.

One of the problems with 'real-world' problems is that they often include a lot of extraneous information to their problems, in order to show relevance. Relevance to the world, but not to the problem. It's easy to focus on this much more comprehensible and memorable material rather than the details that are, in fact, what you need to learn.

So one of the skills involved in mathematics is that of learning to see what matters in word problems.

However, mathematics itself is an exact language and you can't, unlike academic texts, read it for 'gist' — in the math language (as opposed to word descriptions), each word and symbol must be attended to and precisely understood. So reading math is not at all like reading in other subjects.

Even when there are words (not in the context of word problems, but mixed in with symbols), they tend to have specific, precise meanings that are different from their general meanings. Such specific meanings need to be memorized. Indeed, this might be a situation where the linking differences strategy might be useful. By explicitly contrasting the math meaning with the generally-understood one, you may find it easier to remember. For example:

associative:

property by which people or ideas combine together for a common purpose (general)

property by which numbers can be added or multiplied in any order and still yield the same value (math)

Difference:

associative generally means combining together for a common purpose, but in math it refers to numbers combining together in a way that produces the same result regardless of the order of the numbers

Links:

this type of associative relationship relates to a common purpose — general

this type of associative relationship means that order doesn't matter in getting the right answer — math

What about "basic facts", like the times table? In all this talk of conceptual understanding, what's happened to those? Surely you still need to memorize these by rote?

Yes and no.

As with language, some memorization is necessary to get you started, but cementing the knowledge is best done through real-world use. Just as speaking and reading give you the necessary and varied practice to develop your language skills and cement your knowledge of vocabulary and grammar (but you need to begin with memorization of vocabulary and instruction in grammar), so in mathematics you should cement your knowledge of basic facts and principles with varied practice.

Just remember that it's vital, if the practice is going to work to help you memorize, that you actually come up with the answer yourself, even if you have to use your fingers! If you simply refer to a table, or use a calculator, then it's not going to help you.

Exercise 14.3

The following figure demonstrates five principles of triangle geometry, pertaining to the interior and exterior angles of a triangle. An exterior angle is the angle between one side of a triangle and the extension of an adjacent side. The exterior angles have been colored in the diagram. Try to put these five principles into words before going on. The principles are listed after the first example problem.

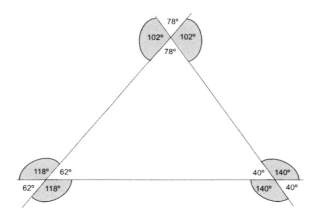

(a) Using as many different approaches as you can think of, calculate X in the following figure. Write down the principle(s) used in each step.

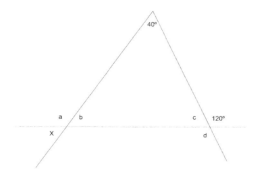

The five principles that might be relevant:

Principle 1: The interior angles of a triangle add up to 180°.

Principle 2: A straight angle (the angle on a straight line) is 180°.

Principle 3: An exterior angle is equal to the sum of the opposite interior angles.

Principle 4: If the equivalent angle is taken at each vertex, the exterior angles always add to 360°.

Principle 5: When two lines cross, vertically opposite angles are equal.

(b) Using as many different approaches as you can think of, calculate X in the following figure. Write down the principle used in each step.

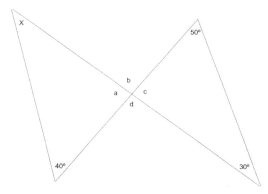

(c) In the following figure, write down all the different ways in which you could calculate X. Note each principle being used in each step.

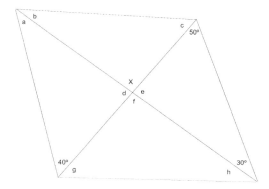

Embodied cognition & reducing cognitive load

Research suggests that too much emphasis on memorization and rote learning, and on speed, impairs math achievement. An emphasis on speed means that working memory is under great pressure. Those who are anxious about mathematics will have less working memory capacity (anxiety and stress tend to 'clog up' working memory), creating more stress, and more distaste of mathematics.

Too high a cognitive load is probably a major reason for the development of math blocks.

For example, fractions have been described as the backbone of mathematics, and also the place where many students' math anxiety begins.

Why? It's been speculated that one reason may be that, when fractions are first introduced, it's on the back of learning basic arithmetic. The young student has learned how to add 2 + 3 and subtract 9 - 6, and has conceptualized what's going on by adding blocks or apples together or subtracting them. They understand the idea and practice of these basic processes. Then the teacher says: we're going to add ¼ and ⅔. Okay, based on what they've already learned, the natural thing to do is to add the top of the fractions together and the bottom: ³⁄₇. Which is of course wrong. But it's alright, because the teacher instructs them that the first thing to do is not to use the rules they've already learned, but instead "to look for the lowest common denominator".

A step too far.

The trouble is that there's no connection between their previous learning and this new learning. The process is the same ("addition", "subtraction", "multiplication"), but now the steps you follow are quite different, and there is no clear conceptual explanation that tells you why.

Which is why an approach has been developed in recent years of connecting the two together by means of a number line. By using a number line, as they did when learning basic arithmetic, students can see that adding fractions is the same as adding whole numbers. Approached the right way, students, even young ones, can easily understand the need for a common unit. From there, it is a small step to the idea of equivalent fractions.

Once comfortable with that, the technical term of "lowest common denominator" can be introduced, and hopefully will find much greater acceptance.

It's all about breaking things down to the smallest steps, and of being consistent with previous learning.

The exact same principles can be applied at higher levels of math.

Diagrams and illustrations, for example, can be very helpful in mathematics, but once again we have to consider cognitive load. Research has found that, while college students with higher mathematical ability benefited from diagrams and illustrations in learning trigonometry, those with poorer skills found them a hindrance to learning (Cooper et al. 2018). Too much information!

Still, with the caveat that some learners may have to work up it, having multiple representations — text, formula, plus graphic — does seem to be the most effective in explaining mathematical problems. That goes back to the idea of approaching a problem from multiple directions, and trying different strategies.

Apart from breaking things down to smaller steps, there is another way of reducing cognitive load: using embodied cognition.

Embodied cognition is, as its name suggests, all about involving the body in your thinking, sharing the cognitive load with that part of you that, as we have seen, has a more durable (if less nuanced) memory.

In math, that can be seen in drawing, in tracing, and in gesture. Research has found that tracing helps in geometry learning (Ginns et al. 2015), while a number of studies have shown that gesturing while working out or explaining problems often helps with the process, and with memory.

One intriguing study with young children found that abstract gesture worked better than concrete gesture, and both worked better than miming (Novack et al. 2014). The children were being taught mathematical equivalence problems, such as

$$4 + 2 + 6 = \underline{} + 6$$

One group picked up magnetic number tiles and put them in their proper place on a magnetic whiteboard. A second group mimed the action without touching the tiles. A third group, however, were taught to produce a V-point gesture with their fingers under two of the numbers, metaphorically grouping them, followed by pointing a finger at the blank in the equation.

I have mentioned this, although it involved young children, because of the specifics of the abstract gesture. The children learned the problems given in the lesson regardless of the method of instruction, but it was only those who used this abstract gesture that were able to generalize the knowledge and apply that to new problems. More support for the value of abstract thinking in understanding mathematics.

Pattern recognition & spatial visualization

Spatial visualization is probably the 'purest' area of skills in this subject area. No need to try and balance abstract thinking and practice here! Practice is all you need.

How do you practice spatial visualization?

Well, as with any practice, by doing it! But if you find spatial visualization within the more abstract world of math too difficult, you could try working up to it. The reason why women, for example, tend to be poorer at spatial memory tasks is that they generally haven't had the extensive practice boys have had in such activities as Lego building. Lego building has indeed been linked to higher mathematical achievement because of this very benefit, for developing visuospatial ability (Nath & Szücs 2014).

There are spatial visualization training exercises around, but if you are really bad at this, or find such exercises too intimidating, I do think something like Lego building is a good idea, because it is concrete, and you're using your body. Another common activity that would probably be helpful in developing your skills is that of cubic block puzzles, such as the soma cube, snake cube, Rubik's cube, etc.

The key factor in choosing an activity is that it be something you can learn to enjoy. Remember how many hours children put into these activities! You don't have to match them to achieve sufficient expertise, but don't expect your abilities to magically improve after spending 15 minutes, or even an hour or two. Skills take time to grow.

Another possible activity, and one that also brings in pattern recognition, is jigsaw puzzles.

Pattern recognition in mathematics is not only something that is visual, however. Pattern recognition is also about recognizing when a problem belongs to a particular category of problems. This, of course, is vital to the task of choosing the right formula to apply to a problem. This sort of pattern recognition is more abstract, but it shares the same elements as more visual patterns: you have to be able to identify which features are important. Improving your ability at this is a matter of varied practice, and making sure you interleave different problem types (as I discussed earlier).

Exercise 14.4

One aspect of spatial visualization is mental rotation. In the following examples, you will see different types of figures, and different instructions. See how much, or whether, your performance varies as a result of these different figures or instructions. Rate each one on a 5-point scale, with 1 representing greater easiness and 5 greater difficulty.

1. Two of these figures are identical. Which one is not?

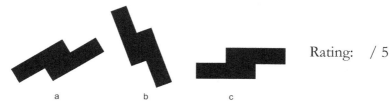

Rating: / 5

a   b   c

2. Three of these figures are identical. Focus on the triangle as you mentally rotate each one to determine which is the odd one out.

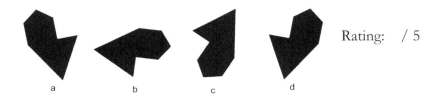

Rating: / 5

a   b   c   d

3. Which of these pairs are mirror images?

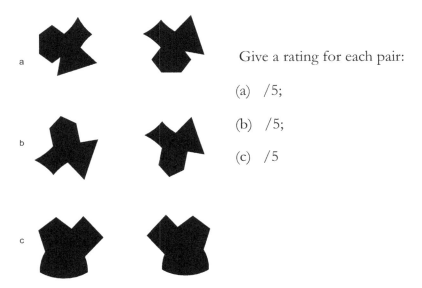

Give a rating for each pair:

(a) /5;

(b) /5;

(c) /5

4. Mentally rotate this normal F to decide which of the three alternatives is backwards.

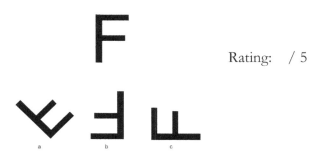

Rating: / 5

5. Which of these pairs are identical? Look closely — they're not as symmetrical as they look!

Give a rating for each pair:

(a) /5;

(b) /5;

(c) /5

6. Imagine that you're grasping the bar at the top of the 5, using that to pull it around in a circle. Which of the three alternatives don't match onto the 5?

Rating: / 5

a   b   c

7. Which of these four figures is not the same as the others?

a   b

Rating: / 5

c   d

8. Raise your arm to match the first figure and imagine yourself rotating. Which of these figures doesn't match the other?

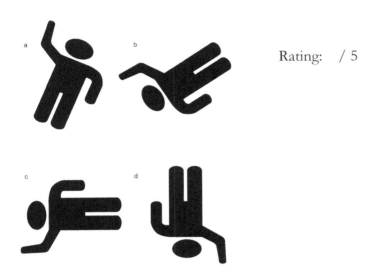

Rating: / 5

9. Which of these clocks show 9 o'clock?

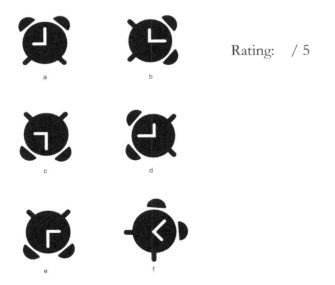

Rating: / 5

10. Which of these figures isn't the same as the others?

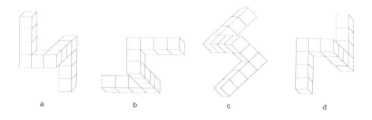

Rating: / 5

11. Focus on the colored squares as you rotate these objects to determine which of these figures isn't the same as the others

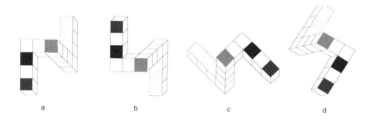

Rating: / 5

12. Which of the three alternatives is a mirror image of the first photo?

Rating: / 5

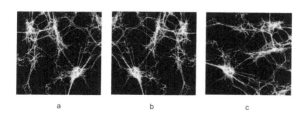

Balancing practice & theory

To a large extent, mathematics is a cognitive skill. The trick to dealing with a cognitive skill is knowing exactly which parts need to be treated as "cognitive" and which as "skill".

I suspect this is more true of mathematics than almost any other cognitive skill. This is because math instruction has always been plagued by this question of the relative value of conceptual understanding and procedural practice. Depending on your age and place of education, you may have spent most of your mathematics education mechanically applying a memorized set of steps, or you may have had a great emphasis on understanding the conceptual foundation with, perhaps, not enough practice in applying these ideas to actual problems.

Both practice and abstract thinking are needed, of course — the trick lies in when and how much. I hope this discussion has given you some help in judging this line in different contexts.

The other trick is knowing how to apply the principles of deliberate practice to those parts that are skill-based.

Here's the bottom line: there's no point in just doing the same task, by rote, over and over again. Yes, practice is needed, and over-practice is needed for mastery. But practice is not simply repetition! Remember the principles of deliberate practice: you need to vary what you're doing. Small variations. Smart variations.

Which means your problems need to extend and connect. Extend to new variations of the problem. Connect to other types of problem.

If something is too difficult for you, see where the problem lies. Can you break the problem down? For example, in the above fractions problem, students found the variant involving decimals most difficult. Is that because they needed more practice in dealing with decimals?

If you make a mistake, use this as an opportunity to monitor your learning. Did you make it because you were careless, or because your knowledge of basic facts was faulty, or because there's something you don't understand? Pinpoint your weakness, then spend time and effort tackling it.

Remember to space out your learning — don't limit your practice of a particular type of problem just to one study session. Interleave your learning within the session (regardless of the instructions given by your teacher or textbook). Use the opportunity to revise previously-practiced problems.

Remember, too, the value of interleaving for math practice.

The main problem — with both language learning and math learning — is finding good resources, since the most effective learning depends on optimal progression through practice exercises, appropriately varied and extended. But I hope that this discussion has given a foundation for knowing what to look for.

Main points

Pay attention to advice about conceptual and general principles; don't simply follow the step-by-step instructions for how to solve a problem. If no such advice is provided, seek it out.

Make sure you practice on a variety of different problems. Try to apply the relevant general principle to each type of problem.

Explain what you're doing to yourself. If you make an error, compare it to the correct solution and explain to yourself where you went wrong.

Where possible, come at problems from different angles, so you have a better understanding of why one approach is better than others.

Remember to space out your learning — don't limit your practice of a particular type of problem just to one study session.

Interleave different types of problem within your study session.

When tackling problems that are expressed in wordy descriptions, teach yourself to distinguish between the details that matter and those that are irrelevant to the mathematical problem.

Pay attention to words that have specific, precise meanings in mathematics that are different from their general meanings. Use the linking differences strategy to help you learn these.

Rather than trying to memorize formulae and "basic facts" (like the times table) solely by rote, support such memorization through varied practice.

Where you are anxious, or find a problem too confusing, try to reduce the demand on your working memory. Break things down to the smallest steps.

Seek out multiple representations (having a concept expressed in words, in numbers, and spatially), but if that's too confusing, train yourself progressively to understand these different representations. Don't overload your working memory.

The demands on your working memory can also be reduced by using your body, by drawing, tracing, or gesture.

Spatial visualization does not require abstract thinking, only practice. If you find it difficult, seek out resources to build your spatial abilities.

Science

"Science" is of course not a single subject area, and the specifics will vary depending on the particular science. However, I will make a few broad generalizations that may help you approach a science subject.

Doing science

Like mathematics, like language, science has two components: the 'doing' and the 'knowing'. Doing science involves lab work, and field observations (for example, star-gazing, tornado chasing, animal tracking, fossil hunting) — to use these two very broad categories. So the skill aspect of science can be seen both in perceptual learning / pattern recognition and the more obviously physical skills involved in doing experiments (think of cooking as a type of chemistry experimentation — fluency in measuring, mixing, heating, etc, all comes with practice).

Remember the principles of deliberate practice — if you're having difficulty with a practical skill:

- break it into smaller components;

- concentrate on the most difficult bits;

- do things slowly until you are skilled enough to build up speed;

- only focus on one aspect at a time.

As for perceptual learning, the main thing is to have faith that practice will indeed give you a level of discrimination ability that may seem unattainable! Remember to start with easier discriminations and build up to harder ones. One way to do this is by participating in citizen science projects, which often provide many opportunities to get the extensive practice that you need to become better at spotting perceptual differences. You can find a list of citizen science projects on my website, at https://www.mempowered.com/resources/citizen-science-links.

Learning basic facts

Most sciences have a core of fundamental facts that need to be memorized. Chemistry, for example, has the periodic table of elements. Physics has formulae. Geology has the geological time scale. Zoology has taxonomies.

Some of these have established mnemonics to help with the memorization task, and I certainly urge you to use these where appropriate. Do remember that mnemonics are there to support your learning, by adding meaning to material that is currently meaningless to you. You still need to use retrieval practice to master the mnemonics!

But also remember that you don't want to have too many mnemonics rattling around in your head. Try first to make the information meaningful to you. Mnemonics are only for what is meaningless.

So, for example, the essence of the Geological Time Scale is that it is an ordered series. Order is essentially meaningless (i.e., arbitrary) — it must be memorized rather than understood. Order is one of the main reasons for the invention of mnemonics. Dates, too, can only be memorized, not understood, and there is a specific type of mnemonic just for that (the coding mnemonic). But the names of the time periods may have some meaning, since there must be some reason for the periods being given these names. Information about the events that characterize such time periods are also likely to have some meaningful connections. The Geological Time Scale is used as a (very detailed) case study in my book *Mnemonics for Study*, so I refer you there if you want more details of when and when not to use mnemonics (I also have an excerpt on my website, at https://www.mempowered.com/mnemonics/memorizing-geological-time-scale).

But in any case, mnemonics only provide a framework. For example, there are various mnemonics around to help you memorize the periodic table. They can be really good for specific bits, but if you try to use mnemonics (and only mnemonics) to memorize the whole table, you are putting far too heavy a load on your memory. Meaning *reduces* the load on your memory. Grasping the essential principles governing the layout of the table will significantly reduce your reliance on mnemonics.

What about physics formulae?

Some simple formulae have mnemonics attached to them, and these can certainly be useful. But for the most part, the best approach to learning formulae is to:

- do a lot of practice in using them

- make sure that practice is varied, spaced out, and interleaved

- try to understand the general principles involved, and explicitly bring them to mind when working a relevant problem.

For example, let's take one of the simplest physics formulae: F=ma (Force = Mass x Acceleration). As is typical, even this very simple formula contains other, implicit, formulae — acceleration is speed divided by time; speed is distance divided by time. So, in this example:

If a 13 kg mountain bike crashes into a person at 20m/s and it takes 2 seconds for the bike to stop, what is the force that the bike hit with?

you need to first calculate the acceleration:

20m/s divided by 2s = 10m/s/s

and then you can calculate the force:

13kg x 10m/s/s = 130N (Newtons)

This seems quite straightforward, but most problems that involve this formula will not be as basic as this, and students have a surprising amount of trouble with less obvious descriptions of a problem. That's because they're trying to apply the formula by rote, and don't have an understanding of the general principles. So what are the general principles? (Do note that I am not a physicist! I leaned heavily on the Physics Classroom, www.physicsclassroom.com, for this, and heartily recommend it.)

The first is that it's not simply force — it's net force. Net force is an unbalanced force. So this is one principle: F=ma only applies where the forces acting upon an object are unbalanced. If the forces were balanced, the object would either not move (if already at rest), or would continue to move at the same speed in the same direction (if already in motion). So it is only if the forces are unbalanced that F=ma applies. Examples of such unbalanced situations are:

- when gravity is weaker than the tension on a vertical rope holding an elevator

- when gravity is stronger than the air resistance holding a leaf up

- when friction slows down a ball rolling down a ramp.

The next important principle is that the net force is the sum of all the forces — *and that this is a vector*. Meaning that you need to apply the principles of vector addition.

The third important principle is that an unbalanced force leads to acceleration, and this acceleration is in the same direction as the net force.

The problem most people have with really understanding this starts with Newton's First Law (F=ma represents the Second Law), that states that force is *not* needed to keep an object in motion. In the world we experience, that doesn't appear to be true. That's because the forces are pretty much always unbalanced. We have no practical experience with a balanced force, so it's counter-intuitive. We have to believe Newton's First Law as an article of faith (that's why it needed a genius to come up with it!). Because you need a very unusual situation (such as outer space) to experience this in action, it may help to play with interactive simulations until you build up a more visceral sense of how things work (the Physics Classroom has some; for more, just search on the internet for Physics Interactives).

It's worth taking a moment to reflect on what it means to *understand* something like this. Understanding here is based very much on practical experience, which has created in you a set of beliefs about how the physical world works. Until you work explicitly to create new experiences that re-write those beliefs, you're going to keep getting answers wrong.

So let's think about what that simple formula is really saying:

- the acceleration of an object is determined by the mass of the object and the net force acting on it

- acceleration is directly proportional to the mass, which means that acceleration will be greater the smaller the mass is (this fits in with our experience, and it's just as important to note when principles match our beliefs and experience, as it is to note when they don't)

- the net force is calculated by working out the vector sum of all the individual forces

- you can't calculate it if you don't know all the forces acting on the object

- vectors involve direction

- if the forces are all acting in the same direction or in direct opposition, the calculation is straightforward

- but if the forces are acting at an angle to each other, then you need to employ trigonometric methods, or scaled vector diagrams (there's a whole separate analysis involved in how to understand those, but I won't go into that).

If you think about these principles when solving your F=ma problems (as opposed to simply applying, or attempting to apply, the formula by rote), you will build up an understanding that will enable you to correctly answer a much greater variety of problems, at varying levels of difficulty.

An important thing to note is that these sort of general principles don't have to be as precise as physics equations and formulae have to be. That is, you can express them a bit more loosely (though not to the point of misleading inaccuracy!), because your aim with them is to obtain a gut-level understanding of the broad concepts involved. That means it's really important to pay attention to any real-world examples your teacher offers, which will help you connect abstract principles and concepts with your own experience.

Understanding science

As regards the conceptual foundations, understanding science is (almost) all about making connections. Learning strategies for this include:

- asking the right questions

- making the right comparisons

- linking differences

- creating concept maps.

I say "almost all" , because apparently one of the biggest problems standing in the way of learning science is, as I touched on in the discussion of F=ma, our misconceptions about how the world works. Not so surprising, when you think about it. If it was so easy to know how everything works that we could do it just wandering through the world, it wouldn't have taken us tens of thousands of year to realize the Earth goes around the Sun!

Correcting our misconceptions thus becomes a crucial element in understanding science. Realizing how new facts contradict 'common sense' is the first and most important step in this.

This challenge needs to be incorporated into our connection making.

Remember that there are two aspects to making connections:

- those you make within a topic, within the new information you're learning about

- those you make between your new information and the information you already know.

It is in that latter information pool, of course, that your potential misconceptions lie. So it is during that type of connection-making that you need to pay careful attention to any discrepancies and contradictions that mean those two information pools (the new and the old) don't fit together as well as they should.

But it is vital that you make those connections with your existing knowledge, which will include familiar experiences. We tend to rank personal experiences very highly in questions of what to believe — but one of the important characteristics of scientists is that they have learned to de-prioritize personal experience. That doesn't mean you should ignore it. Rather, you need to reconcile your experience with the science, which means re-interpreting events in the light of new information.

If you don't clearly and explicitly work out how to reconcile the contradictions, you'll never really believe the science, and you probably won't remember it either.

Additionally, as I indicated when I said that it's just as important to note when principles match our beliefs and experience as it is to note when they don't, making explicit connection to your beliefs and experiences when they are consistent with scientific principles will greatly strengthen your understanding and memory of these principles.

So, how should you go about all this?

Before reading a text, ask yourself what you already believe about the topic, any opinions you already have. Having established this, keep these beliefs and opinions in mind as you read the text. If you come across statements that contradict your beliefs, don't skate over them (we are very good at disregarding information that contradicts our existing beliefs). You want to do the exact opposite of your natural instinct — give these parts extra attention. Do they really contradict your beliefs? Is there a way to reconcile the two pieces of information? Do your existing beliefs need tweaking?

Before reading the text, and during your reading, you should also question yourself about your existing knowledge. It's important that you distinguish between knowledge and opinion — and that's not as easy as you might think. Your existing knowledge provides a structure for your new learning, but if your 'knowledge' is misconceived opinion, that's not going to be a good framework.

Exercise 14.5

Here's an excerpt from the earlier text discussing theories of motivation:

> Another early theory of motivation proposed that the maintenance of homeostasis is particularly important in directing behavior. You may recall from your earlier reading that homeostasis is the tendency to maintain a balance, or optimal level, within a biological system. In a body system, a control center (which is often part of the brain) receives input from receptors (which are often complexes of neurons). The control center directs effectors (which may be other neurons) to correct any imbalance detected by the control center.
>
> According to the drive theory of motivation, deviations from homeostasis create physiological needs. These needs result in psychological drive states that direct behavior to meet the need and, ultimately, bring the system back to homeostasis. For example, if it's been a while since you ate, your blood sugar levels will drop below normal. This low blood sugar will induce a physiological need and a corresponding drive state (i.e., hunger) that will direct you to seek out and consume food. Eating will eliminate the hunger, and, ultimately, your blood sugar levels will return to normal. Interestingly, drive

theory also emphasizes the role that habits play in the type of behavioral response in which we engage. A habit is a pattern of behavior in which we regularly engage. Once we have engaged in a behavior that successfully reduces a drive, we are more likely to engage in that behavior whenever faced with that drive in the future (Graham & Weiner, 1996).

Thinking about this text, list as many examples as you can of your personal beliefs about what motivates you to engage in various behaviors (such as eating, drinking, exercising, working, etc.). Are these beliefs consistent or inconsistent with the drive theory of motivation? Are you more or less inclined to believe in the drive theory because of these beliefs?

Exercise 14.6

The following problems are concerned with heat and temperature. Here are definitions of relevant concepts:

Heat is energy that is transferred because of a difference in temperature.

Temperature is a measure of the average kinetic energy of the particles.

Internal energy is the sum total of the kinetic and potential energies of the particles constituting matter.

1. (This problem is adapted from the Heat, Temperature and Internal Energy Diagnostic Test (Gurcay & Gulbas, 2015).)

A baker bakes two loaves of bread in a wide bakery oven at the same time. The loaves are from the same bread dough, baked under the same conditions and for the same length of time. However, one loaf is bigger than the other. When the loaves are taken out of the oven:

    a.   the bigger loaf will have higher heat

    b.   the smaller loaf will have higher heat

   c.   the two loaves will have equal heat

   d.   it's not possible to compare the heat of the loaves

   e.   the bigger loaf will have a higher temperature

   f.   the smaller loaf will have a higher temperature

   g.   the two loaves will have the same temperature

   h.   it's not possible to compare the temperature of the loaves

The correct answers are (d) and (g). Pick relevant beliefs that might cause students to pick the wrong answer from the following list of common misconceptions:

   i.   Heat and temperature are the same thing.

   ii.   Heat of an object depends on its size.

   iii.   Heat is a property of a particular material or object.

   iv.   Temperature is a property of a particular material or object.

   v.   Temperature of an object depends on its size.

   vi.   The heat of two objects composed of the same material and left in the same environment for a long time depends on the size of the objects.

   vii.   The temperature of two objects composed of the same material and left in the same environment for a long time depends on the size of the objects.

   viii.   Heat flows more slowly through conductors making them feel hot.

The following problems are taken from the Thermal Concept Evaluation (Yeo & Zadnik, 2001).

2. Why do we wear sweaters in cold weather?

   a.   To keep cold out.

   b.   To generate heat.

   c.   To reduce heat loss.

   d.   All three of the above reasons are correct.

The correct answer is (c). Pick relevant beliefs that might cause students to pick the wrong answer from the following list of common misconceptions:

i. Temperature is a property of a particular material or object.

ii. Skin or touch can determine temperature.

iii. Heat and cold are different, rather than opposite ends of a continuum.

iv. Temperature can be transferred.

v. Objects that readily become warm do not readily become cold.

vi. Materials like wool have the ability to warm things up.

vii. Something that's cold contains no heat.

viii. Objects of different temperature that are in contact with each other, or in contact with air at different temperature, do not necessarily move toward the same temperature.

3. Kim takes a metal ruler and a wooden ruler for a pencil case. The metal one feels colder than the wooden one. Why?

a. Metal conducts energy away from the hand more rapidly than wood.

b. Wood is a naturally warmer substance than metal.

c. The wooden ruler contains more heat than the metal ruler.

d. Metals are better heat radiators than wood.

e. Cold flows more readily from a metal.

The correct answer is (a). Pick relevant beliefs that might cause students to pick the wrong answer from the following list of common misconceptions:

i. Something that's cold contains no heat.

ii. Skin or touch can determine temperature.

iii. Perceptions of hot and cold are unrelated to energy transfer.

iv. Wood is naturally warmer than metal.

v.   Temperature is a property of a particular material or object.

vi.   Metal has the ability to attract, hold, intensify or absorb heat and cold.

vii.   Some materials are difficult to heat: they are more resistant to heating.

viii. Heat is proportional to temperature.

4. Sam takes a can of cola and a plastic bottle of cola from the refrigerator, where they have been overnight. He quickly puts a thermometer in the cola in the can. The temperature is 7° C. What are the most likely temperatures of the plastic bottle and cola it holds?

a.   They are both less than 7°C.

b.   They are both equal to 7°C.

c.   They are both greater than 7°C.

d.   The cola is at 7° C but the bottle is greater than 7°C.

e.   It depends on the amount of cola and/or the size of the bottle.

The correct answer is (b). Pick relevant beliefs that might cause students to pick the wrong answer from the following list of common misconceptions:

i.   The temperature of an object depends on its size.

ii.   Heat flows more slowly through conductors making them feel hot.

iii.   Objects of different temperature that are in contact with each other, or in contact with air at different temperature, do not necessarily move toward the same temperature.

iv.   Objects that readily become warm do not readily become cold.

v.   Temperature is a property of a particular material or object.

vi.   Metal has the ability to attract, hold, intensify or absorb heat and cold.

vii.   Plastic is naturally warmer than metal.

viii. Some materials are difficult to heat: they are more resistant to heating.

Perceptual fluency & conceptual understanding

Graphical representations such as those below are often key to science learning.

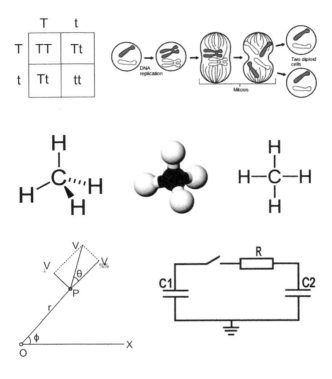

Students tend not to give these the attention they deserve, but to be an effective science student you want to achieve a level of fluency with these that means you can extract the relevant information easily. This is a skill. It is a skill that is best acquired through a combination of conceptual learning and practice.

Research indicates that the best approach to mastery is to first understand how the diagrams work (conceptual learning), then get lots of directed practice to build your fluency in interpreting them (perceptual learning) (Rau & Wu 2018 — note that the chemistry example given below leans heavily on this study).

In both cases, multiple representations are crucial.

In the case of understanding, it helps if you have information that indicates what features are relevant. Otherwise, especially if you're a novice, you're quite likely to pay attention to superficial features that aren't important or helpful. Once you know what you're looking for, explaining the diagram to yourself is a good strategy (although you do need to be careful of this strategy if you're not receiving any feedback).

Perceptual learning requires a very different strategy — here you are best not to think too much! Instead, you want lots of examples that you can categorize or select, as quickly as possible. As I've said, humans are very good at recognizing patterns, and it's something we do at a subconscious level. Conscious thinking is good, but sometimes we're best to step back and let our brains do their thing.

In chemistry, Lewis structures show the bonding between atoms of different molecules, ball and stick models are three-dimensional representations of the same thing, dash-wedge diagrams are a more symbolic way of showing the same information, Bohr models show the electrons on the atomic shells, energy diagrams show electrons in orbitals by energy levels, and orbital diagrams show the spatial arrangement of non-empty orbitals.

In the diagram below, for example, you can see four different ways of representing fluorine. The simple dot diagram shows that fluorine has 7 valence electrons; the Bohr model shows not only the 7 valence electrons on the outer shell, but also the 2 core electrons on the inner shell; the ball-&-stick model tells us that the fluorine molecule contains 2 fluorine atoms, meaning the chemical formula for fluorine can be written as F_2; the energy level diagram shows that there are two electrons in the s orbital at the first energy level ($1s$), two electrons in the s orbital at the second energy level ($2s$), and five electrons in the p orbital at the second level ($2p$).

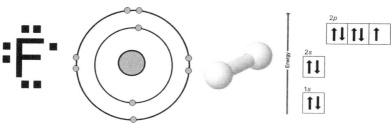

Comparing different ways of representing fluorine gives you a better understanding of the element. Understanding how the different representations connect to each other enables you to better build your fluency in reading and translating them. To acquire this understanding, you need to practice explaining how these representations map onto each other. Some direction helps. So, for example, the following image shows how the dot diagram maps onto the Bohr model. You can see how the valence electrons shown by the dots around the F map onto the electrons on the outer shell in the Bohr model (I haven't filled in all the arrows because it would be confusingly messy, but you can mentally finish the correspondences, and indeed doing so will help you understand it).

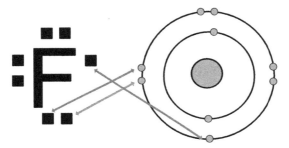

Similarly, an energy level diagram is only one of the ways to represent the electron configuration. We could have expressed it in notation as 1s22s22p5, or as an orbital diagram.

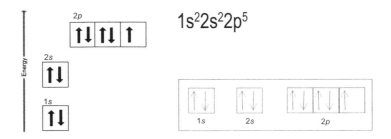

Here, the labels make it easy to make the connections between the different representations (because they are the same across all representations), so we don't need to make them explicit with arrows. But the energy level diagram makes the different energy levels much clearer than in the other representations (because it actually shows them on different levels), and the notation makes the 5 electrons in the 2p orbital much more obvious than in the diagrams using arrows. In other words, studying the representations together, comparing them by looking for the similarities and the differences, gives you a deeper understanding and also helps you on the journey to becoming someone who can look at just one of these representations and mentally visualize the others.

So in this example, the conceptually relevant similarity between the dot diagram and the Bohr model is that they both show the 7 electrons in the outer shell ("valence electrons"). The important difference is that the Bohr model shows the two electrons in the inner shell ("core electrons"), which the dot diagram does not.

The similarity between the energy level diagram and the orbital diagram is that both show the arrangement of the electrons in the shells and subshells. The difference between the two diagrams is one of emphasis rather than information — they both contain the same information, but the energy level diagram displays that information in a way that makes the shells and subshells clearer.

Comparing the energy level diagram and Bohr model:

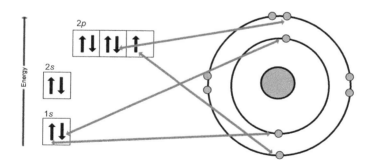

(Again, I haven't filled in all the arrows, because it's already quite a mess! But the point of this is not to produce a pretty picture but simply to sketch out the correspondences.)

So here you could say that the similarity is that both diagrams show the number of electrons and which shell they're on. The difference is that the energy level diagram also shows the subshell, which the Bohr model doesn't.

Having gone through several examples, explicitly mapping the different representations onto each other, and describing how they are similar and different from each other, you might then work on perceptual fluency. One way of doing this is to practice matching different representations with each other. The following exercises demonstrate the process.

Exercise 14.7

For each dot diagram — Bohr model — orbital diagram triplet, specify the conceptually relevant similarities and the important differences between each pair (dot—Bohr; Bohr—orbital; dot—orbital)

(a)

(b)

(c)

Exercise 14.8

In the following items, match the target to its alternate representation among the two choices offered. Try to do it as quickly as possible.

1.

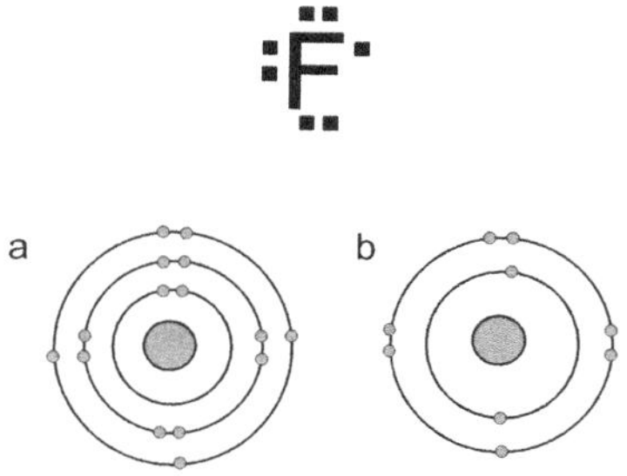

:F̈·

a   b

2.

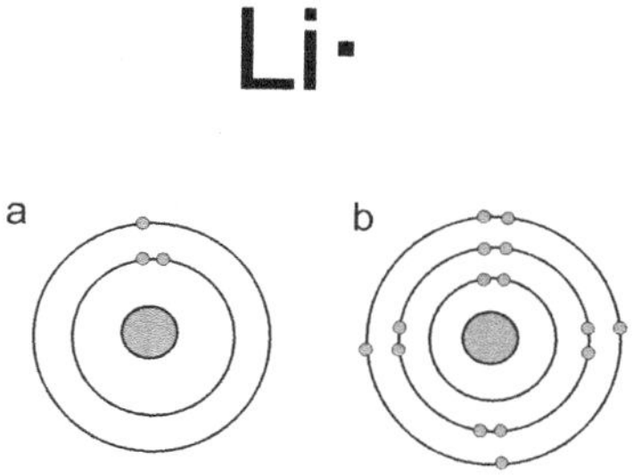

Li·

a   b

3.

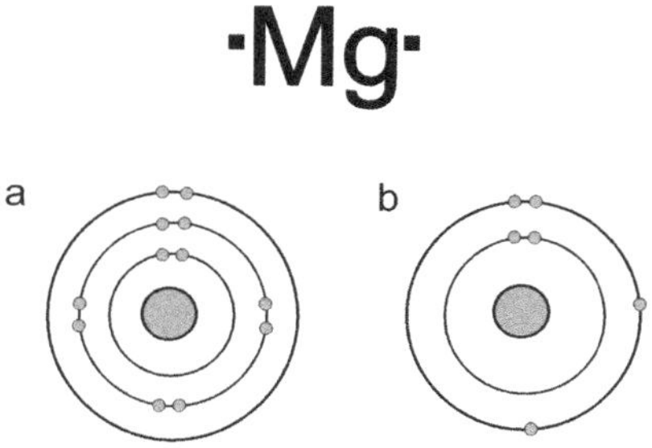

·Mg·

a   b

4.

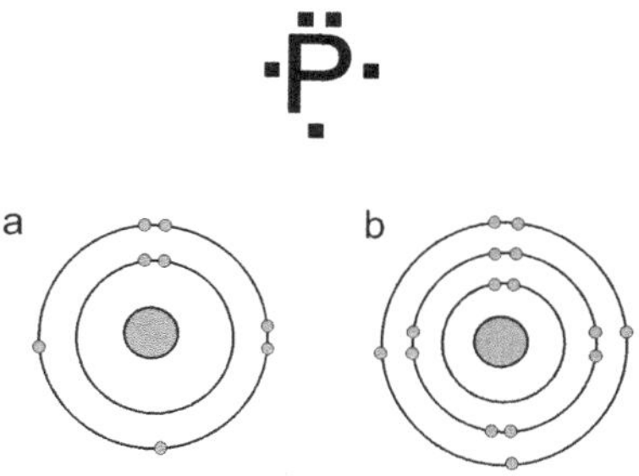

·P̈·

a   b

5.

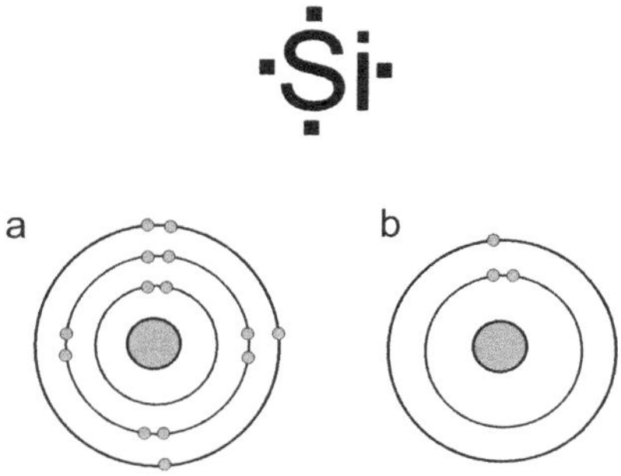

·S̈i·

a   b

6.

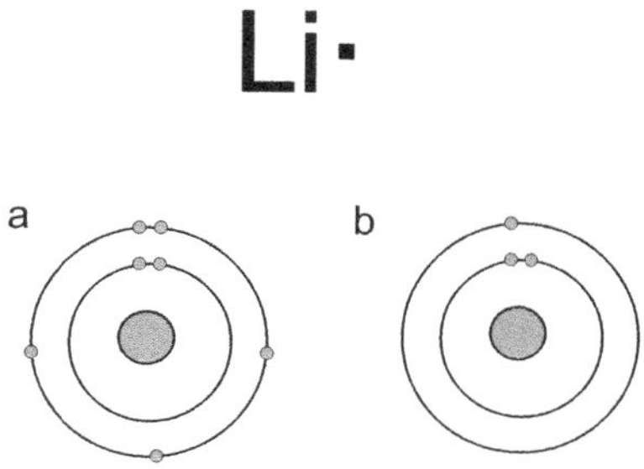

Li·

a   b

7.

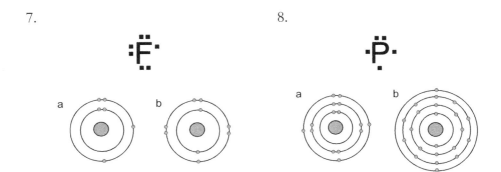

8.

9.

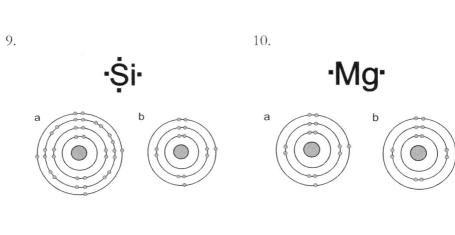

10.

11.

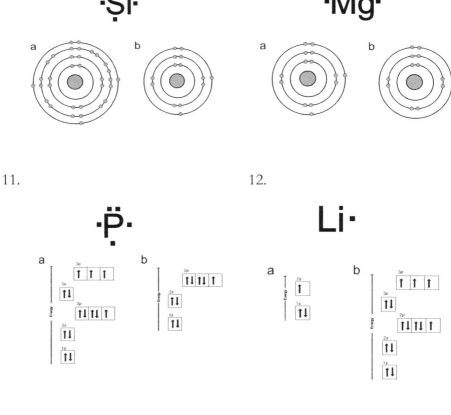

12.

13. 14.

15.

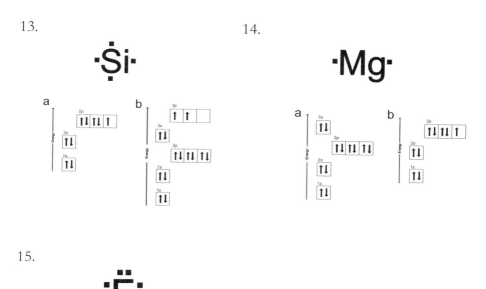

Obviously, these aren't nearly enough to build up perceptual fluency! But I hope they've given you a sense of the task. Remember, when you're doing something like this, you want to start easy and build up to more difficult. If you're finding the task difficult, don't give up, thinking the task is beyond you — just go simpler, and practice at that simple level until you're confident of your mastery, before going on to more difficult examples.

Reading science

As I said earlier, reading is a cognitive skill. But in the same way that throwing a ball is a skill, but throwing a ball in baseball is different from throwing a ball in cricket, and both are different from throwing a ball in football, and all of those are different from throwing a ball in basketball, so reading different types of material are different skills. Reading history is not the same as reading scientific text, and neither are the same as reading a novel.

One aspect, of course, is language. Technical vocabulary is a major stumbling block for many novices approaching scientific text, and here the various strategies I've discussed for learning new words are useful. Do remember that, in academic subjects, many words used have both general meanings and meanings that are specific to the topic. It is vital, when reading science texts, to know what specific meanings the words have, and the linking differences strategy will help you remember these.

But unfamiliar vocabulary is not the only problem. Different subject areas use different formats, and these different ways of organizing text require their own reading skills. I discuss various text structures and strategies for dealing with them at great length in my *Effective Notetaking* book, so I won't delve into that too deeply here. The main point I want to make is very simple — that the problems you might be having in reading scientific text stem from your lack of experience with this type of text. Your skill will greatly benefit from practice.

The right kind of practice, of course!

The right kind of practice means:

- knowing the various kinds of text structure you might come across

- practicing recognizing each kind

- knowing various strategies that are appropriate for those different structures

- practicing applying those strategies.

The main thing to remember about reading for study is that such reading is very much an active process, that involves taking notes, going back and forth between alternative representations (such as pictures, diagrams, graphs, text), and entering into a mental dialog with the text. That is, you have to think, not just receive.

In fact, reading is always an active process, but skilled readers reading easy material are not usually aware of it. But how different is the process of reading scientific text from that of reading a story?

We are programmed for stories. Right from infancy, we are told stories, we pay attention to stories, we enjoy stories. Stories have a particular structure (and within the broad structure, a set of sub-structures), and we develop a lot of practice with that structure. Expository texts (information texts), on the other hand, don't get nearly the same level of practice.

So how much of our difficulty with that type of text is simply down to that extreme difference in practice?

And how much is due to the fact that students never realize that what they're missing is a retrieval structure for the type of text they're studying?

Building an effective retrieval structure

A retrieval structure, a mental model, a situation model, a schema, a script — these are all terms cognitive psychologists have for various instances of what is essentially the same concept: an organized body of knowledge that enables the user to understand a situation or set of facts.

So, we have a 'script' for events like going to the dentist, or going to a restaurant, that tells us what the situation will be like, how other people will act, and what actions we'll be expected to take. A chess master has a huge set of chess patterns stored in his mind, which allows him to quickly grasp what is happening on the board, easily remember briefly-seen boards, play multiple games.

And a mental, or situation, model, is something we build as we read.

Have you ever seen a movie of a book you loved? Been taken aback by a character that was completely different to how you had 'pictured' them — even though you may not ever have realized, until that point, that you had had a picture in mind at all? That's your mental model at work.

When we read stories, we build a little model in our mind of the story — our own little movie. Even though we may not be consciously aware of it, it is that model that enables you to 'follow' the story, to understand that the characters are sitting at the table over a cup of tea, that the heroine is running through the forest, hunting the monster.

We know the patterns of stories, that's why they're so easy to remember. We learned them in childhood, so we don't remember how long, and how much effort it was, to learn them (though if you're a parent, or have much younger siblings, you can probably recall the unbelievable number of times the child would ask to have the same, very simple, story read to them!).

Take that thought with you as you tackle scientific text. You have to practice. But because you are not a small child, who doesn't yet have the knowledge or understanding to do anything more than repeat and repeat and repeat, you have the ability to tackle the learning in a more directed way, reducing the amount of practice needed.

Expository text, text that is about something, needs very different mental models than a narrative, or story, text. Understanding that is the first, critical, step.

A situation model for a narrative is likely to refer to the characters in it and their emotional states, the setting, the action and sequence of events. A situation model for a scientific text, on the other hand, is likely to concentrate on the components of a system and their relationships, the events and processes that occur during the working of the system, and the uses of the system.

Your understanding of the text depends on your ability to build a single, coherent mental model from it. This mental model will build not only on the text, but also on the existing knowledge you already have.

Your success at building a good mental model therefore rests partly of the extent of your previous knowledge, and also partly of the coherence of the text itself.

The extent to which a text is coherent to you is not, however, some fixed quality that is the same for every reader. One factor that governs it is your knowledge of how that sort of text explains things.

One very broad difference between an expository text and a narrative text, in terms of how they explain things, is that stories tend to be explainable, and understood, in terms of goals. This is another reason why stories are so much more comprehensible and memorable — our own thoughts, about our lives and other people, also revolve around goals. The hero goes on a quest to win the prize / the kingdom / the princess. You are trying not to eat that pie because you want to lose weight.

But expository texts are not organized around goals, although many students try to understand them that way, and many teachers try to re-interpret them that way. Expository texts are based around logical or causal connections. The greater difficulty that students often have in following these connections is greatly exacerbated by a common problem in scientific texts: coherence gaps.

Coherence gaps

A text never explains — never *can* explain — every single word and detail. When you read a story, there are a huge number of inferences we make all the time, filling in the details, as it were. Imagine how impossible it would be to tell a story where you had to explain every object, every attribute of every object, every relationship, every emotion …

The extent to which a story is difficult reflects the number of inferences you cannot make easily. If you don't understand what is happening or why it's happening, then there's a 'coherence gap' — the text is not explaining what you need to know, and you can't make the requisite inferences to close that gap.

There's nothing intrinsically wrong with coherence gaps — as I've said, you can't explain everything, so much must be left to the reader to fill in with their existing knowledge and understanding. Moreover, the right amount of coherence gaps adds intensity and engagement to a story, and a desirable amount of difficulty to an expository text (a certain level of difficulty enhances learning, and makes information more memorable).

But what is the 'right' amount? Therein lies the problem. Because the right amount depends on the reader, on their skill and knowledge.

Research has found that students tend to be quite bad at noticing coherence gaps. That's why concept maps are so useful in building understanding — it is not until you try to explicitly describe the connections between concepts that you realize that you don't know. **Noticing coherence gaps, and taking action to close them, is critical in coming to grips with difficult text**.

What sort of action do you need to take? It depends on the nature of the coherence gap.

While narratives involve a lot of predictive inferences (we know the way the story will go), expository texts typically involve a lot of backward inferences. Here's a very simple example to show what that means:

The man hit the dog, so the dog bit the man.

Fair enough, that seems a reasonable cause-and-effect sequence. But what about:

The dog bit the man because the man hit the dog.

And sure, this is still very easy to grasp, because it's such a simple sentence. But did you notice that it was just ever so slightly more difficult to process? The order of events is inverted — we are told the consequence before the action. This means, instead of merrily playing your mental movie (man hits dog, dog bites man), your movie plays (dog bites man, what was that?), replay: (man hits dog, dog bites man). This is a backward inference, because you have the effect before the cause. It's often expressed using the word *because*, but it's not always that easy to spot.

Backward inferencing slows down your reading and understanding of the text. That doesn't mean it's bad, by any means, but it does mean that you need to make allowances for it, and expect to have to look back at the text repeatedly.

The above example was simple not only because the concepts were simple, but because it all took place in one sentence. But for the most part, the backward inferencing required is more separated than that. That's why it puts so much pressure on working memory — the further back you need to refer to, in order to understand what's being said, the more likely that it's gone from working memory.

That's why backward inferencing puts more pressure on those with low working memory capacity. But remember that this isn't, in this context, simply a matter of some fixed IQ-like attribute. Your working memory capacity reflects your expertise. The more knowledge you have on the topic, the more that accessible long-term memory will support your working memory.

In the absence of expertise, your best strategy is to lean heavily on note-taking. Taking notes is one way of expanding our working memory — but when used in this fashion, it's best done as an outline. This is not when you want all the details! Think of these notes as your adjunct working memory. In the same way that too many details or distractions clog up your working memory, pushing out what matters, so this external working memory will become clogged if there's too much information for you to see it at a glance.

But not all coherence gaps are of this type. Many are of the you're-assumed-to-know-this-so-I-don't-need-to-explain-it variety. Here, your first step (after you recognize the nature of the problem) is to decide whether or not this information gap is important. Just because there's something you don't understand doesn't mean you need to understand it! (This will come as a surprise to some students.)

Here's a very short text to help demonstrate what I mean (example adapted from McNamara et al. 1996).

> Mammals have very specialized teeth. There are four types of teeth in mammals: incisors, canines, premolars, and molars. The number and shape of each of these types of teeth are related to the kind of food the mammal eats. Carnivores, such as wolves and lions, have long, pointed canine teeth that are used for tearing, and chisel-shaped incisors that are used for cutting. Herbivores, such as horses and cows, have large, flat premolars and molars. These teeth are used for grinding plant materials.

Here's an annotated version, with various potential coherence gaps attended to [in square brackets].

> Mammals [are successful because they have evolved different kinds of] very specialized teeth [which enables them to eat many different kinds of food]. [This also helps them live in different kinds of environments. Their ability to be more flexible in terms of habitat and types of food means they are less likely to starve if they lose a food source.] There are four types of teeth in mammals: incisors [in humans, these are the four teeth in the center of your top teeth and the four in the center among the bottom teeth), canines [the four pointed ones on each side of the sets of incisors], premolars [the eight flat teeth, two on each side after the canines], and molars. The number and shape of each of these types of teeth are related to the kind of food the mammal eats. [Humans can be omnivorous because they have all these different kinds of teeth.] Carnivores [meat-eaters], such as wolves and lions, have long, pointed canine teeth that are used for tearing, and chisel-shaped incisors that are used for cutting. Herbivores [plant-eaters], such as horses and cows, have large, flat premolars and molars. These teeth are used for grinding plant materials.

Spotting coherence gaps — those that are real rather than potential (that is, they are impeding your understanding of the text) — is a skill that will improve with practice. You will get that practice quite naturally if you simply remember to be alert. When a text is difficult, ask yourself why. Go through it slowly, trying to spot what the problem is. Are there concepts you don't understand properly, words that you don't know or may be misreading? Is the text written in such a way that you have to keep looking back to remind yourself what was said? Is the text badly organized?

This is the third major type of coherence gap. The author, or lecturer, has failed to organize the material in ways that make the information easy to understand. If it's essentially well-organized (that is, the order of information is appropriate), you may be able to correct for its lack of clarity by supplying headings, highlighting important information, etc. If the material is very disorganized, you'll have to rely more heavily on note-taking strategies that will help you re-organize the material.

Again, the first step is to recognize when the problem is of this nature.

Every science is different

Science is a very broad category. Each science will have areas that are fundamental, that you need to ensure you understand if you want to understand the science. Your teacher or textbook will point these out — your job is to take that seriously. You need to focus your efforts on these key areas.

If you're having difficulty understanding those critical topics, you will doom yourself to study-by-rote. And the very important thing to note is that, while most students see rote learning as the easy path, learning by making connections and building understanding, while more difficult initially, is easier in the long term. Indeed, because of the growing load on memory, rote learning is limited in how far it can take you. There is no limit on your ability to learn, if you follow the path of understanding.

Main points

The most important thing to remember is that, whatever science subject you're approaching, it will have several components to it that require different skills — you cannot be 'bad at science'; you may be weak in certain areas.

Science, like mathematics and language, has a skill component and a knowledge component.

Whatever the skill, it will benefit from deliberate practice. Recognize what is a skill; isolate the difficult aspects of it; focus your attention on those difficult bits, tackling them in small steps.

Use mnemonics where necessary, to memorize basic facts, but keep them to a minimum, seeking meaningful connections wherever you can.

Learn formulae through practice, and understanding of the general principles they express.

Learn technical words through use of keyword mnemonics, cognate connections, other meaningful connections, the linking differences strategy, and retrieval practice.

Recognize that science textbooks are written and organized in a way that is probably different from what you are accustomed to, but learning to read and study this text is a skill that will improve with directed practice.

Strategies for gaining understanding of complex topics — like asking questions, making comparisons, linking differences, and drawing concept maps — are all skills, and thus amenable to practice. Use the principles of deliberate practice to build these skills.

Science is about the physical world, which we have been experiencing and learning about since we were born. We have lots of beliefs about the way the physical world works, some of which will be consistent with modern science, and some of which will not. To understand and remember scientific knowledge, it helps a lot if you explicitly make those connections — both to consistent beliefs and inconsistent ones. Consistent beliefs will reinforce your learning. Inconsistent beliefs must be confronted and worked through, if you are to acquire new learning.

Music

Music is different from these other subject areas in that it is primarily a skill, with a much smaller cognitive component. It's for that reason I have included it as an example, since it gives a different perspective on the working together of knowledge and skill.

Part of the cognitive component in learning to play a musical instrument is theoretical knowledge (e.g., what's the C major scale) and, less obvious but more vital, aural schema (mental patterns of how different genres of music 'should' sound). Another part is concerned with specific pieces of music. While playing a specific piece is very much a skill, in that it's a specific motor sequence, it's not *only* a sequence of physical actions. There's also processing that encodes visuospatial information (such as the sight of particular piano keys going down in a particular order), encoding of the temporal rhythm (this isn't only a musical phenomenon

— rhythm is an important part of many motor skills), and of course sound information.

There have been several studies exploring how practice differs between experienced musicians and beginners. For example, almost all experienced musicians get an overview of a new piece first, either by playing it through or examining the score. All of them stress the importance of thinking analytically about the music and playing it very slowly and carefully in the initial stages of learning it. After this, however, there seems to be considerable variation, in, for example, the level of organization and planning, and the extent to which they mark the score.

Here's a list of strategies associated with growing expertise among students (beginner to Grade 8) (Hallam et al. 2012). Notice which ones have to do with pinpointing difficult sections or aspects and dealing with them deliberately:

- Practicing small sections

- Getting recordings of a piece that is being learned

- Practicing things slowly

- Knowing when a mistake has been made

- When making a mistake, practicing a section slowly

- When something is difficult, playing it over and over again

- Marking the score

- Practicing with a metronome

- Recording practice and listening to tapes

- Identifying difficult sections

- Thinking about how to interpret the music

- Doing warm-up exercises

- Starting practice with studies

- Starting practice with scales.

By contrast, the following strategies were *negatively* associated with growing expertise (that is, they became steadily less common as the students became more expert):

- Practicing pieces from beginning to end without stopping

- Going back to the beginning after a mistake

- Immediately correcting errors (that is, 'fixing' a mistake by stopping and immediately trying to play the note correctly, as opposed to stopping at the end of the section, then playing the section again more slowly and with more attention).

It's worth noting that these strategies might well be appropriate right at the beginning, when the student is first learning to play the instrument, but they become less useful as pieces become longer and more complex. It's also likely that at higher levels of expertise (say, among professional musicians), some of the 'good' strategies may be less appropriate.

Similarly, although you can short-cut your path to expertise by using metacognitive strategies, you can't avoid the need to first build up a certain level of basic skill and music knowledge. One reason for that is that playing music, whatever the instrument, requires several concurrent processes. For example, for a violin, there are the finger movements, the movement of the bow, reading the notes, attention to pitch, to rhythm, to intonation, to dynamics. You can't master all of these all at once, and trying to do so will only hurt your learning.

As regards mental practice, here's an example of a training program aimed specifically at pianists, that will give you some idea:

- choose a small section of a piece you're learning (say, 4 bars)

- as you read the score, visualize as precisely as possible the keys on the keyboard corresponding to the written notes

- now visualize the position of your hand, the width of movement of your arm

- bring in the auditory 'images' — that is, hear the notes in your head as you mentally play them

- break down the section into its main components

- feel each single interval, in terms of both movement and sound, starting at a slow tempo

- feel inside your body how the fingers should press the keys, initially using a legato touch

- progressively increase the speed for each component

- occasionally try physically playing the passage, swapping back and forth between mental and physical practice

- near the end of your practice, abandon the legato touch and mentally play fortissimo

- play the whole sequence as a complete movement.

(adapted from Bernardi et al. 2013, who adapted it from Klöppel's 2006 mental training manual)

Review Questions

1. As an adult language learner, I can never hope to sound like a native speaker

   a. true

   b. it depends on how similar the language is to my native language

   c. it depends on how many hours I put into the language

   d. it depends on how good my ear is

   e. it depends on how much deliberate practice I put into listening to and trying to reproduce those sounds that are unfamiliar to me

2. Learning a language is a skill that you can be good or bad at. Y / N

3. Cognates are words that
   a. sound similar
   b. look similar
   c. are meaningfully connected
   d. share a common ancestor
   e. have a similar meaning

4. Grammar rules
   a. should be memorized using flashcards
   b. can be learned using sentence patterns and the principles of deliberate practice
   c. are arbitrary, so should be memorized using mnemonics
   d. don't need to be memorized at all

5. Learning a language
   a. is about learning a lot of words
   b. is mainly about learning a lot of words, but also about learning abstract rules on how to arrange the words into sentences
   c. is a skill
   d. involves different skills plus content knowledge

6. If you get a math problem wrong, your best response is to
   a. do lots more of the same sort of the problem, until you get one right
   b. go over it carefully, to see where you went wrong
   c. compare it to a correct example, and explain out loud what you did wrong
   d. go over the example problem again, trying to memorize the steps
   e. look for the general principle(s) involved, explain how it is expressed in the correct example, and why your incorrect solution wasn't in keeping with that principle

7. The best strategies for learning how to do a type of math problem are to

    a. memorize the formulae and/or steps

    b. practice doing that exact type of problem

    c. work through a correct worked example and think about the general principles involved

    d. work through an incorrect worked example and explain to yourself why it's wrong

    e. practice on many varied problems of that type, and mix it up with problems of other types

8. There is only one correct way to do a math problem. Y / N

9. There may be more than one way you can solve a math problem, but there is a best way. To become a good math student, you should find that best way. Y / N

10. Math concepts are best expressed

    a. in diagrams

    b. in numbers

    c. in words

    d. in numbers and words

    e. in numbers and words and diagrams

11. Reading scientific text is hard because it

    a. contradicts your beliefs about how the world works

    b. is too hard to understand

    c. uses too many words you don't know

    d. is structured and expressed in ways that you don't have much practice in

    e. uses words that mean something different to their usual meaning

12. The best way to learn technical words is to

  a. use cognates

  b. create keyword mnemonics

  c. use the linking differences strategy

  d. use flashcards and retrieval practice

  e. look for meaningful connections

  f. look for or create connections to minimize the amount of retrieval practice needed; apply the linking differences where appropriate; use flashcards and retrieval practice

13. Learning science

  a. is a skill, so if you're good at physics, you'll be good at biology

  b. is easy if you're smart

  c. is easy if you're good at memorizing stuff

  d. requires different skills, some of which you may be more practiced than others

  e. is just like learning any other subject, once you understand the basic concepts

14. Pick the true statements:

  a. There are certain great strategies that are always effective, for all subjects.

  b. Every subject has effective strategies that work best for them, and that works for all students.

  c. Once a student works out what strategies work best for them, they should always use them, for all subjects.

  d. Whether a strategy works well for a student depends not only on that student's way of thinking, but also on their degree of expertise in that subject, so the best strategy may change over time.

Obstacles to effective practice

A brief word about the main obstacles to using effective practice strategies: incorrect beliefs, test anxiety, and failure to set in place the right habits.

Beliefs that stand in the way of effective learning

There's so much research now that makes it clear that spacing and interleaving are far superior to massed / blocked practice, and that testing is far superior to re-reading. Nevertheless, surveys of college students have found that re-reading is the study strategy employed almost all of the time, and teachers continue to teach in blocks, without returning to earlier material until the final exam. Why is that?

A great deal of the problem has to do with the ease of the ineffective strategies. Re-reading is much much easier than testing yourself, and it's easy to fool yourself that you know the material. If you study in a block, you will perform much better on a test at the end of that block than you would if you mixed it up — and the immediate memory is all you know at the time. Spaced, interleaved learning requires (at least initially) faith. But if you try it, you will see the benefits over time.

be even less inclined to practice enough. There are several reasons for that. One is that you may remember learning being so much easier, once upon a time. When the same amount of study doesn't produce the same performance, you may be inclined to believe that age has destroyed your ability to learn. While it's true that age can make learning more difficult, it certainly hasn't ruined your learning ability! You may, however, have to get more serious about using effective study strategies than you remember doing when you were young.

The main problem older adults have is interference. Over time we carve ruts in our mind, along the paths we travel a lot, while other paths have time to become neglected and overgrown. We also accumulate more and more information. No surprise that when we learn something new, it has a greater chance of contradicting older information, or getting entangled with similar information (which can be a plus, but isn't always).

Effective practice, and more frequent practice, is thus more important for older adults. In particular, they need to adopt learning strategies designed to counter the problem of interference. Additionally, recent research suggests that older brains may consolidate new memories more slowly. That means you need to support consolidation as much as possible, which means:

- giving yourself time during the day for new information to 'settle' (stabilize)

- reviewing in the evening before bed

- having 'immersion periods', when you immerse yourself in the topic or language or skill

- widely spacing your learning of different skills or topics.

This advice isn't limited to older students! Any student who has trouble consolidating new information — meaning that, although you seem to master the information when first studying it, your memory of it on the following day is poor — will benefit from following these strategies.

Test anxiety

Many students who do poorly in exams suffer from test anxiety. Unfortunately, being anxious makes it more likely that you will indeed perform badly, because your anxious thoughts are using much-needed working memory resources.

Testing yourself is the best way of reducing your anxiety about testing, giving you reassurance that you know the material, and also providing positive test experiences to counteract the negative experiences you've probably had. Unfortunately, those who suffer from test anxiety may be even more reluctant than other students to use testing as a learning strategy. All I can say is that, if you're in this category, you should force yourself to do it anyway! I assure you that you'll soon reap the rewards of doing so.

Retrieval practice helps protect you from the negative effects of stress and anxiety not only because it may help reduce any negative feelings you have developed in regard to any testing questions, but also because it improves accessibility of the information.

One study that looked at this found that students who learned a series of words and images using retrieval practice remembered the material just as well after an experience of acute stress [15.1]. Those students who used the conventional strategy of re-reading, on the other hand, remembered less well, and were more affected by stress.

If you do suffer from test anxiety, I recommend that you ease up on the demands of my standard recommendations. Make sure you don't stretch your spacing too far — it's more important that you find remembering easy. To make up for shortening the review intervals, increase the number of reviews. As time goes on, and your faith in your own abilities increases, you'll be able to stretch your spacing out further.

Remember: if you don't do well when being tested, it's because the interval before the test was too long, and you haven't reviewed enough for the demands of the material. It's *not* because you are 'stupid'! Respond to failure by re-assessing your strategies. Here's a checklist you may find helpful:

- Do you understand the material sufficiently well? If you haven't done this, try drawing a concept map to test your understanding. If the concepts aren't well-connected, or you can't spell out how they're connected, then you need to study the material further (see my book on *Effective notetaking* for more on this).

- Are there particular concepts that you're having trouble remembering? If they're simple concepts, expressed in a word or phrase, try using a keyword mnemonic to help you remember. If they're more complex concepts, try putting the information in a graphical format, such as a picture or diagram or map (I cover this in *Effective notetaking* as well).

- If the material is a skill or has a skill component, break the skill down into its smallest components, and master each component bit by bit.

Habits can break or make you

We might like to think of ourselves as 'higher' beings, self-willed and self-directed, but the truth of the matter is that we are more programmed than we like to think. Our daily lives tend to be ruled by habit, and this is true even if you think you live a free and non-routine life. Habits can be invisible.

There's nothing wrong with any of this! Habits are what allow us to get through our days without having to make a constant stream of decisions. Without habit, it would be as if every day was a brand new day in a brand new place, with new and possibly frightening choices to make. Habits relieve the pressure on working memory, allowing us to focus on what really matters to us.

So, yay for habits. But habits, as we all know only too well, can be good or bad. And in the context of practice, they can either support practice, or they can sabotage it.

If you don't make a deliberate effort to incorporate your practice into your schedule — to turn it into a habit — then the power of habit is not working for you, but against you.

Scheduling your reviews

So don't assume that planning to review means that it will happen! You need to take more concrete action than simply thinking to yourself: "I'll review that on Thursday". When you study, you need to formally take note of the dates on which you'll review the material. If you use a calendar app on your phone or tablet or computer, then put these reviews into your schedule. If you don't, get a calendar with large squares and write down your review dates. Make sure you note down what material you're reviewing, and which review it is (given that your strategy may change depending on whether it's the first or third or fifth review). If you're planning on long-delayed reviews (as recommended if you want long-lasting learning), then it's particularly important that you write these into your future schedule.

We're all familiar with good intentions. They're easy to keep in the beginning, and even easier to let slide. Writing your intended reviews into your calendar is vital, but may not, in the long-term, be sufficient on its own. You'll find it much more likely that you do those reviews if you build review sessions into your daily routine. If you're a full-time student, or are studying a language, have a particular time of day in which you do your reviews (with some flexibility, to allow for disruptions to your routine). By that, I mean you review something every day (or nearly so). If you're only doing a single course, daily review times would be over-kill, but it's even more vital that you establish a regular schedule. If you set your 'review days' for, say, Monday and Thursday, then you'll get into the habit of thinking of them on those days.

Bottom line

There are a lot of details and specific recommendations in this book, that I hope will help you develop an individualized program that maximizes your learning. But if nothing else, I hope you come away with some 'big picture' ideas firmly in your brain and gut — the knowledge that:

- learning is a matter of using appropriate strategies, not a matter of your personal 'ability'

- more than anything else, successful learning reflects effective practice

- there is no one 'right' way to practice that fits all situations and all people

- practice is the key to increasing your effective 'intelligence' (working memory capacity; ability to understand and reason and remember).

Study productively!

Glossary

axon: a long projection extending from the cell body, that carries the output of the neuron away from it.

chunk: a tight cluster of information able to be treated as a single unit when worked with.

code principle: every memory is a selected and edited code, not a recording of real-world events.

cognitive load: the burden on your working memory system made by information-processing tasks.

consolidation: the process of further editing and stabilizing new memories for long-term storage.

context: the information contained in the situation in which you are encoding or retrieving the target information. It includes the physical environment and your own physical, mental and emotional state, as well as information presented at the same time as the target.

context effect: the degree to which the context in which you are trying to retrieve information matches the context in which you originally encoded it affects how easy it is to retrieve.

declarative memory: factual knowledge; information you can make a declaration or statement about. This contrasts with procedural knowledge, knowledge about how to do something.

dendrite: a branched projection of a nerve cell that conducts electrical stimulation *to* the cell body. The name is derived from the Greek word for tree (dendron).

desirable difficulties: a degree of difficulty, such as reading in a hard-to-read font, that encourages learners to put more time and effort into processing the information, resulting in better learning.

distinctiveness principle: memory codes are easier to find when they can be easily distinguished from other related codes.

domino principle: activating one memory code causes other, linked, codes to be activated also.

encoding: the process of transforming information into a memory code, and placing it in your memory.

frequency effect: the more often a code has been retrieved, the easier it becomes to find.

fluid intelligence: cognitive functions associated with general reasoning and problem-solving; often described as executive function, or working memory capacity. This contrasts with crystallized intelligence, which refers to cognitive functions associated with previously acquired knowledge in long-term store.

hindbrain: the brain develops, in utero, in three separate portions, reflecting evolutionary history: the hindbrain, the midbrain, and the forebrain. The hindbrain (the oldest part of the brain) develops into the cerebellum, the pons, and the medulla.

hypercorrection effect: when students are more confident of a wrong answer, they are more likely to remember the right answer if corrected.

interleaving: interspersing practice of one type with practice of other types.

learnable point: important information expressed concisely in a statement that can be easily turned into a question-&-answer format.

matching effect: a memory code is easier to find the more closely the code and retrieval cue match.

metacognition: your understanding of cognitive processing in general, and of your own cognitive processing.

monitoring: strategies to inform you how well you have learned the information in a memory situation so that you can plan your encoding strategies appropriately.

myelin: the (white-ish) sheathing that insulates axons and facilitates speedy communication among neurons.

network: the structure of memory — memory codes that are connected to each other.

neurotransmitter: a messenger chemical in the brain; it is through neurotransmitters that neurons communicate with each other. Examples are GABA, glutamate, acetylcholine, dopamine, serotonin, norepinephrine.

outcome goals: your objective in carrying out a learning task, in terms of the desired outcome. This contrasts with process goals.

priming effect: a memory code is readier to activate, and so easier to access, when memory codes linked to it have been recently activated.

process goals: specific intermediate objectives that need to be achieved on the way to producing the desired outcome of a learning task.

recall: the retrieval of information from long-term memory.

recency effect: a memory code is more readily activated when it has recently been activated.

recognition: the awareness that you have seen or learned this information before. Multi-choice tests assess recognition rather than recall.

reconsolidation: stable memory codes become labile again (capable of being changed) after reactivation, suggesting that consolidation, rather than being a one-time event, occurs repeatedly every time the representation is activated (that is, retrieved from long-term memory).

retrieval cue: something that prompts you to recall a specific memory.

retrieval context: the situation in which you attempt to remember the information. In the study situation, examples include an exam, multi-choice test, classroom discussion, writing an essay, or a brainstorming session.

retrieval practice: the strategy of repeatedly trying to retrieve the information to be learned.

retrieval-induced facilitation: when retrieval practice improves memory for related, untested information.

retrieval-induced forgetting: when retrieval of information blocks the retrieval of other information.

retrieving: finding a memory code; 'remembering'.

schema: a generalized outline or composite framework that has been constructed from a number of specific examples.

spacing: reviewing learning or practicing a skill at spaced intervals, rather than in one concentrated block.

stabilization: the first stage of memory processing, lasting about six hours, during which new information is particularly vulnerable to being lost.

synapse: the place where one neuron makes contact with another; this contact is not physical, but a specialized receptor sensitive to particular neurotransmitters.

working memory: includes the part of memory of which you are conscious; the "active state" of memory. Information is held in working memory during both encoding and retrieval. Working memory governs your ability to understand, to learn new words, to plan and organize yourself, and much more..

working memory capacity: the amount of information you can hold and work with at one time. Now thought to be 3-5 chunks.

Chapter notes

Chapter 3: Retrieval practice

3.1 Comparison of retrieval practice with other strategies: Re-reading

In a study in which college students were tested on their recall of two short prose passages, each about 250-275 words long, the students studied the texts in one half-hour session. During each of four 7-minute periods, they either read a text, re-read one of the texts, or took a recall test on the text they didn't re-read — meaning that one passage was read twice, while the other was read once and tested once.

When tested a mere five minutes after the study session, the passage read twice was recalled slightly better (the recency effect in action). However, when tested a week later, the passage that had been read once and tested once (not counting the 5-minute-delay test, on which no feedback was given) was remembered decidedly better than the one that had been read twice. Those re-reading scored 81% on an immediate test, but only 42% a week later. Those who read it only once, followed by a test, scored only 75% immediately, but 56% a week later (the difference, I note, between a passing grade and a fail!).

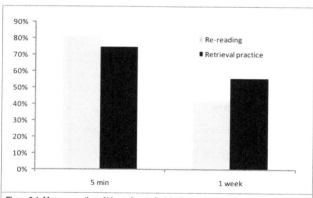

Figure 3.1: Mean proportion of idea units recalled 5 minutes after study and one week after study, for students who re-read compared to those who used retrieval practice. From Roediger & Karpicke, 2006.

In other words, while re-reading gave the immediate illusion of having been learned better, it was forgotten at a much greater rate over time (and bear in mind that this is only after a week; the gap is expected to get wider over time).

In a further experiment, using only one of the two prose passages, some students read and re-read the passage during four 5-minute study periods, while another group studied their passage for three of the periods then were tested during the fourth, and the final group studied their passage during the first period before being given three recall tests.

Again, those students who only re-read the passage had an advantage when tested five minutes after the session. But, as before, the story was different a week later — and the best performers were those who had read the passage only *once*, followed by three tests. Those who only re-read the text scored 83% immediately, but only 40% after a week, while those who read the text only once, followed by three tests, scored 71% immediately but 61% a week later.

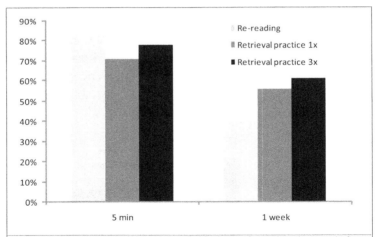

Figure 3.2: Mean proportion of idea units recalled 5 minutes after study and one week after study, for students who re-read compared to those who used retrieval practice once and those who used retrieval practice three times. From Roediger & Karpicke, 2006.

The benefit of retrieval practice is even more dramatic if you use a proportional measure in order to show how much *forgetting* took place. This shows 52% forgetting for the re-reading group compared to only 14% forgetting for the group who only read it once but were tested three times.

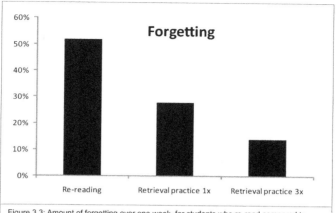

Figure 3.3: Amount of forgetting over one week, for students who re-read compared to those who used retrieval practice once and those who used retrieval practice three times. From Roediger & Karpicke, 2006.

Note that the re-reading group read the passage about 14 times in total, while the repeated testing (retrieval practice) group read the passage only an average of 3.4 times in its one-and-only study session. So, those re-reading experienced the material four times more than the testing group, but still failed to achieve much long-term remembering.

Despite this, those in the re-reading group were much more likely to believe they'd remember the information than students in the repeated-testing group. After all, the text is now very familiar, and when you have made no effort to test your ability to retrieve it, you have no idea how hard that might be.

Roediger, H. L., & Karpicke, J. D. (2006). Test-enhanced learning: taking memory tests improves long-term retention. *Psychological science, 17(3)*, 249–55.

Comparison of retrieval practice with other strategies: Keyword mnemonic

3.2

In the classic study referred to in the text, the keyword group recalled 72% of the words when they were tested on the day following the three study days (40 words were studied each day), compared to 46% by the control group. When they were (without warning) tested again six weeks later, the keyword group remembered 43% compared to the control group's 28%.

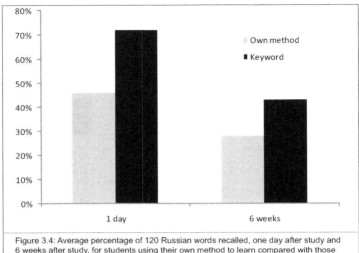

Figure 3.4: Average percentage of 120 Russian words recalled, one day after study and 6 weeks after study, for students using their own method to learn compared with those using the keyword mnemonic. From Atkinson 1975.

Atkinson, R. C. (1975). Mnemotechnics in second-language learning. *American Psychologist, 30(8)*, 821–828.

3.3

One study comparing the learning of 20 German words using either the keyword mnemonic, retrieval practice, or rote repetition, found equal levels of recall a day later for those using the keyword method and those using retrieval practice, with both significantly better than the group average for those using rote repetition (an average of 15 words vs 11).

A follow-up compared the learning of 24 German words in which sets of six words were learned in one of four different ways:

- **Elaboration**: either describing a different English meaning for the word (e.g., "The German for SHARP is SCHARF, scharf also means hot (as in spicy).") or by breaking down a compound word into its components (e.g., "The German for LIGHTHOUSE is LEUCHTTURM, Leuchtturm consists of the two words for shine and tower.").

- **Retrieval practice**: filler pages between each retrieval attempt gave an expanding schedule of 1-3-5-7 (I will discuss practice schedules in a later chapter; what this means here is that there was one intervening filler item before the first retrieval attempt, three items before the second attempt, and so on).

- **Keyword mnemonic**: the English and German words were presented with a description of a suggested image (e.g., "The German for SHARP is SCHARF. Imagine cutting a German flag with SHARP scissors.").

- **Retrieval practice + keyword mnemonic**

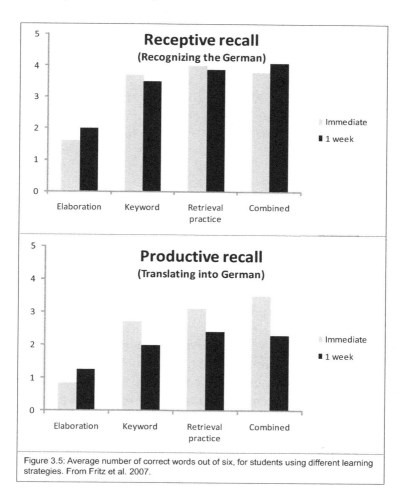

Figure 3.5: Average number of correct words out of six, for students using different learning strategies. From Fritz et al. 2007.

As you can see from the graphs, the elaboration strategy produced significantly worse learning than the others, and this was especially true with the more difficult task of remembering the German on seeing the English.

On the easier task of recognizing the meaning of a German word, there was little difference between the other strategies on the immediate test, but when tested a week later, the combined strategy was significantly better than the others, and retrieval practice produced slightly, but not quite significantly, better recall than the keyword method. (The main problem with this study is that, for practical reasons, the number of words learned by each strategy is so small that it's hard to get a lot of difference between the recall scores.)

For the harder task (translating into German), retrieval practice achieved significantly better remembering than the keyword mnemonic.

Fritz, C. O., Morris, P. E., Acton, M., Voelkel, A. R., & Etkind, R. (2007). Comparing and Combining Retrieval Practice and the Keyword Mnemonic for Foreign Vocabulary Learning. *Applied Cognitive Psychology*, *21*, 499–526.

3.4

In this study, students learned 48 Swahili words by the keyword method, with some students simply 're-studying' the words on practice trials (i.e., keyword method alone), while others practiced retrieving them (keyword + retrieval practice). Those who were given retrieval practice performed almost *three times* better on the final test compared to those given restudy only: 40% correct vs 14%.

A triumph for the use of retrieval practice! But the real interest of this study lies in a further comparison they made. On the final test one week later, students were either given the cue only (the Swahili word), or the cue plus keyword, or the cue plus a prompt to remember their keyword.

The group that used testing as part of their study weren't significantly affected by the cue given in the final test — it didn't matter that much whether it was only the word itself, the word plus keyword, or the word with a reminder to help them recall their keyword. But the group that only restudied the material were significantly helped by being given the keyword as well as the cue. You can see in the graph below how badly the study-only group did when given only the cue, and how much it improved their performance when reminded of the keyword as well.

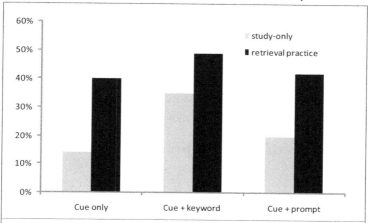

Figure 3.6: Average percentage of items correctly recalled on final test, when given either the cue only, the cue plus the keyword, or the cue plus a prompt to remember the keyword, for students who restudied only compared with those who used retrieval practice. From Pyc & Rawson. 2010.

Moreover, when the researchers looked deeper into the results for the group receiving the prompt, they found that remembering the keyword made a huge difference to recall of the English word:

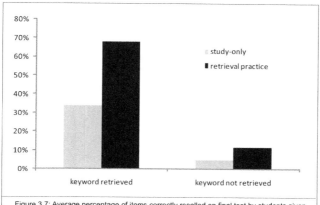

Figure 3.7: Average percentage of items correctly recalled on final test by students given the cue plus a prompt to remember the keyword, as a function of whether or not the keywords were remembered, for students who restudied only compared with those who used retrieval practice. From Pyc & Rawson. 2010.

You can see how recall of the English word depends very heavily on remembering the keyword. But the main point of this graph is the difference between the retrieval practice group and the study-only group when the keyword was remembered: see how the keyword triggered recall of the English word nearly 70% of the time for the retrieval practice group, but only around a third of the time for the study-only group. Why were the keywords so much more effective for the retrieval practice group? It seems likely that they had better keywords — keywords that did a better job of evoking the English words.

Pyc, M.A. & Rawson, K.A. (2010). Why testing improves memory: mediator effectiveness hypothesis. *Science, 330(6002)*, 335.

3.5 Comparison of retrieval practice with other strategies: Concept maps

In one study comparing concept maps and retrieval practice, students studied a short text about sea otters using one of four strategies:

- **study-only:** this group studied the text for five minutes

- **repeated study**: this group studied the text during four 5-minute periods, each period separated by a one-minute break

- **concept mapping**: this group studied the text for five minutes, then were given 25 minutes to construct a concept map from the text, which they had in front of them

- **retrieval practice:** this group were given five minutes to study the text, then given 10 minutes to write down as much as they could recall; they were then given another five minutes to re-study the text, before carrying out a second recall test.

When tested a week later, performance was (as expected) worst in the study-once group, and best in the retrieval practice group — about 50% better than that of the concept mapping group (67% vs 45%).

It's interesting that there was no significant difference between the repeated-study and the concept mapping groups. This suggests that the main benefit of concept mapping (when used in this way, in the presence

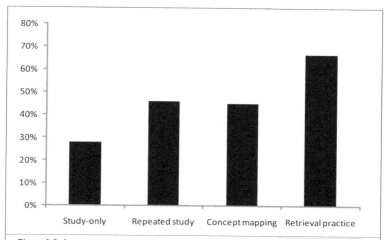

Figure 3.8: Average percentage of correctly answered short-answer questions after studying a science text either over one study period, or on four consecutive periods, or by creating a concept map or using retrieval practice after the initial study period. From Karpicke & Blunt. 2011.

of the text, which is a very important point that I'll discuss later) is simply to increase the time spent with the material. Nothing wrong with that. Drawing a concept map is probably a more interesting way of spending time with the text than simply re-reading it, and it's always worth finding more interesting ways to do things (it increases the likelihood of you doing them!).

As always, when asked, students' beliefs were at odds with the results. Students in the repeated study condition gave the highest predictions for their learning, and those in the retrieval practice condition gave the lowest.

In another experiment, with students employing a concept map strategy on one text and retrieval practice on a different text, retrieval practice once again greatly out-performed concept mapping on the final short-answer test (an average score of 73% compared to an average of 54%) — and, surprisingly, also out-performed it on an alternative final test that involved drawing a concept map (44% vs 28%) (see over for graph).

The study has one other important finding, concerning how the strategies suited individual students. While the great majority of students (101 of the 120; 84%) performed better after retrieval practice, a few (16%) benefited more from concept mapping.

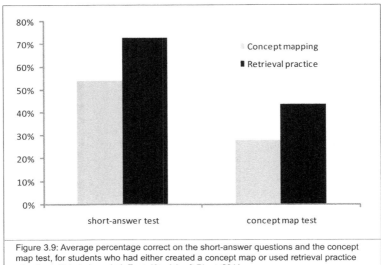

Figure 3.9: Average percentage correct on the short-answer questions and the concept map test, for students who had either created a concept map or used retrieval practice after the initial study period. From Karpicke & Blunt. 2011.

Karpicke, J. D., & Blunt, J. R. (2011). Retrieval practice produces more learning than elaborative studying with concept mapping. *Science*, *331(6018)*, 772–5.

3.6 Benefits for related information

That retrieval practice can improve your memory for untested material (but not just any untested information!) has been shown in a series of three experiments using much longer texts than typically used in lab experiments. The first experiment used a text of 2,700 words, and students either read the article then were tested on it, or read the article and then read the answers to the test questions. Those who were tested were given instructions not to guess, and were given no feedback on the accuracy of their answers. After they'd been tested, they were given the test again, with the questions in a different order. All the students were tested a day later.

Here's the crucial point — each question in the practice test was matched with a related question. For example, the question "Where do toucans sleep at night?" was related to "What other bird species is the toucan related to?" because toucans sleep in the holes created by woodpeckers. While most related pairs appeared in the same paragraph of the article, knowing the answer to one question wouldn't of itself tell you the answer to the other.

So what happened? Those given extra study recalled more of the practice-test questions (79% vs 70%) than those who were tested (remember that those in the testing condition weren't given any feedback on their answers, while those given extra study read the answers to the practice-test questions, so those given extra study had this advantage over the study-test group). However, and this is the interesting bit, the study-test group did better on the related questions (59% vs 49%) — that is, those that hadn't been part of the practice test. Similar findings occurred in the follow-up experiments.

Now I must emphasize that the information actually practiced is, of course, remembered far better than any other. But what this study tells us is that retrieval practice can have benefits that extend beyond the exact information practiced, to information that is related or appears in close proximity to the information practiced.

Chan, J. C. K., McDermott, K. B., & Roediger, H. L. (2006). Retrieval-induced facilitation: initially nontested material can benefit from prior testing of related material. *Journal of experimental psychology. General, 135(4)*, 553–71.

3.7 Forced guessing

This study had students read 80 obscure facts before being tested on them. If they offered an answer, they were asked to rate their confidence in it. If they didn't offer an answer, they were randomly asked half the time to guess. They were told the correct answer in all cases, and were tested again a day later.

In almost all cases, questions answered correctly on the first test were again answered correctly (91%). Only 36% of those initially answered incorrectly were answered correctly on the final test. Only 19% of those questions in which the students were forced to guess, were answered correctly on the final test. This compares to 23% of those questions students were allowed to skip (a non-significant difference).

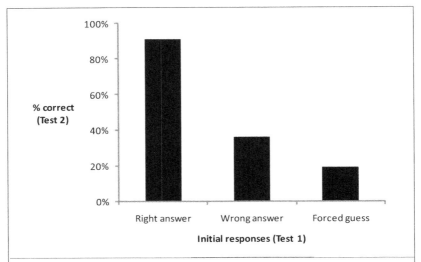

Figure 3.10: Average percentage correct on final test as a function of whether or not the student gave the right answer, the wrong answer, or was asked to guess, on the initial test. From Kang et al. 2011.

There are two particularly interesting findings:

- Those who were more confident of their *incorrect* answers were *more* likely to get the answer correct on the final test.

- Forced guessing didn't make a significant difference, either way.

The relationship with confidence has been found before. It's even got a name. It's called the **hypercorrection effect**, and it's not as counter-intuitive as it may immediately appear. It may be, for example, that greater confidence produces greater surprise when the answer turns out to be wrong, and it is this surprise that makes you more likely to remember it.

On the other hand (and demonstrating that learning is a complex process, in which at any time a number of variables are potentially at work), incorrect answers at the *lowest* confidence level were also associated with better learning, while *correct* responses at the lowest confidence level (which might also be expected to elicit surprise) were *not* better learned.

It seems likely that there is more than one thing going on here. One is surprise; the other might have to do with your familiarity with the general area of knowledge in question. Your knowledge of the topic often affects a strategy's relative effectiveness — this is one reason why we can't just make simple black-and-white rules about what strategies are best to use. In this case, those with more familiarity with the topic might be more willing to offer low-confidence guesses. If they have higher domain knowledge, they'll be better able to acquire new information in it (this is why experts can learn new information in their area of expertise so much more easily than novices — they have a larger and denser network into which new information can slot).

A similar experiment using explanations that required longer answers (e.g., "Why does the moon influence the Earth's tides more than the sun, even though the sun has the greater gravitational pull?") also found no effects of forced guessing.

Kang, S. H. K., Pashler, H., Cepeda, N. J., Rohrer, D., Carpenter, S. K., & Mozer, M. C. (2011). Does incorrect guessing impair fact learning? *Journal of Educational Psychology, 103(1)*, 48–59.

Chapter 4. How often should you practice?

4.1 Task difficulty affects optimal criterion level

In this study, students studied 50 English-Lithuanian word pairs, which were displayed on a screen one by one for 10 seconds. After studying the list, the students practiced retrieving the English words. They were given little time to ponder — they had a mere eight seconds to type in the English word as each Lithuanian word appeared — and those that were correct went to the end of the list to be asked again, while incorrect items had to be restudied (that is, the correct item was displayed on the screen for four seconds, before going to the end of the list for re-testing). Each item was pre-assigned a criterion level from one to five — that is, some words only had to be correctly recalled once or twice before disappearing, while others had to be retrieved three, four or five times.

This basic scenario was played out in two experiments. In the first, students took a recall test and a recognition test two days after the study session. In the second experiment, students were only given a recognition test (in order to eliminate any reminder effect of the recall test), and they were given it one week after the study session.

Both experiments found that higher criterion levels led to better memory.

But the effects were not precisely the same for all tests, emphasizing once again that you really do need to think about how you'll be retrieving the information 'in real life' — different scenarios require different practice, and perhaps different criterion levels.

The graph below shows the average proportion correct on the associative recognition test (in which students simply had to recognize whether the English-Lithuanian word pair was correct or not), the cued English recall test (in which students were presented with the Lithuanian word and had to type in the English word), and the cued Lithuanian recall test (students had to type in the Lithuanian word in response to the English word):

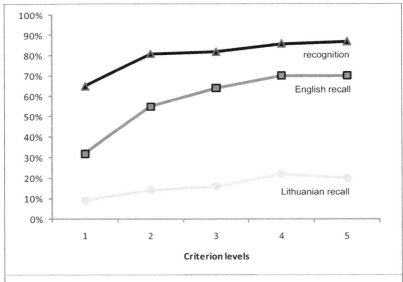

Figure 4.1: Average percentage correct on three types of test as a function of the number of times the item was correctly recalled during practice. From Vaughn & Rawson 2011.

Unsurprisingly, the best performance was on the associative recognition test. You can also see how much better performance is for the cued recall of the English words compared to cued recall of Lithuanian words. Again, this is no surprise.

But what we're interested in is which criterion level produces the best performance. See how, for cued recall of English words, having a criterion level of two (two correct retrievals) is so much better than only one, and that there's a more gradual, and even, progression for 2, 3, and 4 correct retrievals, at which point it plateaus. In other words, it appears that for this sort of situation (remembering the English meaning when presented with the foreign word), the optimum number of correct retrieval attempts on the first study session is four, but the really vital thing to do is make sure you don't stop at only one correct retrieval.

The benefit of that second retrieval attempt is also clear in the easier task of recognizing the correct English-Lithuanian pairs, and here any benefit of additional retrieval attempts is much less evident.

As with cued recall of English, the optimal number for cued recall of Lithuanian words also seems to be four, although the overall level of performance is much lower than it is for English. Given that, I can't help but wonder if the plateau at 4-5 is more apparent than real. It may be that a criterion level of 6 would produce better recall again. It also seems likely that for this much harder task, some additional help (such as the keyword mnemonic) would really help.

Vaughn, K. E., & Rawson, K. A. (2011). Diagnosing Criterion-Level Effects on Memory: What Aspects of Memory Are Enhanced by Repeated Retrieval? *Psychological Science, 22(9)*, 1127-31.

4.2 How many times should you review?

In this study, criterion levels varied from one to four correct retrievals in the initial session. Items also varied in how many subsequent sessions they were practiced. In these one to five testing/relearning sessions, the items were practiced until they were correctly recalled once. Memory was tested one and four months later.

Here are two examples of the short texts: "Sensory memory is a memory system that retains large amounts of sensory input for very brief periods of time"; "Declarative memory is memory for specific facts and events that can be stated verbally".

Students were given 4 minutes to study the whole text (only some 400 words), before proceeding to the retrieval attempts. For these, students were presented with a term and had to type in their definition. Each definition contained several idea units. The students were given feedback to enable them to mark their answers.

The researchers used not only accuracy on the test as a measure of learning, but also the rate of *re*-learning — how many presentations it took for the student to re-learn an item on later review sessions. I applaud this. As the researchers remark, no one — student or teacher — expects a student to remember everything they've ever learned, particularly when (as is sadly only too common), the information is not referred to again for many months, if not years. The ease and speed with which you can refresh your memory is therefore crucial.

The aim of the first experiment was to explore the effects of initial criterion level, the question I have just discussed. However, I'd like to briefly describe the results, partly to provide additional confirmation, but mostly because this experiment shows how initial criterion level interacts with number of study sessions. In this experiment, students were assigned a specific criterion level in the initial study session, and then participated in two review sessions: the first two days after the initial session, and the other some six weeks after that. These sessions began with a trial that served as a cued recall test.

As anticipated, at the 2-day test, recall was better the more times the item had been correctly recalled during the initial study session. See, in the graph below, how a criterion level of two produced distinctly better recall on the 2-day test than a criterion level of one, and a criterion level of three was better still (see next page for graph).

The second experiment, which compared a criterion level of either one or three, and increased the number of review sessions for half the items, showed very clearly the advantage to having three revision sessions rather than just one. Average recall on the final test was less than 40% for items that only had one re-learning session, compared to over 50%

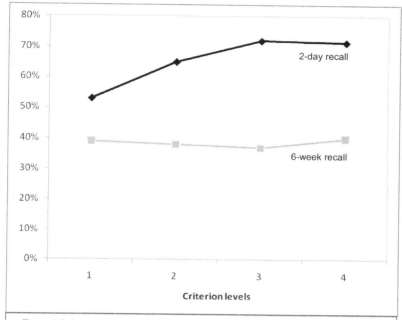

Figure 4.2: Average percentage correct 2 days and 6 weeks after initial study, as a function of the number of times the item was correctly recalled during initial study. From Vaughn & Rawson 2011.

for those that had three re-learning sessions. Notice, too, how poor recall was for those 'control' items that were not revised at all!

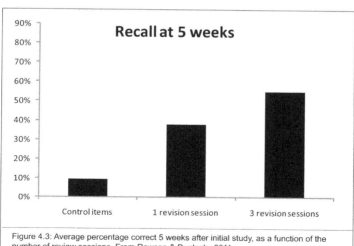

Figure 4.3: Average percentage correct 5 weeks after initial study, as a function of the number of review sessions. From Rawson & Dunlosky 2011.

Interestingly, there was also a clear benefit to having a criterion level of three compared with only one. While this benefit was greatest on the first review session (Day 3), it persisted through to the third review session (Day 10). The benefits for re-learning also continued through all learning sessions.

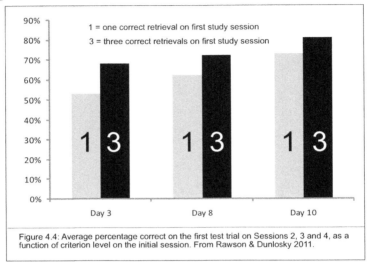

Figure 4.4: Average percentage correct on the first test trial on Sessions 2, 3 and 4, as a function of criterion level on the initial session. From Rawson & Dunlosky 2011.

The final experiment, which involved a greater number of students and more study sessions, confirmed this pattern: the benefit of having three correct retrievals rather than one was much greater on the first test, and got smaller with each subsequent session.

Rawson, K. A, & Dunlosky, J. (2011). Optimizing schedules of retrieval practice for durable and efficient learning: How much is enough? *Journal of experimental psychology: General, 140(3)*, 283–302.

Chapter 5: The advantage of spreading out your practice

5.1

Here's a graph showing how well the postmen were doing after 58 hours of training, which was the point at which the 1-hour-a-day group stopped (performance is measured in terms of speed and accuracy — the measure is number of correct keystrokes per minute):

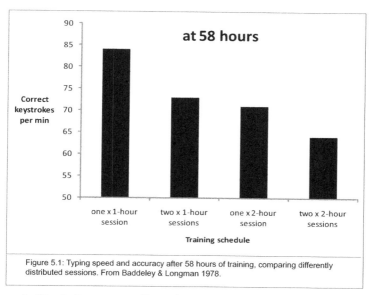

Figure 5.1: Typing speed and accuracy after 58 hours of training, comparing differently distributed sessions. From Baddeley & Longman 1978.

Baddeley, A. D., & Longman, D. J. A. (1978). The Influence of Length and Frequency of Training Session on the Rate of Learning to Type. *Ergonomics*, *21(8)*, 627–635.

5.2 Optimal spacing

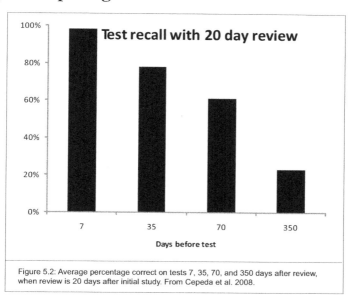

Figure 5.2: Average percentage correct on tests 7, 35, 70, and 350 days after review, when review is 20 days after initial study. From Cepeda et al. 2008.

Cepeda, N. J., Vul, E., Rohrer, D., Wixted, J. T., & Pashler, H. (2008). Spacing effects in learning: a temporal ridgeline of optimal retention. *Psychological Science, 19(11)*, 1095–102.

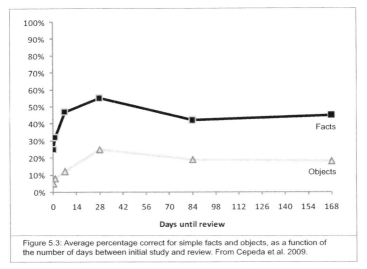

Figure 5.3: Average percentage correct for simple facts and objects, as a function of the number of days between initial study and review. From Cepeda et al. 2009.

Cepeda, N. J., Coburn, N., Rohrer, D., Wixted, J. T., Mozer, M. C., & Pashler, H. (2009). Optimizing distributed practice: theoretical analysis and practical implications. *Experimental Psychology, 56(4)*, 236–46.

Chapter 6. Spacing within your study session

6.1

One study presented Year 2 school-children and college students with words to be learned according to one of the three different schedules. For both the young children and the adult students, learning was the same for words presented massed or clustered. Only spaced words showed better learning (see next page for graph).

In a follow-up experiment, Year 1 school-children were given phonics instruction in very short lessons that were either spaced (three 2-minute sessions per day) or clustered (one 6-minute session per day). After two weeks of teaching, the children were tested. Those who received the spaced lessons showed much more learning than those who had received clustered lessons: 8.3 vs 1.3 points improvement (score at final test

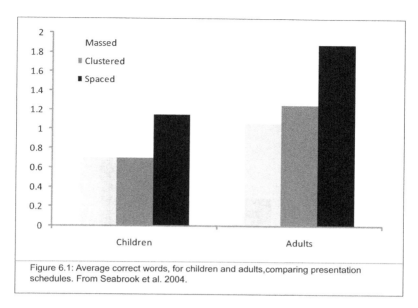

Figure 6.1: Average correct words, for children and adults, comparing presentation schedules. From Seabrook et al. 2004.

minus score at initial test) — a significant difference indeed!

Seabrook, R., Brown, G. D. a., & Solity, J. E. (2005). Distributed and massed practice: from laboratory to classroom. *Applied Cognitive Psychology, 19(1)*, 107–122.

6.2

Remember that optimal spacing is at that point *just before* you'd forget. Too long may be better than too short, but 'just right' is best of all.

An interesting study comparing highly supported self-study of new words with computer study may demonstrate this. The computer study used item-spacing, retrieval practice, and a criterion-level of 2 correct answers. The students were 6th and 7th graders in a poorly performing New York public school. There were four daily training sessions, with new words added each session, and old words revised. See how the students did in the first experiment, when the words to be learned were word-definition pairs (e.g., Ancestor—A person from whom one is descended; an organism from which later organisms evolved.):

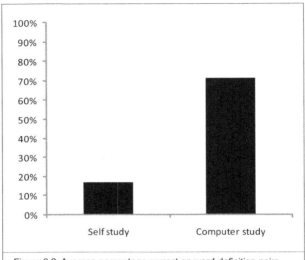

Figure 6.2: Average percentage correct on word-definition pairs, comparing supported self-study and computer-supported study. From Metcalfe et al. 2007.

Mammoth support for the benefits of appropriate practice!

But now let's look at the results of the second experiment, when the words to be learned were English equivalents of Spanish words (the children were native Spanish-speakers):

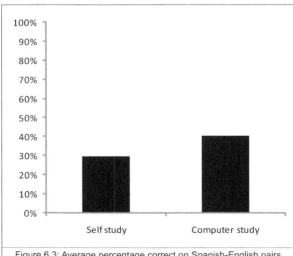

Figure 6.3: Average percentage correct on Spanish-English pairs, comparing supported self-study and computer-supported study. From Metcalfe et al. 2007.

Computerized practice is still of significant benefit, but the benefit is far smaller. Why? Simply because the words to be learned are different? The difference between word-definition pairs and Spanish-English word pairs doesn't seem great enough to produce such a massive difference in performance. Is it because there was no review session (the first experiment included a review session the day before the testing session, while the second experiment didn't). Again, this may well be a factor, but since previous words were always reviewed at each training session, it seems unlikely that the loss of a final review would have such a large effect.

No, I suggest that the principal factor at work here is the number of words to be learned — only ten in each condition in each learning session in the first experiment, compared with twenty in each condition in the second experiment. Given that the training sessions were no longer (five minutes shorter in fact), it seems more likely that the children either couldn't get enough repetition of individual items, or that the longer space between repetitions was too long for them to reliably remember them. Most likely, both are true. This may be supported by the better self-study performance: self-study's greater control of which words to study may have allowed individuals to focus only on a subset of the words, rather than try to learn all of them.

In other words, spaced retrieval practice can only do so much when you're trying to do more than you can handle.

Metcalfe, J., Kornell, N., & Son, L. K. (2007). A cognitive-science based programme to enhance study efficacy in a high and low risk setting. *The European Journal of Cognitive Psychology, 19(4-5)*, 743–768.

6.3 The importance of interleaving for category and type learning

On the next page you can see a graph showing the results when the children were tested in a blocked or interleaved condition.

When students were given the test in which they were told the right formula and only had to apply it (a common situation, unfortunately, in math instruction), the benefits of interleaving were not nearly as great (100% vs. 90%).

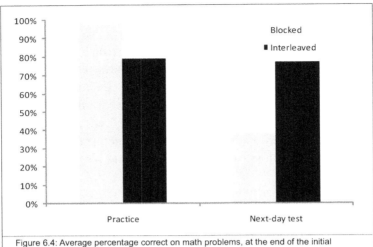

Figure 6.4: Average percentage correct on math problems, at the end of the initial practice session and on the next-day test, comparing blocked and interleaved practice. From Taylor & Rohrer 2010.

The message is clear, and it's reinforced by the type of errors made. With the exception of a single problem that was left unsolved by a single participant, every error on the test requiring the formula to be selected fell into one of two types:

● using the wrong one of the four formulas (discrimination error)

● using a completely different formula (category error).

Only one of these was affected by the type of practice. Blocked practice and interleaved practice produced about the same number of category errors (15% vs. 13%, respectively), but interleaved practice dramatically reduced the frequency of discrimination errors (46% vs. 10%).

Taylor, K., & Rohrer, D. (2010). The effects of interleaved practice. *Applied Cognitive Psychology*, *24*, 837–848.

6.4

In the study in which students practiced typing three different five-key sequences, those who practiced the sequences in separate blocks, working a sequence until they correctly completed it 30 times (blocked practice) learned to type the sequences faster and more accurately than those in the interleaved practice condition, but this advantage of blocking was only significant for the first three blocks, and decreased steadily as time went on. Moreover, when tested the next day, those who had practiced in the interleaved condition were dramatically better than those who had practiced in the blocked condition. Average recall of the sequence was 50% for those in the interleaved group, compared to a mere 17% for the blocked group. The average timing accuracy was 83% vs 43%.

Simon, D. A., & Bjork, R. A. (2001). Metacognition in motor learning. *Journal of Experimental Psychology: Learning, Memory, and Cognition, 27(4)*, 907–912.

6.5

In the first experiment, participants were shown all the paintings by one artist in a consecutive series (block) for six of the artists (massed condition), while the paintings by the other six artists were shown all mixed up, with participants never seeing two paintings by the same artist consecutively (spaced condition). Each painting was displayed for five seconds.

Testing continued through four blocks, each of which showed one painting from each of the 12 artists — in other words, the test itself provided spaced learning. In response to this, the difference between spaced vs massed initial learning declined: on the fourth test block, the difference was less than 10 percentage points (around 64% vs 55%).

In a later experiment, the researchers added another two conditions:

- a variant of the spaced condition, which put cartoon drawings in the spaces (which the participants were told to ignore), so that the spacing

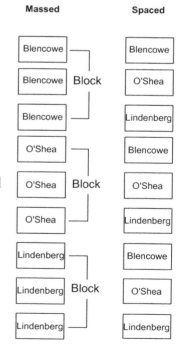

between paintings by the same artist was the same as in the spaced condition, but all the paintings by each artist were presented in the same order as they were in the massed condition.

- a variant of the massed condition, which involved paintings by any artist appearing four at a time.

Only three artists were used. The test took place after a 20 minute filler task (watching a video).

These variants produced no better learning than the massed condition (all three produced average recall scores of around 60%). Improved performance only occurred when the paintings by the three artists were interleaved with each other in the standard spaced condition, with no irrelevant fillers (68%).

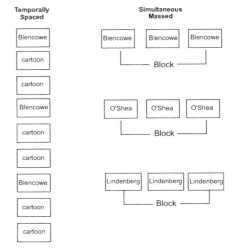

Kang, S. H. K., & Pashler, H. (2011). Learning Painting Styles: Spacing is Advantageous when it Promotes Discriminative Contrast. *Applied Cognitive Psychology, 26(1)*, 97–103.

6.6 Children's brains may work differently

In one study, young people (aged 9, 12, and 17) were trained on a finger-tapping task, then tested on the next two days. Some of the participants were further tested six weeks later. Another group of young students were given the same training, but also received an additional training session two hours later, during which the motor sequence to be learned was the reverse of that practiced in the initial session. They were then tested, 24 hours later, on the first sequence.

Now you'd expect, if you learned one sequence and then learned the reverse, that this would interfere badly with your memory for the first sequence. And so it did, for the 17-year-olds. But not for the 9- and 12-year-olds, who both showed the same performance gain at 24 hours that was seen when students only learned the first sequence.

Moreover, while better performance on the reverse sequence was linked to worse performance on the initial sequence at the 24-hour test for the 17-year-olds (as you'd expect), for the 12-year-olds, the better they were on the reverse sequence, the better they also did on the first sequence.

Dorfberger, S., Adi-Japha, E., & Karni, A. (2007). Reduced Susceptibility to Interference in the Consolidation of Motor Memory before Adolescence. *PLoS ONE, 2(2)*, e240.

6.7 Aging also affects consolidation & interference

In one study, young adults (average age 20) and older adults (average age 58) learned a motor sequence task requiring them to press the appropriate button when they saw a blue dot appear in one of four positions on the screen. The training included several learnable sequences interspersed with random trials, but participants weren't advised of this (this is a test of implicit rather than explicit learning — that is, learning you aren't consciously aware of).

As expected, younger adults were notably faster in their responses than the older group. Less expected was the fact that the older group actually learned the sequences faster than the younger group, even if they couldn't perform the task as quickly. However, on the second session a day later, while the younger adults showed the expected gain in performance from consolidation, the older adults returned to performing at the same level as they had early in the first session.

In other words, the older adults learned perfectly well during the first session, but they failed to consolidate the learning.

This pattern was confirmed in another study comparing younger and older adults, which found that, while the older adults showed improvement on an implicit sequence-learning task after 12 hours, this improvement had disappeared at 24 hours (which isn't to say that all benefit of the earlier training was lost).

Is this because we become slower to consolidate with age? This recalls the idea that children suffer less interference because they can consolidate memories more swiftly. Slower consolidation means older learning hangs around for longer, providing more opportunity for interference with later learning; faster consolidation means new information gets processed quickly, leaving less opportunity for interference.

It may also have to do with the greater interference consequent on the brains of older adults being more richly connected. Indeed, it seems likely that both processes are going on. Greater interference, and slower consolidation.

And there's a third potential factor: changes in time perception. Remember that the brain tries to associate events that occur closely in time — but what does 'closely' mean? To a child, two hours is a very long time — their brain isn't going to try and tie together events two hours apart, not without a great deal of prodding. For an older adult, on the other hand, two hours isn't significant.

Brown, R. M., Robertson, E. M., & Press, D. Z. (2009). Sequence Skill Acquisition and Off-Line Learning in Normal Aging. *PLoS ONE, 4(8)*, e6683.

Nemeth, D., & Janacsek, K. (2010). The Dynamics of Implicit Skill Consolidation in Young and Elderly Adults. *The Journals of Gerontology Series B: Psychological Sciences and Social Sciences, 66(1)*, 15–22.

6.8 Spacing & interleaving for complex material

The study I referred to earlier, that used a web-based module on the search for life on other planets, found only a small benefit to interleaving, and then only for conceptual understanding (that is, learners' ability to answer novel questions involving both mass and distance concepts), not the recall of single facts or integration of facts relating to only one information-set. This speaks, I think, to the difficulty of applying interleaving to complex material.

Richland, L.E., Bjork, R., Finley, J.R. & Linn, M.C. (2005). Linking cognitive science to education: Generation and interleaving effects. *Proceedings of the twenty-seventh annual conference of the cognitive science society.* Mahwah, NJ: Erlbaum.

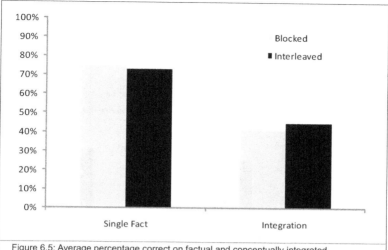

Figure 6.5: Average percentage correct on factual and conceptually integrated questions 2 days after initial study, comparing blocked and interleaved practice. From Richland et al. 2005.

There's a particularly interesting example of spaced learning in the classroom from a U.K. program developed by researchers and teachers, in which very intensive and fast-paced instruction is given in short blocks. Each instruction block is no more than 20 minutes long, and three instruction blocks are spaced by 10-minute distractor activities. There are two critical factors to this strategy:

- each of the three instruction blocks covers the same material, expressed in different ways: the first focuses on presenting the information; the second on recalling it; the third on understanding it

- the distractor activities aren't 'learning' activities, but more physical (creative or active) 'doing' activities (e.g., origami, clay modeling, ball-handling games, light aerobics).

Note the retrieval practice in the second block, while the 'understanding' block also includes recalling the information, in the context of making connections.

In one study, secondary school students (aged 13-15) were taught biology either in traditional classes over four months (a total of 23 hours instruction), or in a single Spaced Learning session. On the later GCSE test, there was no significant difference between the scores of these groups. In other words, one hour of focused, spaced, and practiced instruction, apparently produced as much learning as a term's worth of traditional classes!

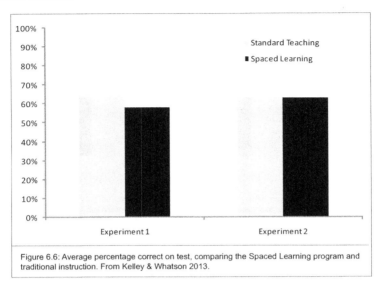

Figure 6.6: Average percentage correct on test, comparing the Spaced Learning program and traditional instruction. From Kelley & Whatson 2013.

[Note that the Spaced Learning students were disadvantaged in the first experiment, by experiencing the second biology course before the first one (traditionally taught) — this was so that any relevant prior knowledge would be minimized. In the second experiment, the courses were run in their normal order.]

In a further experiment, students experienced their normal biology classes, but were then given either the customary one-hour review of the year's material before the exam, or a Spaced Learning lesson of the same duration. Those given the Spaced Learning review scored significantly higher on the biology exam (an average of 63% vs 55%).

I'm sure you noticed how, despite the emphasis on spacing (the program is called "Spaced Learning"), the program includes several other recommendations I've discussed: variable repetition; retrieval practice; connection; time to allow stabilization of the new learning. So, this study isn't only about spacing, but is a demonstration of how these principles can be integrated and used in the classroom. Or, indeed, in private study.

Kelley, P., & Whatson, T. (2013). Making long-term memories in minutes: a spaced learning pattern from memory research in education. *Frontiers in Human Neuroscience*, 7, 1–9.

Learning Futures and Monkseaton High School. Spaced Learning: Making memories stick. https://static1.squarespace.com/static/ 54247a57e4b08e3d52eb03df/t/5440c848e4b01ad919f6fe26/1413531720341/ Spaced+Learning+Guide.pdf

Chapter 12. Learning a skill

12.1 Varied repetition

Those in the random (interleaved) group performed better when tested at the end of training, and showed more than twice as much improvement from training (57% vs 25%). (Do note, however, that blocked practice was still far better than less practice! A control group, that only experienced 12 'acquisition' sessions that were the same for all groups, and not the extra 12 sessions given to the random and blocked groups, only improved by 6%).

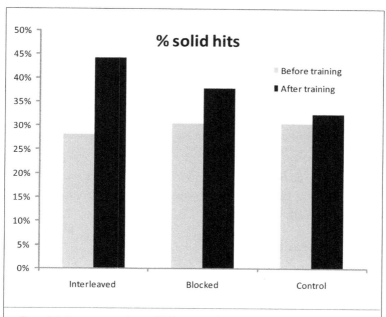

Figure 9.1: Average percentage solid hits, comparing performance before and after baseball training, for interleaved, blocked, and control conditions. From Hall et al. 1994.

Hall, K., Domingues, D., & Cavazos, R. (1994). Contextual interference effects with skilled baseball players. *Perceptual and motor skills*, *78*, 835–841.

12.2 Self-monitoring and goal-setting

The graph shows dart-throwing skill measured by the average of six throws at a target made of seven concentric circles, with each circle ranging from 1 (outermost circle) to 7 (center). The study also included a further condition: some of each goal group recorded their performance as they practiced, either in terms of their scores or their actions, as appropriate. As you can see, whatever the goal, this self-monitoring significantly helped.

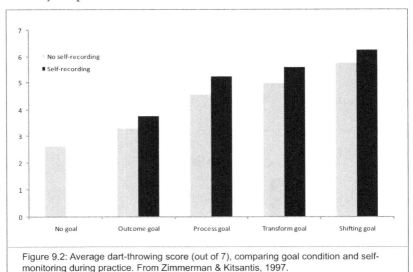

Figure 9.2: Average dart-throwing score (out of 7), comparing goal condition and self-monitoring during practice. From Zimmerman & Kitsantis, 1997.

Zimmerman, B.J. & Kitsantas, A. (1997). Developmental phases in self-regulation: Shifting from process goals to outcome goals. *Journal of Educational Psychology*, *89*, 29-36.

12.3 Mental practice

The study involved 44 right-handed, skilled male golfers. Their putting performance was assessed in a lab environment, where they completed 40 putts with instructions to 'make the ball stop as close to the target as possible' while being recorded by a three-dimensional ultrasound camera. Some of the golfers first watched a video of an expert golfer performing the same task, while a voice-over described key visual and kinaesthetic feelings associated with performing the putt.

Kinesthetic imagery ability was assessed using a self-report questionnaire (the Motor Imagery Questionnaire, MIQ-3). Those with a mean score equal or greater than 6 were classified as good imagers. The questionnaire has 12 items.

McNeill, E., Ramsbottom, N., Toth, A. J., & Campbell, M. J. (2020). Kinaesthetic imagery ability moderates the effect of an AO+MI intervention on golf putt performance: A pilot study. *Psychology of Sport and Exercise*, *46*, 101610.

12.4

The study involved picking up an object using only thumb and index finger, and inserting it into a slot in another distant object. The object was a complicated one, with objects attached to it to make it more difficult to grasp and to force the user to pick it up in a particular way. The object's orientation also changed.

The participant began a trial with their eyes closed (so as not to see the object). After opening their eyes, the mental rehearsal group imagined performing the action, while the other group actually performed it.

The mental rehearsal group did this for the first 180 trials, before physically executing the task for the final 60 trials.

Amplitudes and latencies of event-related potentials (ERPs) were compared across groups at different stages during learning.

It's suggested that mental rehearsal induced changes in neurons in the premotor cortex which in turn, once the body was involved, sped up the appropriate changes across the motor network.

Allami, N., Brovelli, A., Hamzaoui, E. M., Regragui, F., Paulignan, Y., & Boussaoud, D. (2014). Neurophysiological correlates of visuo-motor learning through mental and physical practice. *Neuropsychologia*, *55*, 6-14.

Chapter 13. Cognitive skills

13.1

Preliminary results from the Chess Expertise from Eye Gaze and Emotion (CEEGE) Project, https://www.uni-bielefeld.de/sport/arbeitsbereiche/ab_ii/research/ceege.html

Chapter 14. Specific subjects

Language

14.1

In the study, participants were given nine nonsense words to learn. Each word had two syllables, and fell into one of three categories (A, B, and C), defined by the order of consonant and vowel sounds. The words were repeated in three-word sequences, with one word from each category, and no pauses between the words to show where one word ended and another began.

Participants listened to this spate of words for 10 minutes. One group was told to listen without overanalyzing what they heard. To help with this, they were given the option of completing a puzzle or coloring while they listened. The other group was told to try to identify the words they were hearing.

Both groups were equally successful at segmenting the words, and picking out correct word sequences. In the final test, however, they heard a three-word sequence that included a new word, and were asked to judge whether this new word, which belonged to one of the three categories, was in the correct location. Those who had been asked to pay close attention to the original word stream performed much worse than those who had listened with less attention.

Finn, A.S., Lee, T., Kraus, A. & Hudson, Kam C.L. (2014). When it hurts (and helps) to try: The role of effort in language learning. *PLoS ONE*, *9(7)*: e101806.

Chapter 15 Obstacles to effective practice

15.1 Test anxiety

In the study, 120 students learned 30 words and 30 images. One group studied by taking timed practice tests in which they freely recalled as many items as they could remember. For the other group, items were re-displayed on the computer screen, one at a time, for a few seconds each. Participants were given multiple timed periods to study.

Recall was tested after 24 hours. Half of each group was placed into a stress-inducing scenario, in which they were required to give an unexpected, impromptu speech and solve math problems in front of two judges, three peers and a video camera. Participants took two memory tests, in which they recalled the words or images they studied the previous day. These tests were taken during the stress scenario and twenty minutes after.

Among the retrieval practice group, stressed students remembered an average of 11 items from each set of 30, while non-stressed students remembered an average of 10 items (not a significant difference). Among the re-reading group, stressed students remembered an average of 7 items, and the unstressed students a little less than 9 items.

Smith, A. M., Floerke, V. A., & Thomas, A. K. (2016). Retrieval practice protects memory against acute stress. *Science, 354(6315)*, 1046–1048.

Answers to Review Questions

Chapter 1

1. N
2. b, c
3. All of these
4. a, b, d, e
5. Y
6. a, c, e
7. N
8. a, b, c
9. a, b, c
10. a, b, c
11. b
12. c, e
13. All of these
14. a, b, c
15. c, d

Chapter 3

1. d
2. N
3. f
4. c
5. b, c, e

6. e

7. a, c

8. b

Chapter 4

1. b

2. d

3. d

4. a. i
   b. ii
   c. ii

5. Y

6. b

Chapter 5

1. b

2. a

3. c

4. a

5. c

6. N

7. d

8. d

9. b

10. d

Chapter 6

1. d

2. d

3. c
4. c, d
5. b, c, e
6. a, b
7. a, b, c, e
8. a, b, d
9. a, b, c
10. Y

Chapter 8

1. d
2. c
3. f
4. Y
5. N

Chapter 9

1. a, b, c, e
2. b, c, d
3. e
4. c
5. N

Chapter 10

1. e
2. c
3. d
4. c

5. a

Chapter 11

1. All of these
2. a, d
3. b, c (d is usually true, but not necessarily)
4. a, b, d
5. Y

Chapter 12

1. d
2. b, c, d, e
3. c
4. b, c, f
5. N
6. N
7. All of these
8. a, b, c
9. All of these
10. a, d, e
11. b, e
12. b, c, d
13. b, c, d, e
14. N
15. c, e, f
16. e

Chapter 13

1. a, c
2. b, d, e
3. b, d, e
4. b, c, d, e
5. d

Chapter 14

1. e
2. Y
3. d
4. b
5. d
6. e
7. c, d, e
8. N
9. N
10. e
11. a, c, d, e
12. f
13. d
14. d

Answers to Exercises

Remember that in most cases these "answers" are guides only.

Exercise 2.1

Instinct theory:

- William James (1842–1910) important early figure in psychology in the United States

- theorized that behavior was driven by a number of instincts

    - an instinct is a species-specific pattern of behavior that is not learned

    - debate over what human behaviors are instincts, e.g., mother's protection of baby, hunting prey, liking sugar

    - some instinctive behaviors were experimentally demonstrated to result from associative learning ("Little Albert")

Drive theory:

- deviations from homeostasis create physiological needs, which result in psychological drive states that direct behavior to meet the need and, ultimately, bring the system back to homeostasis

    - homeostasis = tendency to maintain a balance, or optimal level, within a biological system.

    - e.g., when your blood sugar levels drop below normal, hunger (the drive state) directs you to find food; eating removes the hunger, and, ultimately, your blood sugar levels return to normal.

- emphasizes the importance of habits — a behavior that successfully reduces a drive is more likely to be repeated whenever faced with that drive.

- extended to include arousal level as a potential motivator (too little and we become bored, driving us to seek stimulation; too much and we try to reduce it)

- the optimal level of arousal is usually a moderate level, but it depends on the complexity and difficulty of the task to be performed:

- Yerkes-Dodson law holds that a simple task is performed best when arousal levels are relatively high and complex tasks are best performed when arousal levels are lower.

Exercise 2.2

Types of matter: mixtures and pure substances.

A pure substance has a constant composition — any sample will be exactly the same as any other sample.

- Pure substances can be elements or compounds.

- Elements can't be broken down into simpler substances by chemical changes, while compounds can.

- Examples of elements: gold, aluminium, copper

- Examples of compounds: mercury oxide, silver chloride, sucrose

- The properties of compounds can be quite different from the elements that make them, e.g. sodium chloride (salt)

A mixture has two or more types of matter in varying amounts which can be separated by physical changes, such as evaporation.

- A heterogeneous mixture has a composition that varies within itself — e.g. Italian dressing, chocolate chip cookies.

- A homogeneous mixture (solution) is the same throughout — e.g. a sports drink, maple syrup, gasoline.

Only 100+ elements (periodic table), but vast number of compounds, and infinite number of mixtures.

Only 11 elements make up 99% of the earth's crust and atmosphere.

Exercise 9.1

The numbers in brackets indicate ratings — these are not hard and fast! Indeed, several I myself would probably rate differently on another occasion. The point of the exercise is more to think about each word in terms of these criteria, and to get a feeling for what makes a good keyword.

angolo, corner — angle [1-0-1-1=3]

campana, bell — camp [1-1-1-1=4]

collo, neck — collar [1-1-1-1=4]

mano, hand — man [1-1-1-1=4]

mare, sea — mare (horse) [1-1-1-1=4]

Exercise 9.2

ezis, hedgehog — easy, airsick [1-0-1-0=2]

kas, who — case, cast [1-0-1-1=3]

nams, house — name, gnome [1-1-1-1=4]

uguns, fire — egg [1-1-1-1=4]

zirnis, pea — see nest [1-0-1-1=3]

Exercise 9.3

ancora, yet, still — anchor [1-0-1-1=3]

dopo, after — dope [1-0-1-1=3]

fiume, river — fumes [1-0-1-1=3]

strofinare, to rub — strafe, strove, strop [1-0-1-0=2]

sviluppare, to develop — swill, swell up [1-0-1-0=2]

Exercise 9.4

acqua, water — aqua

denti, teeth — dental, dentist

fratello, brother — fraternal

giorno, day — journal

libro, book — library

nave, ship — navigate, naval

pneumatico, tire — pneumatic tire

risposta, answer — response

scarpa, shoe — sharp

sole, sun — solar

Exercise 9.5

angolo, corner — angle

campana, bell — campanology

collo, neck — collar

mano, hand — manual, manuscript

mare, sea — maritime, marine

ezis, hedgehog — echinus, echinid, echinoderm, urchin (sea)

kas, who — quis (Latin)

nams, house — domestic

uguns, fire — ignite, igneous

zirnis, pea — corn, grain

Exercise 9.6

angolo [cue] — angle — corner; **corner** [cue] — angle — angolo

campana [cue] — campanology — bell; **bell** [cue] — campanology — campana

collo [cue] — collar — neck; **neck** [cue] — collar — collo

mano [cue] — manual — hand; **hand** [cue] — manual — mano

mare [cue] — marine — sea; **sea** [cue] — marine — mare

ezis [cue] — echinid — hedgehog; **hedgehog** [cue] — echinid — ezis

kas [cue] — quis — who; **who** [cue] — quis — kas

nams [cue] — domestic — house; **house** [cue] — domestic — nams

uguns [cue] — ignite — fire; **fire** [cue] — ignite — uguns

zirnis [cue] — corn — pea; **pea** [cue] — corn — zirnis

Exercise 9.7

bioturbation, disturbance of sediment by burrowing or other activity of living organisms — biological disturbance, perturbed by organisms, turbid soil — link the bio- to living organisms; link the -turb to disturb, perturb, turbid (turbid links with sediment, since it evokes water made cloudy by disturbed sediment) — bioturbation, bio, life, living organism, plus turb as in disturb, perturb, turbid — disturbance of sediment by a living organism

clastic, consisting of broken pieces of older rocks — as in iconoclastic, iconoclast, a breaker or destroyer of images / icons (several words have this -clastic ending, signifying something that breaks the first part of the word) — clastic, like in iconoclastic, meaning broken, containing pieces of broken rocks, older because clastic is an old word (that's just a way of helping you remember that they're pieces of older rocks)

cryofracture, technique in which an object is rapidly and drastically cooled in order to break it down for internal study or disassembly — cryo- as in cryogenics, plus fracture — cryo-, cryogenics, to do with freezing, so freezing causing breaks — way of breaking up an object by quickly freezing it.

euphony, language which sounds pleasing to the ear, quality of having a pleasant sound — eu- means pleasant, as in euphoria, eulogy (saying nice things about a person); -phone as in microphone, telephone, etc, meaning to do with sound

geophagy, practice of eating earth — geo- meaning earth (geology, geography, etc) plus -phagy (also -phagia, -phagous) meaning eating, e.g., anthropophagy, coprophagous; but if you don't know any of these words, you could make up a mnemonic for the -phagy suffix

hermeneutics, theory and methodology of the interpretation of texts — think of the messenger god Hermes, imagine him translating and explaining the letters he carries to their recipients

orexigenic, something that stimulates appetite for food — relates to anorexic (without appetite), so not an-orexic, so something to do with enjoying eating; -genic means generating, as in carcinogenic — something that generates appetite for food

myelin, white fatty substance that coats nerve axons in the brain — "*my linen* covers my nerves"

paleogeography, the study of the physical landscapes in the past — paleo- as in Paleolithic / Palaeolithic (Stone Age), Paleocene / Palaeocene, paleology / palaeology etc, meaning very old — geography of long ago

tectogenesis, the formation of the highly distorted rock structures characteristic of mountain ranges — tecto- as in tectonics, relates somehow to earthquakes and volcanoes [in my mind], means the structure of the earth's crust [from dictionary]; earthquakes connect it to the distortion, volcanoes to mountains; plus -genesis, meaning origin, source, creation — creation of distorted rock structures found in mountain ranges

Exercise 9.8

Note that all the orders end in -formes, so you don't need to specifically include this in your keywords, just be aware of it; similarly, all the families end in -idae, so ditto.

Percy if you know one, or purse — latrine — tarred kiwi, smoke, trumpeter: Imagine a giant pink purse lying in a latrine block, when a kiwi covered in tar wanders in and pulls a silver trumpet and a cigar out of the purse. Smoking the cigar, he tries to stuff the trumpet down one of the toilets.

leaf — leaf — goose, monk (two "leaf"s will tell you the name is essentially repeated, the only difference being the endings): A giant leaf settles on the head of a monk as he solemnly settles a smaller leaf on the head of a goose

sombrero — central / cent on a leaf — warehouse, rudder: The leaf with the cent on it has a rudder attached, and is scooting around the rain-filled brim of a sombrero toward a toy warehouse.

zero / zebra / Zeus (it's actually named for Zeus) — citadel / city — door with crown on it = king's door: A zebra strikes with his hooves at the King's door to the citadel.

Exercise 9.9

- What species belong to the order Perciformes?

- What families belong to the order Perciformes?

- What order does the family Latridae belong to?

- What order do tarakihi belong to?

- What order do moki belong to?

- What order does the fish species silver trumpeter belong to?

- What family do tarakihi belong to?

- What family do moki belong to?

- What family does the fish species silver trumpeter belong to?

- What species belong to the order Lophiiformes?

- What families belong to the order Lophiiformes?

- What order does the family Lophiidae belong to?

- What order do goosefish belong to?

- What order do monkfish belong to?

- What family do goosefish belong to?

- What family do monkfish belong to?

- What species belong to the order Scombriformes?

- What families belong to the order Scombriformes?

- What order does the family Centrolophidae belong to?

- What order do blue warehou belong to?

- What order do rudderfish belong to?

- What family do blue warehou belong to?

- What family do rudderfish belong to?

- What species belong to the order Zeiformes?

- What families belong to the order Zeiformes?

- What order does the family Cyttidae belong to?

- What order do King dory belong to?

- What family do King dory belong to?

Exercise 10.1

(a)

Differences:

genotype can't be seen, but phenotype can

genotype isn't affected by environment, but phenotype is

Links:

an organisms's properties that can't be seen — genotype

an organisms's properties that can be seen — phenotype

an organisms's properties that are affected by the environment — phenotype

an organisms's properties that aren't affected by the environment — genotype

an organisms's properties that are solely determined by genes — genotype

an organisms's properties that aren't solely determined by genes — phenotype

(b)

Differences:

morphemes carry meaning, but phonemes don't

phonemes are sounds and so are only found in spoken language, while morphemes exist in language however expressed

Links:

the smallest unit of language that carries meaning — morpheme

the smallest sound that distinguishes a word or word element from another — phoneme

(c)

Difference:

proactive interference occurs when previous learning disrupts recall of new information, whereas retroactive interference occurs when new information disrupts recall of previous information

Links:

it occurs when previous learning disrupts recall of new information — proactive interference

it occurs when new information disrupts recall of previous information — retroactive interference

(d)

Differences:

mitosis occurs in body cells, but meiosis only occurs in sex cells

division occurs once in mitosis, but twice in meiosis

mitosis produces two daughter cells, but meiosis produces four

daughter cells produced by mitosis are identical, but those produced by meiosis are not

Links:

this type of cell division occurs only in sex cells — meiosis this type of cell division occurs throughout the body — mitosis

this type of cell division occurs once — mitosis

this type of cell division occurs twice, consecutively — meiosis

this type of cell division produces two daughter cells — mitosis

this type of cell division produces four daughter cells — meiosis

this type of cell division produces identical daughter cells — mitosis

this type of cell division produces non-identical daughter cells — meiosis

(e)

Differences:

the balance of payments records all economic transactions between the residents of a country and the rest of the world, while the balance of trade only looks at imports and exports

the balance of payments includes both visible and non-visible transactions, while the balance of trade includes only visible items (goods)

the balance of payments is always balanced, while the balance of trade may or may not be

Links:

the set of accounts that includes all economic transactions — balance of payments

the set of accounts that includes only imports and exports — balance of trade

the set of accounts that includes both tangible and intangible items — balance of payments the set of accounts that includes only tangible items — balance of trade

the set of accounts that is always balanced — balance of payments

the set of accounts that may be in surplus, in deficit, or balanced — balance of trade

(f) Sometimes there are more than two highly similar concepts!

Differences:

speed is measured by distance travelled divided by time passed, while velocity is specified by an object's speed and direction of motion, and momentum is specified by an object's velocity and its mass

speed is scalar, while velocity and momentum are vector qualities

Links:

distance travelled divided by time passed — speed

distance travelled divided by time passed, taking into account direction — velocity

distance travelled divided by time passed, taking into account direction and the object's mass — momentum

speed + direction — velocity

velocity + mass — momentum

this property takes mass into account — momentum

these properties take direction into account — velocity, momentum

these properties don't take mass into account — speed, velocity

this property doesn't take direction into account — speed

this property is scalar — speed

these properties are vectors — velocity, momentum

Exercise 10.2

Q: When did the Hundred Years War begin?

A: 1337

Q: Which countries was the Hundred Years War between?

A: England and France

Q: Who created the first steam engine?

A: Thomas Savery

Q: When was the first steam engine created?

A: 1698

Q: What is the second most common element in the Earth's crust?

A: Silicon

Q: How far back have we found signs of cockroaches?

A: 280 million years

Q: Which is older — cockroaches or dinosaurs?

A: Cockroaches

Q: How far back is our oldest evidence of dinosaurs?

A: 200 million years

Q: What are mafic rocks?

A: Igneous rocks that are high in magnesium and iron

Q: What elements are characteristic of mafic rocks?

A: Magnesium and iron

Q: What type of rock are mafic rocks?

A: Igneous

Q: Who was Cassius Dio?

A: A famous Roman historian

Q: When did Cassius Dio live?

A: In the 2nd century

Q: Name a Roman historian of the 2nd century

A: Cassius Dio

Q: Name the longest river in Mongolia.

A: Orkhon River

Q: Where is the Orkhon River found?

A: Mongolia

Q: Name a surviving member of the Rhynchocephalia

A: Tuatara

Q: The tuatara belongs to what Order?

A: Rhynchocephalia

Q: Where is Disko Island?

A: Greenland

Q: What's the name of the Basque language?

A: Euskara

Q: Who speaks Euskara?

A: The Basque

Exercise 10.3

Q: Who was William James?

A: An important 19th century figure in psychology in the United States

Q: What was William James' theory of human behavior?

A: That behavior is driven by a number of instincts

Q: Who invented instinct theory?

A: William James

Q: Define an instinct

A: A species-specific pattern of behavior that is not learned

Q: What's the term for a species-specific pattern of behavior that is not learned?

A: An instinct

Q: Name some supposed human instincts

A: A mother's protection of baby, hunting prey, liking sugar

Q: What are two problems with instinct theory?

A: That people can't agree on specific instincts; that some instinctive behaviors have been shown to be learned

Q: What's drive theory?

A: A theory of human behavior that says physiological needs come from deviations from homeostasis, causing psychological drive states that direct behavior to meet the need, bringing the system back to homeostasis

Q: What's homeostasis?

A: The tendency to maintain a balance, or optimal level, within a biological system

Q: Give an example of homeostasis

A: Hunger caused by a drop in blood sugar. Hunger drives us to eat, raising blood sugar back up.

Q: Habits are important in which theory of human behavior?

A: Drive theory

Q: Define a habit in the context of drive theory

A: A behavior that successfully reduces a drive is more likely to be repeated whenever faced with that drive

Q: Which theory recognizes arousal as a potential motivator?

A: Drive theory

Q: What's the Yerkes-Dodson law?

A: That a simple task is performed best when arousal levels are relatively high and complex tasks are best performed when arousal levels are lower

Exercise 10.4

Q: What are the two main types of matter?

A: Mixtures and pure substances

Q: What type of matter has a constant composition?

A: Pure substances

Q: There are two types of pure substance. What are they?

A: Elements and compounds

Q: What type of matter is an element?

A: A pure substance

Q: What type of matter is a compound?

A: A pure substance

Q: What's the main difference between an element and a compound?

A: Elements can't be broken down into simpler substances by chemical changes, while compounds can

Q: Name 3 elements

A: Gold, aluminium, copper

Q: Name 3 compounds

A: Mercury oxide, silver chloride, sucrose

Q: Do compounds have the same properties as the elements they are made of?

A: Not necessarily

Q: What's the difference between a pure substance and a mixture?

A: Any sample of a pure substance will always be the same as any other sample, but because a mixture has varying amounts of different types of matter, samples may not be identical

Q: What are the two types of mixture?

A: Heterogeneous and homogeneous

Q: A chocolate chip cookie is an example of what type of mixture?

A: Heterogeneous

Q: Maple syrup is an example of what type of mixture?

A: Homogeneous

Q: Something that contains at least two types of matter in varying amounts, and whose composition varies within itself, is what?

A: A heterogeneous mixture

Q: Something that contains at least two types of matter in varying amounts, and whose composition is the same throughout, is what?

A: A homogeneous mixture

Q: If something can be broken down into simpler substances, what type of matter is it?

A: A compound or a mixture

Q: If something can't be broken down into simpler substances, what type of matter is it?

A: A pure substance

Q: Name 2 examples of a heterogeneous mixture

A: Italian dressing, chocolate chip cookies

Q: Name 3 examples of a homogeneous mixture

A: A sports drink, maple syrup, gasoline

Q: What's the difference between a mixture and a compound?

A: A compound has constant properties and composition, while a mixture doesn't

Q: Are there more compounds or mixtures?

A: Mixtures

Q: What type of matter do most substances belong to?

A: Mixtures

Q: How many elements are there?

A: Over 100

Q: How many elements make up 99% of the earth's crust and atmosphere?

A: 11

Exercise 11.1

Focal question: Compare instinct theory & drive theory as explanations of human motivation

Key concepts:

motivation: (not explained in the context of this excerpted text, but Relationships make it clear that this overreaching concept is needed)

instincts: species-specific; not learned

learned behavior: (added after doing the concept map, when it became apparent it was needed)

homeostasis: balance within a biological system

drive states: psychological state created by deviations from homeostasis

habits: repeated behaviors that reduce a drive state; learned from experience

optimal arousal level: potential motivator; depends on complexity and difficulty of task

Relationships:

instincts, drive states, and **arousal level** can all provide **motivation**

drive states are responses to deviations from **homeostasis**

habits are learned responses to **drive states**

Concept order (most general to most specific):

motivation

- instincts

- homeostasis

  ▪ drive states

- habits

- arousal level

  ▪ Yerkes-Dodson law

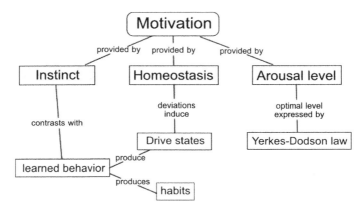

Exercise 11.2

Types of matter: mixtures and pure substances.

A pure substance has a constant composition — any sample will be exactly the same as any other sample.

- Pure substances can be elements or compounds.

- Elements can't be broken down into simpler substances by chemical changes, while compounds can.

- Examples of elements: gold, aluminium, copper

- Examples of compounds: mercury oxide, silver chloride, sucrose

- The properties of compounds can be quite different from the elements that make them, e.g. sodium chloride (salt)

A mixture has two or more types of matter in varying amounts which can be separated by physical changes, such as evaporation.

- A heterogeneous mixture has a composition that varies within itself — e.g. Italian dressing, chocolate chip cookies.

- A homogeneous mixture (solution) is the same throughout — e.g. a sports drink, maple syrup, gasoline.

Only 100+ elements (periodic table), but vast number of compounds, and infinite number of mixtures.

Only 11 elements make up 99% of the earth's crust and atmosphere.

Focal question: How to classify basic types of matter

Key concepts:

pure substance: matter with a constant composition

element: a type of pure substance that can't be broken down into anything simpler

compound: a type of pure substance that's made up of simpler substances

mixture: contains at least two types of matter in varying amounts

heterogeneous: variable composition

homogeneous: composition is the same throughout

Relationships:

pure substances can be **elements** or **compounds**

mixtures can be **heterogeneous** or **homogeneous**

Concept order (most general to most specific):

matter

- pure substance

  - element

  - compound

- mixture

  - heterogeneous

  - homogeneous

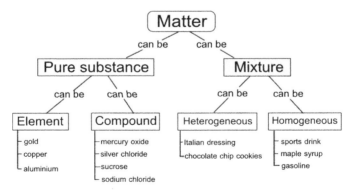

notice how the concept map includes the examples — remember that the focal question, key concepts, relationships, etc, are there to provide the framework for your concept map, they are not the sum total of it. The examples are not key concepts, but they are important to help you remember the differences, because we remember concrete things better than abstract categories

Exercise 11.3

Learnable points:

Microeconomics focuses on individuals, households, and businesses. It asks questions such as

- how people spend their budgets, decide how much to save, whether to borrow, how much to work, etc., and

- how firms make decisions about their products, their pricing, their financing, their staff levels.

Macroeconomics looks at the economy as a whole, focusing on broad issues such as

- production growth

- unemployment rate

- inflation

- export-import levels

- government deficits

The most important measures of macroeconomic health are improved living standards, low unemployment, low inflation.

Monetary policy is determined by the nation's central bank (e.g. the Federal Reserve), and concerns bank lending, interest rates, and capital markets.

Fiscal policy is determined by the nation's lawmakers (Congress, Parliament, etc), and concerns government spending and taxes.

Q & A:

Q: What part of the economy does microeconomics cover?

A: Individuals, households, and businesses

Q: What part of the economy does macroeconomics cover?

A: Broad issues of the economy as a whole

Q: Household spending would be covered in microeconomics or macroeconomics?

A: Microeconomics

Q: Mortgages would be covered in microeconomics or macroeconomics?

A: Microeconomics

Q: Inflation would be covered in microeconomics or macroeconomics?

A: Macroeconomics

Q: The unemployment rate would be covered in microeconomics or macroeconomics?

A: Macroeconomics

Q: Staffing decisions would be covered in microeconomics or macroeconomics?

A: Microeconomics

Q: Individual decisions about whether to work part-time or full-time would be covered in microeconomics or macroeconomics?

A: Microeconomics

Q: Budgeting would be covered in microeconomics or macroeconomics?

A: Microeconomics

Q: The export-import balance would be covered in microeconomics or macroeconomics?

A: Macroeconomics

Q: Government deficits would be covered in microeconomics or macroeconomics?

A: Macroeconomics

Q: A firm's decisions about financing would be covered in microeconomics or macroeconomics?

A: Microeconomics

Q: A firm's decisions about product pricing would be covered in microeconomics or macroeconomics?

A: Microeconomics

Q: What are the most important measures of macroeconomic health?

A: Improved living standards, low unemployment, low inflation

Q: Who determines fiscal policy?

A: Legislators / Congress / Parliament

Q: Who determines monetary policy?

A: The central bank / Federal Reserve / Reserve Bank

Q: Bank lending is part of fiscal policy or monetary policy?

A: Monetary policy

Q: Interest rates are part of fiscal policy or monetary policy?

A: Monetary policy

Q: Financial capital markets are part of fiscal policy or monetary policy?

A: Monetary policy

Q: Taxes are part of fiscal policy or monetary policy?

A: Fiscal policy

Q: Government spending is part of fiscal policy or monetary policy?

A: Fiscal policy

Focal question: How to distinguish micro- and macro-economics

Key concepts:

microeconomics: focuses on individuals, households, and businesses

macroeconomics: looks at the economy as a whole, focusing on broad issues

monetary policy: concerns bank lending, interest rates, and capital markets

fiscal policy: concerns government spending and taxes

Relationships:

economics is divided into **microeconomics** and **macroeconomics**

monetary policy and **fiscal policy** are the concern of **macroeconomics**

Concept order (most general to most specific):

- microeconomics
- macroeconomics
  - monetary policy
  - fiscal policy

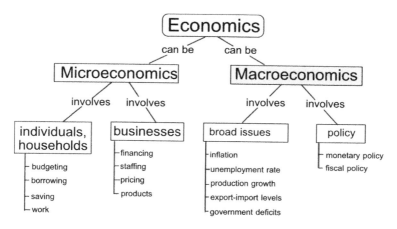

Exercise 13.1

1. Example 2. The second splits the information; the first example is integrated.

2. Example 1. Although the second example may seem better, as it has more information, the student has to split their attention between the figure and the text. Too much information often makes it difficult to integrate it all. Additionally, by labelling and ordering two steps, the steps are made clear and explicit, again reducing cognitive load.

3. Example 1

Exercise 13.2

Missing: c, d

Redundant: b, e

Exercise 13.3

As always, the purpose of this exercise is to get you to think. Remember that motor skills, cognitive skills, and information learning with a skill element, all exist on a continuum, which means the distance between one and another can be quite small. In some cases, it is quite easy to argue one way or another.

a. motor skill

b. cognitive skill

c. cognitive skill

d. motor skill

e. declarative learning

f. cognitive skill

g. motor skill

h. cognitive skill

i. cognitive skill

j. cognitive skill

k. cognitive skill

l. motor skill

m. cognitive skill

n. declarative learning

o. declarative learning

Exercise 13.4

Examples given only

a. knowledge of music pieces, music theory, learning how to read music

b. knowledge of the road code, of the parts of the car and what they do

c. knowing the names and requirements of different plants, k

d. knowing vocabulary, rules of grammar

e. knowledge of recipes and ingredients, of kitchen safety rules

Exercise 13.5

Examples given only

a. achieving fluency in bowing and fingering, in reading music, in playing specific pieces

b. coordinating gear changes and acceleration / braking movements, automatizing action sequences involved in starting and stopping, coordinating steering and acceleration / braking movements, coordinating visual information about parking spaces and steering movements, learning to see and quickly interpret exterior movements (other vehicles, pedestrians, etc)

c. pruning, use of tools, recognizing water needs, perceiving weeds, handling plants, sowing seed

d. achieving fluency in putting words together into sentences

e. developing a feel for how to put ingredients together, and what they look and feel like at certain process stages, learning to recognize when something is 'done', becoming fluent in certain recipes or processes

Exercise 14.1

First of all, I would recognize that it is confusing, and why it's confusing. Because possession is usually shown through use of an apostrophe, I would make careful note of the fact that **its** is an exception to that particular rule. But having noted that, I would put the emphasis on recognizing when it's time to use an apostrophe. That's because it's an easier rule to use. I would phrase it as: if it makes sense to replace the **its** with **it is**, then use an apostrophe. The apostrophe is taking the place of the missing letter.

Then I'd try to spot examples when **its** is appropriate, because **it's** is much more common, and I want to get used to seeing it as a correct usage, and *recognizing* when it is a correct usage. For a while, I might also say **it is** to myself when I see **it's**. That will strengthen the connection between those two.

When I write, every time I write **its** I will say to myself: can I replace that with **it is**? If I can, I'll use an apostrophe. If I can't, I'll check that **its** is followed by something that belongs to **it**. This is to reinforce the idea that **its** (without an apostrophe) indicates possession.

Exercise 14.2

Pick a language (other than your native one) that you have some familiarity with and interest in. Identify the elements of the language that need different types of practice, and say how you would go about learning them. Be as specific as possible.

Exercise 14.3

Principle 1: The interior angles of a triangle add up to 180°.

Principle 2: A straight angle (the angle on a straight line) is 180°.

Principle 3: An exterior angle is equal to the sum of the opposite interior angles.

Principle 4: If the equivalent angle is taken at each vertex, the exterior angles always add to 360°.

Principle 5: When two lines cross, vertically opposite angles are equal.

(a)

c=60: 180-120=60 (a straight angle is 180°)

40+60=100

b=80: 180-100=80 (interior angles of a triangle add up to 180°)

X=80 (vertically opposite angles are equal)

OR:

c=60: 180-120=60 (a straight angle is 180°)

40+60=100

a=100 (exterior angle is equal to the sum of the opposite interior angles)

X=80 (a straight angle is 180°)

OR:

b=80: 120-40=80 (exterior angle is equal to the sum of the opposite interior angles)

X=80 (vertically opposite angles are equal)

OR:

d=120 (vertically opposite angles are equal)

b=80: 120-40=80 (exterior angle is equal to the sum of the opposite interior angles)

X=80 (vertically opposite angles are equal)

(b)

c=100: 50+30=80; 180=80=100 (interior angles of a triangle add up to 180°)

a=100 (vertically opposite angles are equal)

100+40=140

180-140=40 (interior angles of a triangle add up to 180°)

X=40

OR

c=100: 50+30=80; 180=80=100 (interior angles of a triangle add up to 180°)

b=80 (a straight angle is 180°)

80-40=40 (exterior angle is equal to the sum of the opposite interior angles)

X=40

OR

c=100: 50+30=80; 180=80=100 (interior angles of a triangle add up to 180°)

d=80 (a straight angle is 180°)

80-40=40 (exterior angle is equal to the sum of the opposite interior angles)

X=40

(c)

e=100: 50+30=80; 180-80=100 (interior angles of a triangle add up to 180°)

X=80: 180-80=100 (a straight angle is 180°)

OR

e=100: 50+30=80; 180-80=100 (interior angles of a triangle add up to 180°)

f=80: 180-100=80 (a straight angle is 180°)

X=80 (vertically opposite angles are equal)

OR

50+30=80

X=80 (exterior angle is equal to the sum of the opposite interior angles)

OR

e=100: 50+30=80; 180-80=100 (interior angles of a triangle add up to 180°)

d=100 (vertically opposite angles are equal)

X=80: 180-100=80 (a straight angle is 180°)

(d)

X=80 therefore e=100, d=100, f=80 (a straight angle is 180°)

a=40 (interior angles of a triangle add up to 180°)

b+c=100

g+h=100

Exercise 14.4

1. a

2. d

3. b, c

4. a

5. a, b (if you're confused by my answers, look closely at the E and see how the bottom stroke comes out slightly further than the top stroke)

6. a, c (the strategy I suggested is deliberately not the best strategy for this example — how would you have done it if you'd just been asked for the answer?)

7. a (the difference between the male and female heads makes this very easy, if rather than rotating the figure you simply noted whether the female was on the left or right)

8. b

9. a, b, e

10. d

11. a (did the addition of colored squares help you at all with this task?)

12. b

Did you notice that some of these figures lent themselves to different strategies than others? The task is called mental rotation, but did you always mentally rotate the figure, or did you sometimes (or always) pick particular elements of the figure to compare? Did you find some of these more difficult than others? Do you know why?

The purpose of this exercise is two-fold — not only to demonstrate one aspect of spatial visualization, that you might test yourself on, but also to demonstrate the value of varied practice. Do you think you learnt more from this exercise than you would if all the examples had been of one type?

Exercise 14.5

Some sample beliefs that might affect your belief in the drive theory of motivation:

Consistent with drive theory:

I eat when I'm hungry.

Men have sex to relieve their sexual tension.

If we need to drink, we'll feel thirsty.

When I'm cold, I seek warmth.

Inconsistent:

I don't know why I eat so much.

Sex is sometimes used as a means of having power over another person.

I'm really bad at knowing when I need to drink.

I don't really like running, but I know it's good for me.

I like to bask in the sun even though I get too hot.

Exercise 14.6

You don't have to get all of these, or exactly these, to achieve the point of this exercise! The point is to think about how various commonsense beliefs can affect your understanding.

1. ii, iv, vi, vii

2. i, iii, v, vi

3. ii, iv, v, vi

4. i, ii, iii, v, vi, vii

Exercise 14.7

For each dot diagram — Bohr model — orbital diagram triplet, specify the conceptually relevant similarities and the important differences between each pair (dot—Bohr; Bohr—orbital; dot—orbital)

(a) dot—Bohr: both show the single electron in the outer shell. The Bohr model shows the two electrons in the inner shell, which the dot diagram does not. Also, the Bohr model shows that the outer shell is the second shell (all we know from the dot diagram is that lithium has only one electron in its outer shell, we don't know how many shells there are).

Bohr—orbital: both show the two electrons in the first shell, and the single electron in the second shell. Since there are no electrons in the p subshell, there is no important difference between the two diagrams, except that the energy level diagram makes it much clearer that there are no electrons in the p subshell.

dot—orbital: both show the single electron on the outer shell. The energy level diagram also shows the two electrons in the first shell.

(b) dot—Bohr: both show the two electrons in the outer shell. The Bohr model shows that there are three shells, with the expected two electrons in the inner shell, and eight electrons in the second shell (of course, all we really need to know is that there are three shells — this tells us that there will be two in the first shell and 8 in the second).

Bohr—orbital: both show the electrons in the three shells, but the energy level diagram also tells us that the 8 electrons in the second shell are divided into two electrons in the s subshell and 6 in the p subshell.

dot—orbital: both show the two electrons on the outer shell. The energy level diagram also shows the 10 electrons in the other shells, and how they're divided into subshells.

(c) dot—Bohr: both show the four electrons in the outer shell. The Bohr model also shows that there are three shells, with the expected two electrons in the inner shell, and eight electrons in the second shell.

Bohr—orbital: both show the electrons in the three shells, but the energy level diagram also shows how the electrons on the second and third shells are divided into subshells: two electrons in the s subshell and 6 in the p subshell in the second shell; two electrons in the s subshell and two in the p subshell in the third shell. Moreover, it is

dot—orbital: both show the four electrons on the outer shell. The energy level diagram also shows the 12 electrons in the other shells, and how they're divided into subshells — particularly that the two electrons in the 3p subshell are unpaired.

Exercise 14.8

1. b

2. a

3. a

4. b

5. a

6. b

7. b

8. a

9. b

10. b

11. a

12. a

13. b

14. a

15. b

References

Allami, N., Brovelli, A., Hamzaoui, E. M., Regragui, F., Paulignan, Y., & Boussaoud, D. (2014). Neurophysiological correlates of visuo-motor learning through mental and physical practice. *Neuropsychologia, 55*, 6-14.

Allen, S. E. (2012). Memory stabilization and enhancement following music practice. *Psychology of Music, 41(6)*, 794–803.

Atkinson, R. C. (1975). Mnemotechnics in second-language learning. *American Psychologist, 30(8)*, 821–828.

Baddeley, A. D., & Longman, D. J. A. (1978). The Influence of Length and Frequency of Training Session on the Rate of Learning to Type. *Ergonomics, 21(8)*, 627–635.

Bae, C. L., Therriault, D. J., & Redifer, J. L. (2019). Investigating the testing effect: Retrieval as a characteristic of effective study strategies. *Learning and Instruction, 60*, 206–214.

Bernardi, N. F., De Buglio, M., Trimarchi, P. D., Chielli, A., & Bricolo, E. (2013). Mental practice promotes motor anticipation: evidence from skilled music performance. *Frontiers in human neuroscience, 7*, 451.

Brown, R. M., Robertson, E. M., & Press, D. Z. (2009). Sequence Skill Acquisition and Off-Line Learning in Normal Aging. *PLoS ONE, 4(8)*, e6683.

Carney, R. N., & Levin, J. R. (2003). Promoting higher-order learning benefits by building lower-order mnemonic connections. *Applied Cognitive Psychology, 17*(5), 563–575.

Cash, C. D. (2009). Effects of Early and Late Rest Intervals on Performance and Overnight Consolidation of a Keyboard Sequence. *Journal of Research in Music Education, 57(3)*, 252–266.

Cepeda, N. J., Coburn, N., Rohrer, D., Wixted, J. T., Mozer, M. C., & Pashler, H. (2009). Optimizing distributed practice: theoretical analysis and practical implications. *Experimental Psychology, 56(4)*, 236–46.

Cepeda, N. J., Vul, E., Rohrer, D., Wixted, J. T., & Pashler, H. (2008). Spacing effects in learning: a temporal ridgeline of optimal retention. *Psychological Science, 19(11)*, 1095–102.

Chan, J. C. K., McDermott, K. B., & Roediger, H. L. (2006). Retrieval-induced facilitation: initially nontested material can benefit from prior testing of related material. *Journal of experimental psychology. General, 135(4)*, 553–71.

Charness, N., Krampe, R. & Mayr, U. (1996). The role of practice and coaching in entrepreneurial skill domains: an international comparison of life-span chess skill acquisition. In K. Anders Ericsson (ed.), *The road to excellence: The acquisition of expert performance in the arts and sciences, sports and games.* Mahwah, NJ: Lawrence Erlbaum.

Cooper, J. L., Sidney, P. G., & Alibali, M. W. (2018). Who Benefits from Diagrams and Illustrations in Math Problems? Ability and Attitudes Matter. *Applied Cognitive Psychology, 32(1)*, 24-38.

Dorfberger, S., Adi-Japha, E., & Karni, A. (2007). Reduced Susceptibility to Interference in the Consolidation of Motor Memory before Adolescence. *PLoS ONE, 2(2)*, e240.

Ericsson, K.A. (1996). The acquisition of expert performance: An introduction to some of the issues. In K. Anders Ericsson (ed.), *The Road to Excellence: The acquisition of expert performance in the arts and sciences, sports, and games.* Mahwah, NJ: Lawrence Erlbaum.

Ericsson, K.A., Krampe, R.Th. & Tesch-Romer, C. (1993). The role of deliberate practice in the acquisition of expert performance. *Psychological Review, 100*, 363-406.

Feltz, D.L. & Landers, D.M. (1983). The effects of mental practice on motor skill learning and performance: A meta-analysis. *Journal of Sport Psychology, 5*, 25-57.

Finn, A.S., Lee, T., Kraus, A. & Hudson, Kam C.L. (2014). When it hurts (and helps) to try: The role of effort in language learning. *PLoS ONE, 9(7)*, e101806.

Fritz, C. O., Morris, P. E., Acton, M., Voelkel, A. R., & Etkind, R. (2007). Comparing and Combining Retrieval Practice and the Keyword Mnemonic for Foreign Vocabulary Learning. *Applied Cognitive Psychology*, *21*, 499–526.

Ginns, P., Hu, F.-T., Byrne, E., & Bobis, J. (2015). Learning By Tracing Worked Examples. *Applied Cognitive Psychology*, *30(3)*, 160-9.

Gurcay, D., & Gulbas, E. (2015). Development of three-tier heat, temperature and internal energy diagnostic test. *Research in Science & Technological Education*, *33(2)*, 197–217.

Hall, K., Domingues, D., & Cavazos, R. (1994). Contextual interference effects with skilled baseball players. *Perceptual and motor skills*, *78*, 835–841.

Hallam, S., Rinta, T., Varvarigou, M., Creech, A., Papageorgi, I., Gomes, T., & Lanipekun, J. (2012). The development of practising strategies in young people. *Psychology of Music*, *40(5)*, 652–680.

Hannon, B., Lozano, G., Frias, S., Picallo-hernandez, S., & Fuhrman, R. (2009). Differential-associative Processing: A New Strategy for Learning Highly-similar Concepts. *Applied Cognitive Psychology*, *24(9)*, 1222-1244.

Hannon, B. (2012). Differential-associative processing or example elaboration: Which strategy is best for learning the definitions of related and unrelated concepts? *Learning and Instruction*, *22(5)*, 299–310.

Hussain, Z., Sekuler, A. B., & Bennett, P. J. (2011). Superior Identification of Familiar Visual Patterns a Year After Learning. *Psychological Science*, *22(6)*, 724 –730.

Ikeda, K., Castel, A. D., & Murayama, K. (2015). Mastery-Approach Goals Eliminate Retrieval-Induced Forgetting The Role of Achievement Goals in Memory Inhibition. *Personality and Social Psychology Bulletin*, *41(5)*, 687–695.

Kang, S. H. K., & Pashler, H. (2011). Learning Painting Styles: Spacing is Advantageous when it Promotes Discriminative Contrast. *Applied Cognitive Psychology*, *26(1)*, 97–103.

Kang, S. H. K., Pashler, H., Cepeda, N. J., Rohrer, D., Carpenter, S. K., & Mozer, M. C. (2011). Does incorrect guessing impair fact learning? *Journal of Educational Psychology, 103(1)*, 48–59.

Karpicke, J. D., & Blunt, J. R. (2011). Retrieval practice produces more learning than elaborative studying with concept mapping. *Science, 331(6018)*, 772–5.

Kelley, P., & Whatson, T. (2013). Making long-term memories in minutes: a spaced learning pattern from memory research in education. *Frontiers in Human Neuroscience, 7*, 1–9.

Kornell, N. (2009). Optimising Learning Using Flashcards: Spacing Is More Effective Than Cramming. *Applied Cognitive Psychology, 23(9)*, 1297–1317.

Kornell, N., & Bjork, R. A. (2008). Optimising self-regulated study: the benefits — and costs — of dropping flashcards. *Memory, 16(2)*, 125–36.

Margulieux, L. E., & Catrambone, R. (2016). Improving problem solving with subgoal labels in expository text and worked examples. *Learning and Instruction, 42*, 58–71.

McNamara, D.S., Kintsch, E., Songer, N.B. & Kintsch, W. (1996). Are Good Texts Always Better? Interactions of Text Coherence, Background Knowledge, and Levels of Understanding in Learning From Text. *Cognition and Instruction, 14(1)*, 1-43.

McNeill, E., Ramsbottom, N., Toth, A. J., & Campbell, M. J. (2020). Kinaesthetic imagery ability moderates the effect of an AO+MI intervention on golf putt performance: A pilot study. *Psychology of Sport and Exercise, 46*, 101610.

Metcalfe, J., Kornell, N., & Son, L. K. (2007). A cognitive-science based programme to enhance study efficacy in a high and low risk setting. *The European Journal of Cognitive Psychology, 19(4-5)*, 743–768.

Mwangi, W. & Sweller, J. (1998). Learning to Solve Compare Word Problems: The Effect of Example Format and Generating Self-Explanations. *Cognition and Instruction, 16(2)*, 173-199.

Nath, S., & Szücs, D. (2014). Construction play and cognitive skills associated with the development of mathematical abilities in 7-year-old children. *Learning and Instruction, 32*, 73–80.

Nemeth, D., & Janacsek, K. (2010). The Dynamics of Implicit Skill Consolidation in Young and Elderly Adults. *The Journals of Gerontology Series B: Psychological Sciences and Social Sciences, 66(1)*, 15–22.

Novack, M. A., Congdon, E. L., Hemani-Lopez, N., & Goldin-Meadow, S. (2014). From Action to Abstraction Using the Hands to Learn Math. *Psychological Science, 25(4)*, 903–910.

Pyc, M. A, & Rawson, K. A. (2010). Why testing improves memory: mediator effectiveness hypothesis. *Science (New York, N.Y.), 330(6002)*, 335.

Rau, M.A. & Wu, S.P.W. (2018). Combining Instructional Activities for Sense-Making Processes and Perceptual-Induction Processes Involved in Connection-Making Among Multiple Visual Representations. *Cognition and Instruction, 36(4)*, 361-395.

Rawson, K. A, & Dunlosky, J. (2011). Optimizing schedules of retrieval practice for durable and efficient learning: How much is enough? *Journal of experimental psychology: General, 140(3)*, 283–302.

Reinhart, R. M. G., McClenahan, L. J., & Woodman, G. F. (2015). Visualizing Trumps Vision in Training Attention. *Psychological Science, 26(7)*, 1114–1122.

Richland, L.E., Bjork, R., Finley, J.R. & Linn, M.C. (2005). Linking cognitive science to education: Generation and interleaving effects. *Proceedings of the twenty-seventh annual conference of the cognitive science society.* Mahwah, NJ: Erlbaum.

Richman, H.B. et al. (1996). Perceptual and memory processes in the acquisition of expert performance: The EPAM model. In K. Anders Ericsson (ed.), *The road to excellence: The acquisition of expert performance in the arts and sciences, sports and games.* Mahwah, NJ: Lawrence Erlbaum.

Roediger, H. L., & Karpicke, J. D. (2006). Test-enhanced learning: taking memory tests improves long-term retention. *Psychological Science, 17(3)*, 249–55.

Rohrer, D., & Taylor, K. (2007). The shuffling of mathematics practice problems improves learning. *Instructional Science, 35*, 481-498.

Seabrook, R., Brown, G. D. A., & Solity, J. E. (2005). Distributed and massed practice: from laboratory to classroom. *Applied Cognitive Psychology, 19(1)*, 107–122.

Shibata, K., Sasaki, Y., Bang, J. W., Walsh, E. G., Machizawa, M. G., Tamaki, M., Chang, L.-H., & Watanabe, T. (2017). Overlearning hyperstabilizes a skill by rapidly making neurochemical processing inhibitory-dominant. *Nature Neuroscience, 20(3)*, 470-475.

Simon, D. A., & Bjork, R. A. (2001). Metacognition in motor learning. *Journal of Experimental Psychology: Learning, Memory, and Cognition, 27(4)*, 907–912.

Smith, A. M., Floerke, V. A., & Thomas, A. K. (2016). Retrieval practice protects memory against acute stress. *Science, 354(6315)*, 1046–1048.

Starkes, J.L. et al. (1996). Deliberate practice in sports: What is it anyway? In K. Anders Ericsson (ed.), *The road to excellence: The acquisition of expert performance in the arts and sciences, sports and games*. Mahwah, NJ: Lawrence Erlbaum.

Tarmizi, R. A., & Sweller, J. (1988). Guidance During Mathematical Problem Solving. *Journal of Educational Psychology, 80(4)*, 424–436.

Taylor, K., & Rohrer, D. (2010). The effects of interleaved practice. *Applied Cognitive Psychology, 24*, 837–848.

van Gog, T. & Rummel, N. (2010). Example-based learning: Integrating cognitive and social-cognitive research perspectives. *Educational Psychology Review, 22*, 155-74.

Vaughn, K. E., & Rawson, K. A. (2011). Diagnosing Criterion-Level Effects on Memory: What Aspects of Memory Are Enhanced by Repeated Retrieval? *Psychological Science, 22(9)*, 1127-31.

Ward, M., & Sweller, J. (1990). Structuring Effective Worked Examples. *Cognition and Instruction, 7(1)*, 1–39.

Wulf, G., Shea, C. & Lewthwaite, R. (2010). Motor skill learning and performance: a review of influential factors. *Medical Education, 44*, 75-84.

Yeo, S., & Zadnik, M. (2001). Introductory thermal concept evaluation: assessing students' understanding. *The Physics Teacher, 39(8)*, 496–504.

Zimmerman, B.J. & Kitsantas, A. (1997). Developmental phases in self-regulation: Shifting from process goals to outcome goals. *Journal of Educational Psychology, 89*, 29-36.

Made in the USA
Las Vegas, NV
07 June 2022

49943964R00213